Civil War on Race Street

Southern Dissent

Florida A&M University, Tallahassee
Florida Atlantic University, Boca Raton
Florida Gulf Coast University, Ft. Myers
Florida International University, Miami
Florida State University, Tallahassee
University of Central Florida, Orlando
University of Florida, Gainesville
University of North Florida, Jacksonville
University of South Florida, Tampa
University of West Florida, Pensacola

Southern Dissent
Edited by Stanley Harrold and Randall M. Miller

The Other South: Southern Dissenters in the Nineteenth Century, by Carl N. Degler with a new preface (2000)

Crowds and Soldiers in Revolutionary North Carolina: The Culture of Violence in Riot and War, by Wayne E. Lee (2001)

"Lord, We're Just Trying to Save Your Water": Environmental Activism and Dissent in the Appalachian South, by Suzanne Marshall (2002)

The Changing South of Gene Patterson: Journalism and Civil Rights, 1960–1968, edited by Roy Peter Clark and Raymond Arsenault (2002)

Gendered Freedoms: Race, Rights and the Politics of Household in the Postemancipation Delta, 1861–1875, by Nancy Bercaw (2003)

Civil War on Race Street: The Civil Rights Movement in Cambridge, Maryland, by Peter B. Levy (2003)

Civil War on Race Street

The Civil Rights Movement in Cambridge, Maryland

Peter B. Levy

Foreword by Stanley Harrold and Randall J. Miller, Series Editors

University Press of Florida
Gainesville Tallahassee Tampa Boca Raton
Pensacola Orlando Miami Jacksonville Ft. Myers

08 07 06 05 04 03   6 5 4 3 2 1

Library of Congress Cataloging-in-Publication Data
Levy, Peter B.
Civil war on Race Street: the civil rights movement in Cambridge,
Maryland / Peter B. Levy; foreword by Stanley Harrold and Randall J.
Miller, series editors.
p. cm. — (Southern dissent)
Includes bibliographical references and index.
ISBN 0-8130-2638-5 (cloth: alk. paper)
1. African Americans—Civil rights—Maryland—Cambridge—His-
tory—20th century. 2. Civil rights movements—Maryland—Cam-
bridge—History—20th century. 3. Cambridge (Md.)—Race rela-
tions. I. Title. II. Series.
F189.C345L485 2003
323.1'196073075227'09046—dc21 2003040189

The University Press of Florida is the scholarly publishing agency
for the State University System of Florida, comprising Florida A&M
University, Florida Atlantic University, Florida Gulf Coast Univer-
sity, Florida International University, Florida State University, Uni-
versity of Central Florida, University of Florida, University of
North Florida, University of South Florida, and University of West
Florida.

University Press of Florida
15 Northwest 15th Street
Gainesville, FL 32611–2079
http://www.upf.com

There is no real peace in Cambridge, nor can there be real peace until there is justice. This white man's peace is for our people a slave's peace. We have nothing to gain from a peace with a system that makes us less than men.

Gloria Richardson (1963)

Contents

Tables and Figures

Series Foreword

In the large literature on civil rights, historians have begun to remap the routes and character of the movement. No longer does a single narrative or chronology hold sway. The older and still generally popular narrative turned on Dr. Martin Luther King, Jr., and nonviolent resistance. It suggested that with the passage of the Civil Rights Act of 1964 and the Voting Rights Act of 1965, the principal purposes of the movement had been achieved. Though racism remained, legalized racial discrimination had been defeated and a better day for racial relations and social justice beckoned. In such a telling, the black power rhetoric and violence of the mid-1960s and later seemed a denial of the movement rather than an integral part of it. The traditional chronology dated the beginnings of civil rights "direct action" from Rosa Parks's refusal to give up her seat on a Jim Crow bus in Montgomery in December 1955. The ensuing Montgomery bus boycott provided both a real and a symbolic demonstration of church-based African-American social power that attracted national media attention and won a victory over segregation on the buses and in the courts. All that followed by way of activism supposedly came from that critical moment.

Historians know that such a neat narrative misses much of the dynamics of the civil rights movement. Rather than one movement, they argue, many civil rights movements were under way. Some antedated World War II, and all had their own particular personalities and interests. Without discounting the importance of King and Parks, historians insist that understanding civil rights demands a close look at localities other than Montgomery, Birmingham, and Selma. That understanding also requires recognition that no single person or interest group spoke for the movement or for which particular civil rights needed to be secured. Such an understanding further demands an appreciation of what those who opposed the movement in various places expected of civil rights and of themselves.

Peter Levy understands all this, and more. In *Civil War on Race Street*, he restores Cambridge, Maryland, to prominence as one of the most important, and in its day most visible, sites of civil rights ideas and activism. Previously eclipsed by the traditional narrative that sets the story in the Deep South, Cambridge emerges in Levy's account as pivotal in forcing the Kennedy administration to engage civil rights directly, in thrusting forward black insistence on economic justice and autonomy as vital goals of civil rights, and in giving dramatic life and voice to black power.

As Levy recounts, during the 1960s Cambridge stood at the vortex of changing expectations of civil rights. In 1963 demonstrations there revealed the depth of black anger and frustration over poverty, poor housing, substandard and segregated schools, and racial discrimination in employment and public services. Whites in Cambridge prided themselves on the town's supposedly "progressive" history of race relations. They pointed to black enfranchisement in Cambridge as proof that their community was not like the bully South of Ross Barnett or Bull Connor. But Cambridge whites lived in a world apart from blacks in work, faith, and family and completely misread black aspirations. The 1963 demonstrations exploded myths of black passivity as blacks demanded jobs and justice. Especially significant about the Cambridge demonstrations of 1963 was the role of Gloria Richardson, a Cambridge native and graduate of Howard University, where she had seen a wider world of possibility. She called for black pride and no compromise with racism and forged a coalition of students and local working-class residents to press for civil rights and to assert their collective power as a people. After disturbances in town and the smashing of some windows, police moved in to put down the rioters. Martial law ensued. Attorney General Robert Kennedy then negotiated a settlement that promised open accommodations, new public housing, school integration, and attention to unemployment.

Cambridge, though, remained a city under siege. National guardsmen stayed there until May 1964, while blacks' and whites' distrust of one another grew. Extremists on either side of the racial divide used Cambridge to gain national attention for their causes. George Wallace, for one, brought his message of segregation and states' rights to a cheering throng there. The Student Nonviolent Coordinating Committee (SNCC) participated in counterdemonstrations that resulted in a showdown with the National Guard. These confrontations in Cambridge provided a training of sorts for Stokely Carmichael, Cleveland Sellers, and others who went south for "Freedom Summer." The arrival of H. Rap Brown of SNCC in

July 1967 signaled a new phase of black radicalism. He mocked nonviolent tactics and urged a crowd of three hundred young blacks to stop loving and start shooting whites who abused them. Such talk, white authorities later charged, ignited a riot and arson that burned down two city blocks. In the public awareness of civil rights, Cambridge became synonymous with black militancy and riot. Events elsewhere soon grabbed national attention and pushed Cambridge off the front page and almost out of history—until now.

Among Levy's many contributions in *Civil War on Race Street* are his deconstruction of the myths of Cambridge and his careful reconstruction of the interests, individuals, and incidents that make the town so important. He points to the several civil wars under way in Cambridge between races and classes and within them. Levy presents the civil rights story within a larger context of social and economic change in the town, the Chesapeake Bay region, and the nation. He shows that civil rights had very specific meanings depending on place and perspective.

One such meaning is that civil rights activism was not the work of men only. Black women exercised leadership in Cambridge. Through Gloria Richardson, Levy brings fully into view the importance of women to the civil rights movement, not only as foot soldiers in boycotts and sit-ins but also as strategists and spokespersons for the cause. Richardson's unflinching stands on social justice and economic improvement forced the hand of the federal government as well as pressing local officials and power brokers. She did not act like a woman was supposed to do in the face of male authority. The internal dynamics of women and men working out the means and ends of civil rights in Cambridge suggest a reason to revisit civil rights activity elsewhere.

Also significant in Levy's account is the importance of geography. Cambridge's history was tied to the Chesapeake and the Eastern Shore of Maryland, which had bred a very particular economy and culture. But its proximity to Washington, D.C., and its growing ties to the outside after World War II brought it nearer to people in government, journalism, and commerce than most southern places were. Trouble in supposedly progressive Cambridge could not be passed off as Deep South extremism. And it was too close to the nation's capital to be ignored.

By reinserting Cambridge and the upper South into the history of civil rights, Levy's *Civil War on Race Street* enlarges and complicates the narrative of southern dissent. Levy reminds us that the story of civil rights must be simultaneously plural and singular: plural in the many competing interests in one place, and everywhere, and in the multiple definitions of civil rights; singular in the centrality of racism and economic inequity as the root causes of civil rights activism anywhere. He shows that unless we understand civil rights in the terms of those who were in the struggle, and those who opposed it, we will never understand civil rights at all.

Stanley Harrold and Randall M. Miller
Series Editors

Acknowledgments

One of the great joys of writing a book is the ability to thank the numerous people who have offered their help. From its first inception to the final copyediting of the text, I have met and benefited from the advice of more individuals than I can count. Unfortunately, this book has taken me so long to research and write that I have forgotten the names of many who provided sound guidance and enthusiastic support. This includes the numerous archivists and librarians who helped me locate material, especially those at the Maryland Room of the Enoch Pratt Free Library, the Marlandia and Rare Books Collection at the University of Maryland, the Manuscript Division of the Library of Congress, the Martin Luther King Center, Maryland State Archives, National Archives, State Historical Society of Wisconsin, Dorchester County Public Library, and the staff at York College's Schmidt Library. To the librarians and archivists as well as the tens of others who have contributed to this work, a collective thank-you.

Fortunately my memory has not totally failed me yet, so I can at least acknowledge the tremendous debt of gratitude I owe to a number of people who have read all or parts of this manuscript, in one form or another, and who helped me strengthen it in innumerable ways. Those outside the academic world will probably never understand how important such collegiality is, especially since in almost all cases it is provided without charge. But let me suggest that without the help I received from the following individuals, it is unlikely that I would ever have completed this work.

Timothy Gilfoyle and Cheryl Greenberg, whom I befriended in graduate school and with whom I have remained friends as we have watched our families grow, read the entire manuscript and offered both encouragement and extremely constructive criticism. I cannot thank them enough for their continued support. I first encountered Randall Miller, one of the editors of the Southern Dissent series, while working on another book and immediately recognized his superb editorial skills. I have been fortunate to benefit from his insight and red pen again as well as from the very thorough reading his co-editor Stanley Harrold gave my manuscript. Alana Jeydel had been at York College less than a week when I asked if she would be willing to review a draft of my book. In spite of the fact that she was a new faculty member and had to develop a slew of new courses, conduct her own research, and settle into the community, she agreed to do so. I especially benefited from her expertise on the theory of political mobilization. Doug Rossinow and an anonymous reader for the University Press of Florida reviewed the manuscript as well, saving me from making numerous errors and tightening my argument considerably. Barbara Tischler, Doron Bet-Atar, and Alan Draper offered sound commentary on sections of this work that were presented at the meetings of the Organization of American Historians and the Southern Labor Studies Association. I also benefited from the comments made in response to readings of sections of my study by participants of the Washington and Hagley Center seminars, organized by James Banner and Roger Horowitz, respectively.

In addition, my colleagues and students at York College have been a constant source of support. I would especially like to acknowledge the contributions made by students in my courses on the history of the civil rights movement, including mock editorial reviews by Karsten Lovorn and Tom Perrin. Phil Avillo, who served as my department chair for the past dozen years, has done everything in his power to allow me to pursue my research. I also benefited from the financial support of York College, in the form of a Enhancement Committee summer research stipend and funds granted by the Research and Publication Committee. The dean and my department granted me release time to work on this project.

The editorial staff at the University Press of Florida has been an absolute joy to work with. Meredith Morris-Babb's enthusiasm and professionalism deserve special acknowledgment. I owe a debt of gratitude to the men and women who agreed to be interviewed for this study. Gloria Richardson and Enez Grubb, in particular, consented to be interviewed and communicated via E-mail and regular mail on repeated occasions. Both of them are remarkable women who deserve recognition as true freedom fighters.

Last, I must give my profoundest thanks to my family. I think my son Brian was still in utero when I first went in search of a "second book" project. He is now a young teen and asking probing questions about the world, many of which I cannot answer. My daughter Jessica is one of the hardest workers I know. Her drive, in school and on the playing field, has served as a constant inspiration for me to continue working on this project. And my wife Diane is a highly respected attorney, a world-class editor in her own right, and a wonderful lifelong companion, all rolled in one. To them and to my extended family, thank you for the support and expert advice you have offered me.

Introduction

The Cambridge experience is not merely of local interest. On the contrary, the factors which created the crisis . . . are present in practically every place in the United States where there is a sizeable Negro population. It is only the convergence of a number of factors which have made the crisis come earlier and more intensely than in other areas.

Cambridge Nonviolent Action Committee (1963)

On July 13, 1963, shortly after returning from a grand tour of Europe, where he delivered his famous *Ich bin ein Berliner* speech in Germany, visited his ancestral homeland of Ireland, and enjoyed a private audience with the new pope, President John F. Kennedy held his first press conference in months. Beaming with self-confidence boosted by his triumphant journey, he responded to a variety of questions, including several regarding civil rights. Prior to his trip, civil rights demonstrations had reached an all-time peak in number and volume. Turmoil in Birmingham, Alabama, had captured the nation's attention like few other events in American history. So, too, had the assassination of NAACP leader Medgar Evers, in Jackson, Mississippi, and the federal government's showdown with Alabama Governor George C. Wallace over the integration of the University of Alabama. Whereas Kennedy's initial reaction to the civil rights movement had been timid, in the spring of 1963 he staked out an aggressive, pro–civil rights stance. Most important, on June 11, 1963, shortly before he left for Europe, President Kennedy delivered a moving televised address on the "Negro revolt," as it was often called at the time. "The heart of the question" raised by this revolt, Kennedy asserted, was "whether all Americans are to be afforded equal rights and equal opportunities." So as to allow America to "fulfill its promise," the president announced he would submit to Congress a proposal for sweeping civil rights legislation to ensure that "race had no place in American life or law."[1]

Civil rights protests continued unabated during his journey abroad, as did plans for a massive March on Washington. Hoping to ascertain whether his opinions of the movement had shifted while he was abroad, reporters at the July 13 press conference made specific inquiries into his views on the ongoing "Negro revolt," especially the upcoming march. "Do you think that the [civil rights] demonstrations which are taking place are a handicap to you?" one reporter inquired. "No," the president emphatically replied. "We want citizens to come to Washington," he added in reference to the upcoming March on Washington, "if they feel that they are not having their rights expressed." This statement, in fact, represented a stronger endorsement of the upcoming demonstration in the nation's capital than he had given prior to his trip.[2]

Unprovoked by further questions from the press, however, Kennedy proceeded to single out for criticism demonstrations in Cambridge, a port town of 13,000 on Maryland's Eastern Shore. Activists in Cambridge, Kennedy emphasized, had "almost lost sight" of why they were protesting. "I think they go beyond . . . protest. They get into a very bad situation where you get violence, and I think the cause of advancing equal opportunity only loses."[3]

Four days after Kennedy warned that the protests in Cambridge had gone astray, the National Guard marched into Cambridge to restore order, encamping itself on Race Street, the name of the road that literally divided the white and black sections of the town. (The street was actually named after a mill race; some in town thought the name derived from the fact that horse races were once held on it.) Shortly thereafter, U.S. Attorney General Robert Kennedy and Gloria Richardson, the militant leader of the Cambridge Nonviolent Action Committee (CNAC)—the organization that had orchestrated the civil rights protests in Cambridge—met to see if they could arrive at a settlement that would bring an end to the turmoil that had been raging off and on for nearly two years. After eight hours of grueling negotiations they emerged to announce that they had reached an "agreement." Not only did the pact meet nearly all of the demands that CNAC had been making for over a year; it represented the most direct intervention of the Kennedy Administration in the racial affairs of a single community, paling its involvement in Birmingham, Alabama, and Jackson, Mississippi, two cities that have received much study by civil rights scholars.[4]

Several months later, Cambridge again garnered national headlines when a group of pro-segregationists, who were not party to the negotiations with Robert F. Kennedy, forced a referendum on the agreement. Specifically, they challenged the town's decision to outlaw racial discrimination in public accommodations. As a result of their efforts, Cambridge became the first and only city in the nation to have a direct vote on integration.[5] Supporters of the anti-discriminatory measure pleaded with the community to vote against the referendum on the grounds that a victory for the pro-segregationists would result in renewed racial turmoil and deliver a crushing blow to the town's efforts to rebuild its economy. (Unemployment in Cambridge was twice the national average.) State and local officials, including the town's mayor and several other prominent citizens, presumed that Cambridge's blacks, who enjoyed the franchise, would vote in favor of the anti-discriminatory measure. Shortly before Cambridge went to the polls, however, Gloria Richardson and CNAC called upon blacks to boycott the election on the grounds that they should not have to "beg for freedom," that human rights were human rights that should not be left to the whim of the white majority. Richardson and CNAC also complained that the battle over the referendum diverted attention from the main problems of the black community, jobs and housing.[6]

While moderates and liberals, black and white, in Cambridge and nationwide, expressed little surprise over the pro-segregationist campaign, they were astonished by Richardson's and CNAC's call for a boycott and they blamed her for the defeat of the public accommodations measure at the polls. At a time when many civil rights activists were risking their lives to desegregate lunch counters and to win the franchise, they could not fathom why Richardson and CNAC would counsel blacks to refuse to exercise their vote to integrate public accommodations. *Time* magazine called Richardson a "zealot"; writing for the *Saturday Evening Post*, Robert Liston explained that Richardson merely sought to further her "fame and power." And Anthony Lewis, in one of the first and otherwise favorable histories of the civil rights movement, lambasted Richardson for betraying the principles of the movement.[7]

In May 1964, about six months after the special election, George Wallace, the most famous symbol of white resistance, traveled to Cambridge to speak to upward of 2,000 supporters at the arena of the all-white Volunteer Rescue and Fire Company, one of the groups that had orchestrated the referendum. Wallace hoped his appearance in Cambridge would help him win the upcoming Democratic presidential primary in Maryland. Already, the Alabama governor had performed surprisingly well outside the old Confederacy. Stripping his speech of any blatant racist remarks, such as his signature declaration, "segregation now, segregation tomorrow, segregation forever," Wallace warned that the growing power of the federal government endangered long-cherished American liberties. Pending civil rights legislation threatened the right of association and trampled on the private property protections guaranteed by the U.S. Constitution. If Americans did not draw the line, Wallace exclaimed, they would soon lose all of their liberties.[8]

While Wallace spoke inside the arena, civil rights activists from up and down the eastern seaboard assembled outside. Intent on displaying their opposition to the politics of white backlash, the protesters, led by Gloria Richardson, confronted an equally large force of national guardsmen on Race Street. For nearly a year, the National Guard under the command of General George Gelston enjoyed favorable relations with CNAC. On this occasion, however, the nephew of Maryland Governor J. Millard Tawes was in charge. Lacking Gelston's patience and rapport with CNAC, he ordered the demonstrators to disperse. When they did not, he placed Richardson under arrest and ordered the Guard to spray the remaining protesters with tear gas. Chaos followed. Those who did not flee were arrested. Later that night a two-year-old black boy who lived nearby died. Even though a county coroner listed congenital heart failure as the cause of death, some activists insisted that blacks were being gassed to death. Just as important, Richardson's refusal to back down and her willingness to defy the wishes of the National Guard left a lasting impression on many of the activists who had come to Cambridge to protest against Wallace, including Stokely Carmichael, Cleveland Sellers, and H. Rap Brown, three up-and-coming leaders within the Student Nonviolent Coordinating Committee (SNCC). Over the course of the next three years, Carmichael, Sellers, and Brown would help transform SNCC, an organization founded on the principles of nonviolence and interracial unity, into a champion of "black power."[9]

In 1967, H. Rap Brown, the newly elected militant chairman of SNCC, accepted an invitation to speak in Cambridge to help rejuvenate the local movement, which had diminished significantly in size and vigor, due partly to the departure of Gloria Richardson in the fall of 1964. Brown had not been in Cambridge since 1964, yet many of the issues of concern to the Black Action Federation, the successor of CNAC, were familiar to him. For about an hour, he lambasted white "honkies" and extolled the virtues and achievements of African Americans. He condemned the police, white landlords, and the federal government and concluded his address as he had begun it, with fiery rhetoric. "Like I said in the beginning, if this town don't come around, this town should be burned down."[10]

Later that same night, a fire erupted at the Pine Street Elementary School, across the street from where Brown had spoken. On the orders of Police Chief Brice Kinnamon, who feared sniper fire, the Volunteer Fire Company refused to enter the all-black Second Ward to douse the blaze. As a result, two square blocks of the community burned to the ground. At dawn, with the embers still smoldering, Maryland's governor, Spiro T. Agnew, rushed to Cambridge from his vacation home at nearby Ocean City. Visibly upset, Agnew immediately called for Brown's arrest for inciting a riot and condemned black radicals, nationwide, for their incendiary language. Heretofore a moderate "Rockefeller" Republican, Agnew quickly became a symbol of the emerging new right. Richard Nixon, for one, took note of Agnew's ability to voice the frustration of large segments of the white population and tapped Agnew as his vice-presidential running mate in 1968.[11]

Remarkably, in spite of all of these developments, Cambridge has received little attention from historians or other students of the civil rights movement. A dozen leading works on the civil rights movement, including Taylor Branch's exhaustive two-volume chronicle of the "civil rights years," devote no more than a paragraph to Cambridge.[12] One encyclopedia even mistakes Cambridge, Maryland, for Cambridge, Massachusetts.[13] None of President Kennedy's biographers or specialists on his civil rights record have explored what motivated him to single out Cambridge for criticism; nor have they considered why the administration intervened so fully in the community's racial affairs. Most scholars who mention Cambridge only discuss the "Brown riot" of 1967, and they do so only as part of their broader discussion of black power and urban rioting. Some even cite the Brown riot as the most obvious example of the causal relationship between black power and rioting. Ironically, as we shall see, the most sophisticated contemporary analysis of the disorder suggested that Brown did not cause a riot because a riot never really took place.[14]

The failure of historians and other students of the civil rights movement to pay attention to Cambridge, however, should not lead us to conclude that the movement there was of little significance. On the contrary, as is suggested by the aforementioned vignettes, Cambridge offers many compelling reasons for investigation.

First, like all case or community studies, this one allows us, as John

D'Emilio has written, to "challenge, or confirm, broad generalizations and master narratives of the past by testing them 'on the ground.'" It provides students with a concrete feel for the forces that gave rise to the civil rights movement and a sense of the impact, or lack thereof, of the movement on a micro rather than a macro level. It also contributes to our theoretical understanding of the civil rights movement and social movements in general.[15] Put somewhat differently, since Cambridge was not unique (as CNAC recognized; see epigraph, p.1), its story sheds light on the broader history of the civil rights movement, adding to the growing body of literature that has enhanced our understanding of the black freedom struggle, including its impact on the everyday lives of ordinary citizens. Cambridge also provides particular insight into the interaction between the local, regional, and national aspects of the struggle for civil rights.

Second, Cambridge attracts our attention because the movement there was led by a remarkable middle-aged woman, Gloria Richardson. Although she is largely forgotten except by specialists in the field of civil rights studies, contemporaries recognized her as a true giant. For example, organizers of the March on Washington paid special tribute to her along with Rosa Parks, Daisy Bates, Diane Nash Bevel, and Mrs. Medgar Evers, as one of the "women of the movement"; and Robert Kennedy credited her with deepening his understanding of the goals of the civil rights revolution. Unlike many other women of the movement whose stories scholars have begun to explore, Richardson did not simply organize behind the scenes or serve as a symbol of the struggle. Rather, she led, in the fullest sense of the term, as forcefully and as effectively as any of her male counterparts. At the peak of her fame, Richardson remarried and moved to New York City to live with her husband, an act that may have contributed to her relative obscurity in the historical record but makes her even more interesting in retrospect.[16] Her departure provides one more reason for studying Cambridge, because it allows us to consider the role and significance of leaders to the movement more fully than if she had never left.[17]

Third, Cambridge's story stands out because it was not part of the Deep South. Until the urban riots of the latter half of the 1960s, many northerners believed that the "race problem" was restricted to the South, particularly to the states of the old Confederacy. Reared on stories about the Montgomery bus boycott and the confrontations in Birmingham, Selma, and the Mississippi Delta, many Americans still hold this belief. While recent studies have begun to paint a more sophisticated picture of the movement, orthodox histories of the movement, which are the ones most people are most likely to know, have divided the United States into neat geographical categories, the North and the South, and have largely left unexplored the civil rights movement that erupted in the border states, in communities that were neither northern nor southern but a combination of both. (Many recent local or regional works, ironically, have reinforced this geographical conceptualization of the movement because they focus on communities in the Deep South.) Similarly, by sticking to a linear or chronological description of the movement, the orthodox version assumes that the fight for economic and cultural equality and the turn to black power took place, in the North, after the battle against Jim Crow. But as a growing number of recent monographs have suggested and as this study shows, the goals of the civil rights movement were not universal, and local varieties and priorities and possibilities governed definitions of civil rights and strategies to achieve them.[18]

Fourth, what makes Cambridge even more intriguing is that prior to the 1960s it had a reputation as a community with a progressive racial record. Cambridge did not join the wave of resistance to the *Brown* decision. Community leaders pointed with pride to the fact that blacks enjoyed the franchise and had been represented on the town council as far back as 1881. Annapolis was the only city in Maryland to elect a black to office before Cambridge, and blacks have held office in Cambridge for consecutive terms for a longer period of time than probably in any city in the nation. In 1960, NBC newscaster Chet Huntley described Cambridge as a "model city" in terms of race relations. In spite of this record, or perhaps because of it, by 1963 Cambridge was the home of one of the most vibrant locally based civil rights initiatives in the nation and had earned a new reputation as a "cauldron of hate."[19]

Last, Cambridge provides us with the opportunity to understand better the contrasting fortunes of the new right and radical left. When H. Rap Brown accepted an invitation to help rejuvenate the movement in Cambridge, in July 1967, the new left appeared to many to be the new major force in American politics. Some even predicted that the nation was ripe for a revolution, or at least the dawning of a new age. In contrast, many felt that conservatism was dead in America, based in part on Barry Goldwater's devastating defeat in 1964. But as we will see, it was the new right, embodied by Spiro Agnew, who proved far more attractive to the wishes of large numbers of Americans. Even more so than George Wallace, who made a key campaign stop in Cambridge, in 1964 Spiro

Agnew reflected and articulated the views of the budding new right. Intuiting Agnew's appeal, Richard Nixon selected him as a running mate, and we would be well served to follow those political instincts by exploring the specific circumstances that precipitated Agnew's political transformation and emergence as a national symbol and that signaled the new left having reached its zenith.

The Contours of History

This is a place where the word "Mammy" is still taken seriously and the race is so far back that it has illimitable potential—like me.
Langston Hughes (upon his first visit to the Eastern Shore of Maryland, 1929)

On my first visit to Cambridge in 1990, while perusing the vertical files at the Dorchester County Public Library, I struck up a conversation with the reference librarian. During the course of our discussion, she informed me that she had resided in Cambridge for decades yet still was considered an outsider. I do not think I understood the significance of her statement until I returned to Cambridge for my final research trip ten years later. On this occasion, I was taking a "tour of the civil rights movement," offered by the Harriet Tubman Coalition, a nonprofit organization that had been founded in Cambridge in the 1980s. My tour guide was Enez Grubb, a veteran of the civil rights movement. After walking down Race Street, the location of many of the protests of the 1960s, Grubb and I ventured over to Pine Street, which ran parallel to Race Street about two blocks away. In the heart of the all-black Second Ward, Pine Street had once been the home of tens of black-owned businesses. As we meandered down the street on a beautiful late-summer day, she identified exactly who had worked and lived where in the 1950s. We began with the edifices that once housed Charles Cornish's bus company and the St. Clair Funeral Home; the names belonged to two of the primary figures of the civil rights years. We passed by the former homes of William Jews (currently one of the most prominent black businessmen in America), the Bethel AME Church, and an assortment of one-time beauty and barber shops, shoeshine parlors, Laundromats, pool rooms, and luncheonettes before stopping across from where the Pine Street Elementary School and Greene's Savory, a prominent nightspot, had once stood. Both these buildings had burned to the ground during the "Brown riot" of 1967, yet Grubb had no difficulty describing their interiors and recollecting the names of her teachers at the school and some of the bands that had performed at Greene's complex. After introducing me to two elderly gentlemen, who recalled their work at the Phillips Packing Company, long since shut down, Grubb remarked that not only did everyone know everyone else in the Second Ward; everyone was probably interrelated.[1]

The highlight of the tour came with a visit to the Waugh Methodist Church, one of the places where civil rights activists used to gather for mass meetings prior to marching downtown to stage sit-ins. Established prior to the Civil War by free blacks, Waugh was the spiritual home of many of the most prominent figures of the civil rights years. With a red brick exterior and whitewashed walls and dark wooden pews on the interior, the church is both stately and simple in construction and design. An impressive organ sits behind the altar; in the rear of the church stand the balconies, which had often been packed to the rafters during mass meetings. As Grubb explained, she and Frederick Jackson would often lead the mass meetings in song and then the congregants would march out of Waugh's front doors, which opened onto Pine Street, and head for Race Street singing freedom songs. As we headed for the doors, I could still read the lists of names that had long become familiar to me through my study of the civil rights movement in Cambridge. The names were not listed on commemorative plaques but rather on bulletin boards, which reflected their ongoing involvement in the community. As the reference librarian had hinted and the names on the bulletin board confirmed, Cambridge was a community where continuity was the rule.

Obviously, any study of the civil rights movement must take into account the ways in which the modern phase of the black struggle for freedom was shaped by the past. But Grubb's remark and vivid memory of Pine Street in the 1950s, and our stop at Waugh Church, in combination with my recollection of the reference librarian's statement that she still was considered an outsider, drove home the point that one cannot begin to understand the civil rights movement in Cambridge without first considering its history, the forces that shaped and gave rise to the movement, beginning with the arrival of the first slaves in the seventeenth century and stretching all the way to construction in the 1950s of the Chesapeake Bay Bridge, which broke down the community's longtime isolation from the surrounding world.

The history of Cambridge can be divided into three phases, each of which had its distinguishing characteristics and left a mark on the community. In the first phase, Cambridge developed into a racially caste-based society, with whites acquiring a sense of caste superiority over both enslaved and free blacks. I use the term *caste* rather than simply *race* because *caste* better captures the way in which individuals are born with a specific status in society, a status they inherit and cannot alter, no matter their individual merits. Long after the Civil War, the legacy of this racially caste-based society was deeply embedded in the mores and social relations of Cambridge. This can be called the "Old South era."

In the second phase, which began in the latter decades of the nineteenth century, Cambridge grew into a major industrial center, the hometown of the Phillips Packing Company, one of the largest producers of canned foods in the nation. Caste did not disappear during this era, but class distinctions became just as important in the life of the community. The term *class* is best understood as depicting socioeconomic relationships between distinct groups of people. Theoretically, one's class, unlike one's caste, can change, and the line between working class and middle class remained fairly permeable, especially for whites. The concept of class in Cambridge and its environs is complicated by the fact that well into the twentieth century, many members of the working class made a living in preindustrial endeavors, laboring as watermen, muskrat hunters, and small farmers or some combination of the three. By nearly all objective measures these workers and their families were part of the working class. Yet, because of the nature of their work and faith in self-reliance, they did not see themselves as such, although the industrial elite did. On occasion, black and white workers united to challenge the rule of the upper class, in spite of the persistence of caste distinctions. I refer to this period as the "New South era."

The third phase in Cambridge history began following World War II. An assortment of forces, ranging from the collapse of the largest employer in the region, the Phillips Packing Company, to the construction of the Chesapeake Bay Bridge, destabilized the community and paved the way for a challenging of traditional caste and class relations. While community leaders sought to fill the vacuum left by the collapse of the Phillips Packing Company and to take advantage of Cambridge's newfound access to the markets of major metropolises of the eastern seaboard, they found themselves vulnerable to challenges from below. This can be called the modern era. Whether Cambridge has entered a new postmodern era remains unclear.

The Old South Era

In 1684 the General Assembly of Maryland established Cambridge as the county seat of Dorchester County, which at the time extended north and westward from the Choptank River on the Eastern Shore of Maryland to New Sweden (Delaware). Situated on the Chesapeake, the town serviced the surrounding plantations, large and small, and acted as the region's economic and political hub. Attracting lawyers and merchants who profited from this trade, Cambridge grew slowly during the later part of the seventeenth century and more rapidly during the second half of the eighteenth century. During the American Revolution, Cambridge became the headquarters for the Continental Army on the Eastern Shore of Maryland. One of its leading citizens, John Henry, served in the Continental Congress (1777–89), later becoming one of Maryland's first senators (1789–98) and then its governor.[2]

The region was settled by a mixture of Englishmen, French Huguenots, Scotch, and Irish. Throughout the seventeenth century the vast majority of them were white indentured servants. From early in its history, Cambridge and its environs also became the home of captives shipped from Africa and their descendants. In 1699 the ship *African Galley* brought twenty-two enslaved black persons to Cambridge's port. They were not the first Africans in the area; others had migrated to the Eastern Shore from Virginia, some as free blacks. In the first half of the eighteenth century the slave population grew slowly. As of 1755, slaves constituted only 11 percent of the population—a smaller segment than in several northern port towns. Thenceforth, the black population, slave and free, expanded rapidly. In 1790, the year of first federal census, Dorchester County had a total population of just less than 28,000, about one-third being black, all but 500 enslaved. Between 1790 and 1860 Dorchester County's black population increased from just under 6,000 to nearly 9,000, of whom about half were free.[3]

The boom in the free black population was the result of three intertwined developments: the American Revolution and the rise of Methodism, both of which undercut the ideology of natural racial superiority, and the depletion of the soil by tobacco, which made slavery less profitable. In 1790 barely 500 free blacks resided in Dorchester County; by 1860 they numbered 4,500. By the outbreak of the Civil War more free blacks than slaves lived in Dorchester County.[4]

Table 1.1. Population of Dorchester County, 1704–1860

Year	Total	White	Black	Enslaved	Free
1704	2,312	2,113 (91%)	199 (9%)	—	—
1755	3,475	3,088 (89%)	387 (11%)	—	—
1790	16,494	10,010 (63%)	5,865 (37%)	5,337	528
1810	18,108	10,415 (58%)	7,693 (42%)	5,032	2,661
1830	18,686	10,685 (57%)	8,001 (43%)	5,001	3,000
1860	20,467	11,654 (57%)	8,807 (43%)	4,123	4,684

Not surprisingly, the growth of the free black population in the late eighteenth and early nineteenth centuries deeply concerned many of the region's leading citizens, who routinely fretted about what would happen when the most obvious caste distinction—the fact that only individuals of African descent could be enslaved—disappeared. Governor John Henry railed at the "evil societies [and] individuals of certain religious orders" who favored manumission. He warned that the growth of the free black population could easily lead to another revolution, in which the "African might turn the tables and become the master." To defend against such a threat, he demanded the formation of a strong militia made up of whites of all classes.[5] Just as important, Henry and other whites of the elite did what they could to perpetuate a sense of racial caste consciousness in the absence of slavery. To this end, in 1783 the Maryland state legislature stripped free, property-owning blacks—of whom there were very few—of the right to vote. Eight years later the Maryland legislature granted all white males the franchise, including those who did not own land. The "right" to participate in the militia, which was reserved to whites, reinforced white caste consciousness while simultaneously addressing the security concerns of the white elite in case of a black uprising.[6]

Fears about the presence of a large class of free blacks and the ways in which these people could undermine the caste system characterizing the social order in the region affected the Methodist Church too, although it initially took a staunch anti-slavery stance. Methodism arrived on the Eastern Shore in the latter years of the eighteenth century and spread rapidly in the early decades of the nineteenth century. One historian referred to the Eastern Shore as the "Garden of American Methodism," because Methodists quickly became the largest religious affiliation for both blacks and whites in the region. Blacks soon discovered, however, that most white Methodists, in spite of egalitarian theology and rhetoric, did not treat them as equals. Beginning in the 1820s, black Methodists began to push for their own church—either within the white-controlled Baltimore or Philadelphia conference or by establishing their own independent or black-controlled conference. Whites resisted both efforts and effectively checked a split of the Methodist church along racial lines until after the Civil War. Methodist bishops made sure that church trustees remained white, and state authorities passed laws requiring the presence of a white preacher or policeman at black services. On the few occasions when black religious leaders sought to establish an independent black church, they were physically stopped from doing so. For instance, in July 1830, two black Bethel ministers, representing an independent conference, came to Dorchester County to organize an African Methodist Episcopal Church. When they spoke to a group of free blacks, a mob of whites attacked them. Two black homes were burned to the ground. Some blacks were arrested for disturbing the peace; no whites were.[7]

Caste distinctions also developed out of the desire of lower-class whites to protect and maintain their limited economic advantages. As new industries and opportunities appeared, white workers sought to protect their "right" to employment. For instance, an 1836 act banned black men from captaining a boat above a certain size. Just as important, the absence of statutes outlawing racial discrimination in employment allowed for the segmentation of the labor market along racial lines. By 1850, 78 percent of all blacks in Dorchester County worked as laborers, whereas only 19 percent of whites did. While there were 133 white carpenters, there were only four black carpenters. Discriminatory educational practices further limited black employment opportunities. Until Reconstruction, there were no schools for black children in Dorchester County. As a result, in 1860 only 15 to 20 percent of the free black population was literate, compared to about 90 percent of whites.[8]

Land records further reveal the significance of racial castes in the region. While free blacks constituted a significant proportion of the population on the eve of the Civil War, they owned an infinitesimal amount of property. Out of about $5.2 million worth of landholdings, free blacks owned less than 1 percent. While the per capita holding of whites was $478, it was less than $14 for free blacks just before the Civil War. Only ten out of almost 4,700 free blacks owned $500 worth of land.[9]

This does not mean that Dorchester County was a paradise for the majority of whites. A good deal of evidence suggests the opposite. In contrast to Baltimore and western Maryland, Dorchester County was not linked to the rail system and did not develop any significant manufacturing establishments prior to the Civil War. This limited the economic opportunities available to whites, particularly those who did not own land or owned only small tracts. Most whites in the region sustained themselves by harvesting a mixture of staple crops and small amounts of tobacco and by supplementing their diet by hunting and fishing. Soil erosion limited farmer productivity and the lack of rail connections restricted the market accessible to all of the region's residents. Declining farm output, in turn, decreased the allure and importance of Cambridge's port, which at the time of the American Revolution had rivaled the port of Baltimore. One sign of the region's economic stagnation was Dorchester County's inability to attract newcomers. Between 1790 and 1850 the white population in the county increased less than 1 percent, though it doubled in the state as a whole.[10]

During the Civil War, when the nation split into extremes, Dorchester County remained, by in large, in the middle. The bulk of whites in the county did not want to defend the institution of slavery or advance racial equality. In the election of 1860, Lincoln won only thirty-four votes in the county and five in the city of Cambridge. Southern firebrand John Breckenridge received 1,185 votes in the county. Yet the majority of whites supported John Bell, the Constitutional Union candidate. Although a good number of Dorchester County's whites served in the Confederate Army— or aided its efforts—more of them mustered behind Colonel James Wallace, who sided with the Union, and the county remained in Union hands throughout the war. When Lincoln issued the Emancipation Proclamation, white support for the war diminished. Still, emancipation did not prompt the majority of the region's white citizens to support the Confederate cause.[11]

Prior to emancipation, blacks of Dorchester County responded to their situation in different ways. Some sought to leave the area, either as runaways, in the case of slaves, or as migrants, in the case of free blacks. The most famous runaway was Harriet Tubman, born in Bucktown, Dorchester County, not far from Cambridge. She returned to the region on several occasions to help free others. A number of free blacks advocated colonization, migrating to Africa. Thomas Fuller, a native of Cambridge, helped found the Cambridge African Colonization Society in 1851. Along with six other free blacks from Dorchester County he attended an 1852 colonization convention in Baltimore County. Believing that caste barriers would never disappear, Fuller and other advocates of colonization deemed immigration the best alternative for blacks. After the convention, Fuller traveled to Liberia in West Africa. He did not stay, but another free black from the region, Stephen Benson, made Liberia his home, becoming its second president.[12]

The majority of blacks in Dorchester County, free and enslaved, remained in the region. Prior to the Civil War they made minimal progress in bettering their lives. Not much changed during the conflict. But in the aftermath of the war, blacks began to create the institutions and organization and to attain the skills and resources they needed to challenge the racial status quo. In 1865, three blacks from Dorchester County attended the state Republican Convention, where they promoted black suffrage, something they gained with the ratification of the Fifteenth Amendment. With the help of the Freedmen's Bureau, four schools for blacks were established in Dorchester County, among them the Stanley Institute headed by Benjamin Jennifer, Jr., one of the most prominent free blacks in the region. This school began to train a core black elite, many of whose families would remain leaders in town for decades. The first literate blacks in the area had learned to read and write prior to the Civil War at a Sunday school at the black Waugh Chapel. They went on to teach in the first black schools. Black churches grew in number and size as well, including the construction of the Bethel AME Church in 1879 and the formation of the first all-black Baptist church. Meanwhile, the Waugh Methodist Episcopal Church, founded in 1826 and affiliated with a conference of churches headquartered in Philadelphia, grew into the largest all-black congregation in the region, with over three hundred members by the end of the nineteenth century.[13]

Blacks remained second-class citizens during Reconstruction, suggesting that the Civil War alone did not topple the Old South. The 1870 census showed that there were eighty-four black laborers but only eight white laborers in Cambridge. There were no black merchants, clerks, lawyers, printers, or teachers, while sixty-two white men worked in these occupations. Sixty percent of all white men worked in occupations in which there were no black workers. Caste lines were just as sharp among women. Eighty-five percent of all white women listed in the 1870 census were not part of the wage labor force. In contrast, a majority of black women worked for wages. All but one black woman worked as domestic servants, presumably for white women in Cambridge. In contrast, only one-third of all white females in the labor force worked as domestics; the rest held a variety of jobs from dressmaker to boardinghouse keeper.[14]

The inferior caste status of blacks was so pervasive that it influenced the white community's recollection of the past. Elias Jones's *History of Dorchester County*, published in 1925, contained more than six hundred pages on the history of the county but only two and a half pages on blacks, despite the fact that blacks made up about one-third of the population. In his section on prominent citizens, Jones included biographies of John Henry, Colonel Wallace, and other notable white men and some white women. He did not include a description of Harriet Tubman or Thomas Fuller or any other black man or woman. In a book largely devoted to the pre–Civil War era, Jones wrote less than two pages on the institution of slavery. He included three times as many pages about "county folklore and the superstitions" of whites, such as folk remedies for curing warts. More-over, he romanticized slavery when he discussed it at all. "Inhuman cru-elty was rare," Jones asserted, in spite of the fact that physical brutality was a mainstay of the institution of slavery as described by Frederick Douglass, who was reared twenty miles north in Talbott County. Neither Jones's revised history of Dorchester County, published in the mid-1960s, nor studies of the region by Calvin Mowbray or Thomas Flowers, both written in the 1980s, added significantly to Jones's initial brief depiction of black life in Cambridge.[15]

The lack of official or white acknowledgment of the contributions of blacks to the history of the region, however, did not mean that blacks shared Jones's views of the past. On the contrary, they were well aware of Harriet Tubman's exploits, that the founders of Liberia came from the region, and that free blacks had established their own churches and schools. They also knew that these same black churches were a product of protest against a caste system marking black people as inferiors.

The New South Era

In 1886, *Atlanta Constitution* editor Henry Grady delivered his famous speech on the "New South," in which he championed the birth of a new society based not on agriculture but on free labor and manufacturing, par-ticularly of goods derived from southern soil. Grady did not predicate the development of the New South on a rearrangement of caste relations, believing that both whites and blacks would benefit from a move away from the economy of the Old South. While there is no evidence that Cambridge's town leaders heard or read Grady's speech, Cambridge experienced an economic and social transformation that would have made Grady proud. Indeed, even as Grady was proselytizing about the virtues of a New South, Cambridge was in the midst of an oyster boom that established the foundation for its industrial development. As a result, by World War I, Cambridge was no longer a provincial port that shipped cash crops grown in the region. Rather it had grown into an industrial city, dominated by the Phillips Packing Company, which specialized in the production of canned fruits and vegetables. Although the community still had a small rural-town feel, so much so that Annie Oakley adopted it as her home, the majority of the workforce was employed in manufacturing and the town was run by an industrial elite. Caste distinctions remained important in Cambridge, but class emerged as one of the keys to understanding its trajectory.

Cambridge owed its transformation to several factors. Even before the Civil War, many if not most of the region's farmers turned away from tobacco production to grain crops. This eased the way to the planting of fruits and vegetables, especially tomatoes. By World War II, Dorchester County was the third leading producer of tomatoes in the nation. The construction of a railroad in 1867 from Seaford, Delaware, to Cambridge, Maryland, opened new economic markets for these products. Cambridge already had economic access to Baltimore via the ships and ferries that traversed the Chesapeake Bay. The "oyster rush" of the post–Civil War years sped up Cambridge's rebirth as a center of food processing. By the end of the nineteenth century, over one million bushels of oysters were shucked annually in Cambridge, ranking it second in the nation to Baltimore in oyster production. Cambridge businessmen also marketed other products of the great estuary, including crabs and muskrat furs and meat—muskrats were plentiful in the marshlands that occupied about one-third of the county.[16]

Capitalizing on these trends—hungry eastern markets, readily available cheap labor, and produce—Albanus Phillips, Levi Phillips, and William Winterbottom established the Phillips Packing Company in 1902. All three had already tapped the food market before joining together. Albanus Phillips operated a large Chesapeake Bay schooner and worked for an oyster wholesaler in Baltimore. Levi Phillips owned several large schooners that shipped oysters and other goods to the West Indies. And Winterbottom worked in oyster packing and in the coal business.[17]

Starting with one plant on the west side of the Cambridge harbor, the Phillips Packing company grew steadily, focusing increasingly on canned vegetables and less and less on oysters. By 1950, the Phillips Packing Company owned and operated nineteen separate plants on the Delmarva (Delaware, Maryland, and Virginia) Peninsula. At the end of World War II, Phillips produced more than fifty varieties of canned foods, including one-eighth of all of the canned tomatoes in America. In addition to packing food goods, the company manufactured its own tin cans. Phillips made good profits even during the depression. Between 1944 and 1947 the company employed more than four thousand workers, about half of them in Cambridge. During World War II, Phillips was the leading producer of C-rations in the nation, one of the two main ways food was packaged for the military.[18]

The Phillips company's political influence paralleled its economic fortunes. Augustus and Levi Phillips were power brokers in Maryland's Republican Party. Their business partner William Winterbottom enjoyed nearly as much influence within the Democratic Party. His name became synonymous with one of the two main political factions in the region. The other faction was known as the Harrington faction, named after a one-term governor of Maryland and native of Cambridge. Through World War II the Winterbottom faction won nearly every city and county election and controlled the mayor's office, the town council, judgeships, and the county commission.[19]

The *FTA News*, the newspaper of the Food and Tobacco Workers, the union that attempted unsuccessfully to organize packing workers at Phillips after World War II, aptly captured Phillips company prowess.

Cambridge might well be named Phillipsburg. The Phillips family dominates the city politically and economically. In addition to the packing plants, Cambridge's only major industry, Phillips owns the city's largest wholesale and retail hardware store and the city's largest gasoline and fuel-oil distributing service. Phillips' workers, under fear of punishment, are expected to eat Phillips soup, feed their pets Phillips Dog Food, burn Phillips Vim Pep gas, split their wood with a Phillips axe, and decorate their homes with Phillips paint. The present Dorchester County Sheriff is ex-captain of Phillips guards, and most other officeholders, Democrat and Republican, owe their election to Phillips backing. Even the churches are not exempt from Phillips influence.[20]

Whereas the overall population of the county stagnated, Cambridge continued to grow. Most new arrivals came from the surrounding region, not from other parts of Maryland or the Deep South. As of 1947, only one Eastern Shore county had more manufacturing workers than Dorchester County—Wicomico County, where most worked for Campbell's Soup. Even though the majority of the Cambridge labor force did not work directly for the Phillips Packing Company, indirectly a majority of workers were dependent upon it. Phillips was by far the largest manufacturing employer and the main purchaser of farm goods in the region. Small farmers, especially in comparison to those of other parts of the country, enjoyed fairly high or stable prices throughout the twenties and thirties due to the demand for their produce. Yet at the same time they became increasingly dependent on a single purchaser. Money generated by the Phillips Packing Company flowed into the shops and services of the community, from the chain stores and movie theaters that operated on Race Street to the numerous black-owned businesses that were located on Pine Street.[21]

For blacks, the growth of Phillips Packing Company was a mixed blessing. More so than whites, blacks depended on the Phillips Packing Company for jobs. While they faced fewer restrictions on their employment opportunities in the twentieth century than they had in the nineteenth, blacks were still disproportionately employed as unskilled laborers or operatives rather than in the skilled trades or in retail or white collar jobs. Work in the food processing plants was extremely volatile. Unemployment was nearly ten times as high in the late spring as it was in the early fall, when the tomatoes were harvested. In contrast, in Easton, which did not have a large processing plant, unemployment was only about two and a half times as high in spring as in fall and tended to be lower on a yearly basis. Not only did workers in the processing plants make less money per hour, about 30 percent less than at other manufacturing jobs in the region; they also did not work as many hours per year. White factory workers enjoyed more stable hours than blacks because they were more likely to be employed in the making of cans, which was less seasonal, or in manufacturing other than food processing. To make it through the down times, many blacks migrated out to the country to pick beans, tomatoes, and other fruits and vegetables at harvest time and then sought employment in the packing plants. Moreover, black families sustained themselves by having all members of the family work. Many more black than white women worked in the packing plants and as domestics. Still, compared to blacks in the Deep South, who faced a crumbling cotton economy, blacks in Cambridge faired reasonably well.[22]

The growth of the black population, nearly all of whom lived in the Second Ward, gave rise to a substantial black middle class. As already suggested, black-owned business that catered to the all-black Second Ward prospered in the first half of the twentieth century. This consisted of "approximately 40 [black] merchants," according to one source, including barbers, grocers, butchers, and restaurant owners. By the beginning of the twentieth century, Cambridge also supported black teachers and ministers and a black doctor. The sons and daughters of many of these businessmen and professionals attended college and, in some cases, returned to Cambridge to conduct their parents' businesses.[23]

The black community also sustained numerous cultural institutions, ranging from black baseball teams, which competed with other black teams on the Eastern Shore, to a wide assortment of fraternal organizations, such as the Elks, Odd Fellows, Knights of Pythias, and their own branch of the American Legion. In addition to their churches, blacks in Cambridge took great pride in their bands, such as the Merry Concert Band, which traveled all over the state. (For more on the church, see chapter 2.) For Fourth of July parades, representatives of these black institutions would march down Race Street, displaying feelings of pride and instilling the same among members of the black community, who sat or stood on one side of Race Street while whites congregated separately on the other side.[24]

Moreover, partly because Cambridge elected its council members by ward and because of the influence of the Phillips Packing Company, blacks in Cambridge enjoyed political rights about which their southern counterparts could only dream. As noted earlier, not only did blacks retain their vote; they enjoyed representation on the town council. "By 1894," writes C. Christopher Brown, "Cambridge's single-member district system," whereby the five town councilmen represented the city's five wards, "had produced four different black commissioners [councilmen]." The most famous of these was H. Maynadier St. Clair, son of Cyrus St. Clair, a successful butcher. St. Clair was first elected in 1894. Except for a two-year gap, he remained the Second Ward's councilman until his retirement in 1946. Annapolis was the only Maryland community to elect a black to public office prior to Cambridge, and the Annapolis black official lost his seat when the city "reformed" its method for choosing town council members.[25]

St. Clair rarely, if ever, criticized the Phillips Packing Company, believing it would help uplift the black community. To an extent, his views resembled those of Booker T. Washington. Like Washington, St. Clair enjoyed a good deal of respect, especially among the town's black citizens. He entertained such notables as Mordecai Johnson, president of Howard University, and Duke Ellington. His son, Frederick St. Clair, attended Harvard Law School. Yet, unlike Washington's, St. Clair's accommodationist stance did not necessitate surrendering the vote. The establishment of a "colored" library, construction of new schools (including Maryland's first black high school near Baltimore in 1916 and later the Frederick D. St. Clair High School, which opened in 1932), and his appointment as chairman of the town council's committee on lights and water testified to the efficacy of St. Clair's approach.[26]

However, St. Clair did not or could not topple other caste barriers. Nearly all of Cambridge's blacks lived in the Second Ward; even though they constituted about one-third of the population in 1950, they had only one vote on the town council. In the early years of the twentieth century, the region's political leaders blocked "reforms" that would have disenfranchised blacks. At the same time they enacted a law that legally maintained residential segregation. This law was rescinded in 1957. Years later some black leaders looked back upon this as a Faustian deal, arguing that it gave blacks the appearance of political rights while guaranteeing white control. Yet, at the time and through St. Clair's lifetime, there is no evidence that any black leaders felt this way.[27]

While St. Clair took pride in the new high school he prodded the city to construct, black schoolchildren in Dorchester County did not receive an equal education. Rather, they attended inferior schools that had a worse teacher-to-pupil ratio than and received only 55 percent of the funding of white schools. Even though there were blacks on the police force, they were unofficially restricted to patrolling the black community. In addition, even elite blacks faced the sting or humiliation of social segregation. For example, the town council dined together before meetings, with the exception of St. Clair. He had food brought to his home and had to dine alone. The black middle class also had to travel to Baltimore to gain adequate health care because the local hospital did not admit them.[28]

Nor was St. Clair able to desegregate the many social institutions and organizations around which much of life in Cambridge revolved. Ironically, according to many observers, one of Cambridge's most endearing qualities was its civic spirit, manifested by numerous voluntary organizations ranging from Elks and Lions clubs to the Eastern Star and American Legion. During World War II, these community organizations rallied Cambridge citizens behind food, blood, and scrap metal drives; afterward, they welcomed home their war heroes in victory parades and celebrations. Cambridge even supported several baseball teams, some of which were affiliated with the minor leagues of major league baseball while others were all-volunteer in makeup. All of these organizations (and teams), including the American Legion, however, were segregated.[29]

The voluntary organization that perhaps best symbolized Cambridge's small-town boosterism and its racial exclusivity was the Volunteer Rescue and Fire Company (RFC). Founded in 1882 by a veteran of the Confederate Army, the Cambridge Rescue and Fire Company took great pride in its record of having doused many potentially calamitous fires, always for free, including three that nearly destroyed the town around the turn of the century. Novelist and Cambridge native John Barth recalled that children learned to call out "Fire whistle, Dad," knowing that their fathers would respond "at all hours of the day and night." (Barth's father, a candy store owner and Orphan's Court judge known as "Whitey," was a longtime member of the force.) When they were not responding to calls, Barth continued, the volunteers busied themselves helping other communities establish their own fire companies.[30]

The RFC maintained an active force of seventy-five. In addition, the company had "exempt" and "honorary" members, who numbered around four hundred in the years following World War II. In addition to fighting fires, the RFC played an important social and political role. In 1955, the fire company built a large indoor arena; three years later it opened an even more impressive swimming pool, the largest to the east of the Mississippi River, according to several local publications. These facilities were open to all classes of members as well as their families. In 1965, the RFC's pool had 2,327 adult members, or approximately one-third to one-half of the city's population. The RFC hosted Halloween parades for Cambridge's white children, and its arena served as the site of the community's annual Outdoor Show, where community members displayed a variety of skills. (Among other things, they competed for the title of fastest muskrat skinner.) The RFC sponsored and/or hosted Cambridge's annual minstrel show, which was held through the mid-1950s. As the *Democrat and News* observed, locals looked forward to this show that brought back "memories of the nation's loveable and carefree days of the Deep South." Recognizing the RFC's prominence, candidates for office routinely courted its endorsement. Several city and county leaders were officers of the RFC before being elected to public office. One federal government report even described the RFC as a local Tammany Hall.[31]

The Rescue and Fire Company remained all-white until the mid-1980s. No law mandated that the RFC exclude blacks. At the same time, no prominent political leader proposed enacting a law that would compel the voluntary organization to desegregate. On one occasion, in the mid-1950s, a black person applied for membership and was rejected. This rejection, on the questionable grounds that the RFC's membership was full, did not produce an outcry from the black community. Charles Cornish, who succeeded St. Clair as the Second Ward's councilman, issued no demands for change, in spite of the fact that the RFC was housed in the same building as City Hall and regularly received funds from the town government to purchase new equipment.[32]

Paradoxically, blacks in Cambridge simultaneously enjoyed close or intimate relationships with whites and were invisible to them during this era. Many, if not most elite and middle-class white families hired black household help. Some of these "maids" had been born in slavery or were the offspring of former house servants. In numerous instances, whites who had grown up in the region observed that their maids were "part of the family." John Barth recalled that he was taught to swim by his "Colored Mattie." Franklin Pierce reminisced fondly about his "Aunt Liza," who was older than his mother and enjoyed the respect of all of the Pierces even after her hundredth birthday.[33]

Yet, blacks were excluded from virtually every social activity in town—with the exception of those held in public spaces, such as the Fourth of July fireworks and Veterans Day and V-J Day parades. Whites assumed that the "Outdoor Show Queen" or "V-Jay Day parade princess" would be white. Likewise, the masters of ceremonies and honorees at these events were never black. Nor did Cambridge's whites ever query their maids about their real feelings. Instead they relied upon minstrels, whites in blackface, to fashion their notions of past and present race relations.

This said, while caste did not disappear during the New South era in Cambridge, the growth of the Phillips Packing Company produced a growing class consciousness that had the potential to override caste barriers, as became evident in 1937 with the eruption of a massive strike. On the morning of June 22, 1937, tin workers spontaneously shut down the company's can-producing plant and then selected a delegation to present their grievances to Theodore Phillips, vice president and son of the co-founder of the corporation. Phillips refused to assure them that the company would address their concerns, so the delegation called upon other workers to walk out. Within a day, between fifteen hundred and two thousand employees, black and white, joined the picket line and issued a set of demands that included a forty-cents-an-hour minimum wage, an eight-hour day, and the right to organize a union. In spite of the divisions between the AFL and CIO, leaders from both federations—Tin Can Makers (AFL) and the United Cannery, Agricultural, Packing and Allied Workers of America (UCAPAWA-CIO)—quickly rushed to Cambridge to offer their aid. Anna Neary of the Maryland state labor federation presided over a meeting that attracted upward of fifteen hundred workers in a field adjoining one of the Phillips Packing Company's plants, where she pledged her backing. Delegates at UCAPAWA's founding convention in Denver (which included one worker from Cambridge) likewise promised their support.[34]

Novelist John Barth, who witnessed this walkout as a boy, described it in *The Last Voyage of Somebody the Sailor*. "The word *pickets*, lately much spoken in our house . . . I associated with the fenced camps of migrant Negroes who picked tomatoes all summer for Albany Brothers [Phillips Packing Company], but the ones we saw now outside the first cannery building, standing in dungareed groups or walking up and down with placards, were white men," Barth wrote. "I was thrilled and frightened. The pickets had beaten workers and truck drivers who had tried to cross their lines. . . . The most pickets were at the main plant entrance, but as it was Sunday, not much was happening there." Over at another plant, Barth continued, was an "overturned tomato truck surrounded by pickets at the foot of the idle Lifter." This machine, which usually conveyed cases of tomatoes from truckbeds to the upper floors of the warehouse, looked like "a gutted elephant." It lay on its side in the hot sunshine, "its ripe load hugely spilled and stinking. Squashed early tomatoes flooded the macadam from shoulder to shoulder; baskets both shattered and intact were scattered everywhere. The truck's windshield panes . . . were smashed into twin webs of cracks, like the eyes of comic-strip characters stunned or killed."[35]

Clashes of this sort occurred all across the nation during the mid-

1930s, revealing the class divisions that existed in America. On many occasions, as was the case in Cambridge, these strikes overcame caste or racial divisions. While exact figures on the racial makeup of the Phillips strikers are unavailable, by all accounts both blacks and whites joined the strike. William Downs and Frederick Jones, two black residents of Cambridge, served on the original negotiating team and later joined the United Cannery workers as organizers. Samuel Le Compte, a veteran truck driver for the Phillips Packing Company, and other white labor activists welcomed Downs and Jones because they saw racial unity as a necessary condition to winning the strike.[36]

Whereas the nationwide wave of unrest gave rise to a vibrant labor movement elsewhere, the Phillips Packing Company easily crushed the strike in Cambridge. While racial divisions had some impact on the outcome, the company's absolute economic and political power proved a far more salient factor. The company courted the support of black councilman H. Maynadier St. Clair by promising secure employment for his constituents if he supported the company. Like Booker T. Washington, St. Clair distrusted unions and sided with the company. While black strikers did not break ranks because of St. Clair's support of the company, neither did they challenge his leadership in upcoming elections. Overnight, National Guard units arrived to protect trucking convoys that shipped Phillips products. Local authorities arrested several leaders of the walkout and convicted them on a variety of trumped-up charges, from drunkenness to disorderly conduct. On the advice of a leading Baltimore law firm and local counsel Laird Henry, Jr., a descendant of one of the nation's revolutionaries, the Phillips Packing Company devised a sophisticated legal and public relations campaign to marginalize the strike leaders and punish those who supported the union. (Henry was subsequently rewarded with a judgeship.) Even though the Phillips Packing Company historically condemned unions, it quickly recognized the Cambridge Workers Association (CWA), which plant supervisors and local merchants established within days of the walkout. After announcing its recognition of the CWA, the company reopened its gates and offered a raise to anyone who would return. Faced with repression in the streets and a rival company union in the plant, strike leaders capitulated, calling off the walkout.[37]

The company exhibited its might in two trials held after the workers returned to work. In one trial, a judge controlled by William Winterbottom, a co-owner of the Phillips Packing Company, found strike leader

Frederick Jones guilty of assaulting a police officer and sentenced him to seven years in prison. In fact, all Jones had done was place a hand on the officer's shoulder to get his attention. In another trial, charges were dismissed against a truck driver who ran over and killed George Cephas, a black picketer. In response to an order issued by the National Labor Relations Board, the Phillips Packing Company disbanded the Cambridge Workers Association, but shortly afterward a new "independent" union appeared. Named the Dorchester County Workers Association, or DORCO, it was also a company union, but Phillips lawyers made it much more difficult to prove this in a court of law. DORCO and the company quickly signed a collective bargaining agreement, which remained in effect throughout the war years.[38]

While the strike was a startling event, it passed quickly, like a summer hailstorm. Local historians made no record of the event, and conventional wisdom held that it had been caused by "outside agitators" who were foreign to the community. Cambridge's *Democrat and News*, for example, explained that the strike was the work of "Communists." Elderly blacks displayed little memory of the event, especially in comparison to their knowledge of other unrecorded developments, such as Harriet Tubman's exploits. Nonetheless, the failure of the strikers to win what so many other workers were winning across the nation—a modicum of decency and respect—left unresolved several key issues that would loom large in years to come. Most important, the defeat of the strike left in place deep class cleavages and resentments. Furthermore, the resolution of the strike via the heavy hand of the Phillips Packing Company raised the possibility that social disorder could accompany the collapse of the company itself. What would happen if the Phillips Packing Company, the agent of social stability and order, disappeared? Could the local elite rally Cambridge citizens around a campaign to rebuild the community's economy or had they forfeited their chance to lead by siding with the Phillips Packing Company during the 1937 strike? And would race relations among black and white workers worsen if they ceased working side by side or at least for the same boss?

The Modern Era

These were not mere academic questions. After World War II the Phillips Packing Company entered a period of decline. No single factor caused this. The company's reputation as a fierce opponent to unions, which resulted in an AFL boycott of Phillips products, diminished sales. But larger changes in the food processing industry, from the introduction of frozen foods to mergers and market consolidations, more directly undermined the company's position. From 1947 to 1963 the number of plants processing canned fruits and vegetables fell 25 percent nationwide. The stronger, more diversified firms survived this restructuring. Others, such as Phillips, saw earnings plummet from a high of $3.64 a share in 1947 to a low of $0.02 a share in 1956. In 1957, Consolidated Foods (now Sara Lee), a diversified food processing, wholesale, and retail establishment headquartered in Chicago, acquired Phillips. Sara Lee consolidated its operations, closing redundant or inefficient plants and expanding other ones. As a result, by 1962, the remnant of the former Phillips Packing Company employed only between two hundred and four hundred people, about one-tenth of the number that had worked in the Phillips plants fifteen years earlier.[39]

Declining profits and sales and a smaller workforce produced a concomitant decrease in the company's political power. In 1950 Frederick Malkus, a native of Cambridge, graduate of the University of Maryland law school, and a World War II veteran, mounted a successful challenge to Winterbottom's control of the Democratic Party, winning a seat in the state senate, a post he held until his retirement in 1995. In his own words, he "beat" Phillips by building a coalition of rural farmers, muskrat hunters, and watermen. As state senator he essentially controlled the appointment of key county officials, the so-called green bag appointments, including the school superintendent and local judges.[40]

At the same time, the Phillips company's decline created among blacks a sense that the political situation was ripe for a challenge to the racial status quo and unleashed latent rivalries within the black community. Such rivalries began to emerge before 1960, as evidenced by the 1958 race for the town council seat of the Second Ward, the most highly contested political election in fifty years. William Downs, one of the black leaders of the 1937 strike, challenged Charles Cornish for the town council seat. Even though Downs lost by a two-to-one margin, he won three times as many votes as he had four years earlier, indicating that his message—that "the Negro in Cambridge is not in focus with the times"—was starting to strike a responsive chord.[41] Malkus's victory and Downs's challenge to Cornish did not signal the total collapse of the Phillips company in the political arena. Yet they suggested that municipal politics was entering a period of transition or flux, a condition critical to the emergence of the civil rights movement.[42]

Economic survival, not political mobilization, however, tended to consume the community, black and white, as the 1950s drew to a close. While *Life* magazine and others celebrated the good life and affluence, the citizens of Cambridge found themselves mired in a bona fide depression. Blacks were particularly hard hit by the company's troubles since it was their main source of employment, especially during the peak canning seasons. Unemployment statistics revealed the severity of the situation. In 1963 the unemployment rates in the city for white males and females stood at 7.3 percent and 7.9 percent, respectively, about twice the national average. The unemployment rates for black males and females was nearly four times as high, at 29.5 percent and 29.3 percent, respectively—and blacks in Cambridge depended upon the wages of women more heavily than did whites. The economic situation was so bad that Dorchester County easily qualified as a distressed area under the federal Area Redevelopment Act, a designation most commonly associated with Appalachia and big city ghettos. To make matters worse, Cambridge was losing its reputation as the "queen city" of the Eastern Shore to Salisbury and Ocean City, Maryland, both of which were benefiting from the completion of the Chesapeake Bay Bridge.[43]

While Gloria Richardson, the granddaughter of Maynadier St. Clair, continued to find work at her family's drugstore, she found little time or opportunity to engage in political activity. Divorced from her first husband and laboring twelve to eighteen hours a day to earn enough money to feed her two daughters, she was too busy to engage in protests in the street. Other black families were in similar circumstances or feared adding their voices to the cry for racial equality, lest they endanger their marginal economic situation. For instance, Charles Cornish, who owned and operated the bus service that transported black children to all-black schools throughout the region, found time to praise the town's reputation for good racial relations, in part because he did not want to jeopardize his business and middle-class status by decrying the racial status quo. Ironically, when he was first elected in 1946, following Maynadier St. Clair's retirement, Cornish was seen as a more aggressive and independent candidate than his opponent, Maynadier's son Herbert. By 1958, however, Cornish had adopted an accommodationist stance like his predecessor, partly because the downturn of the economy made his situation more precarious. Helen Waters, the black representative on the Dorchester County school board, owned a beauty shop that catered to whites and thus, like Cornish, she could not afford to alienate her customers. Perhaps if the economy had been performing better she could have supported herself, as had other black barbers through much of the twentieth century, on the paychecks of Second Ward black residents. But the collapse of Phillips made such an independent course more problematic for Waters and others.[44]

Remarkably, in spite of the economic situation, or perhaps because of it, many of Cambridge's leading citizens remained upbeat. A deep sense of the past contributed to the tremendous faith that the town's leaders had in their ability to rebuild the city. Some local businessmen even saw the decline of the Phillips Packing Company as an opportunity to escape from the iron grip of a single industry, to diversify and prosper economically and socially. In particular, Herman Stevens, Philip Williamson, Don Holdt, and Robert Davis, known locally as the "four horsemen," aggressively pursued every business lead. In sales pitches to potential employers, they argued that the decline of Phillips presented a golden opportunity for industries choosing to locate in Cambridge. The company's collapse, they noted, had created a large class of unemployed and underemployed workers who constituted a ready-made supply of cheap labor. Former Phillips plants could be bought cheaply and converted to meet the needs of their new owners in a fraction of time it would take to construct new plants elsewhere. Cambridge citizens, they added, accustomed to industrial work, would prove far more productive than workers in more rural areas that lacked an industrial tradition. In their sales pitches, the four horsemen also emphasized Cambridge's history of non-unionism and amicable race relations. To drive home this point, they introduced outside business leaders to Charles Cornish and Helen Waters, who assured white businessmen that Cambridge was not like the Deep South. The four pledged that the town's political leaders would do whatever was necessary, from providing tax breaks to improving public infrastructure, to help new businesses prosper. Some of their efforts paid off. Bumble Bee Tuna, Chung King, and other food processors moved into spaces vacated by Phillips, with expectations of expansion in the near future. Nearly two decades later, when much of the nation faced a similar situation, *Maryland Magazine* revisited the history of the four horsemen to show how "economic teamwork" could overcome seemingly insurmountable adversity.[45]

Yet neither the four horsemen nor Cornish recognized the extent to which racial calm depended on the existence of the Phillips Packing Company. With Phillips gone, what would maintain the old social order? Would blacks accommodate themselves to caste restrictions forever? Would working- and lower-class whites, who had long seen their political and economic aspirations limited by the company, use its demise as an opportunity to vent their class frustrations? And if protests erupted, would new businesses be able to restore order with the ease that Phillips had in 1937?

To complicate matters further, the decline of the Phillips Packing Company coincided with a dramatic shift in the relationship between Cambridge and the surrounding region. The construction of the Chesapeake Bay Bridge shifted Cambridge's spatial boundaries, rapidly integrating it into the megalopolis of the mid-Atlantic states. Had it not been for this shift, the movement in Cambridge might not have taken place, or it would probably have taken place at a different time and in a different manner than it did.[46]

"Until just recently," local historian John Wennersten writes, "the Eastern Shore was one of the most geographically isolated regions" in the nation. "It was difficult to get to and difficult to leave." Over the years the region attracted few migrants, grew slowly, and matured as a separate society. Most residents traced their roots to the colonial migration from England or Ireland or to the African slave trade. The residents of the Eastern Shore retained a strong provincialism, a distaste for government intervention, and a rugged individualism, partly due to their work as fishermen, oyster dredgers, small farmers, and muskrat hunters.[47]

Many communities across America shared Cambridge's provincialism. But modernity came to these communities gradually. In Cambridge it arrived in an unusual hurry. In the 1930s, the Choptank River, which separated Dorchester County from the upper Eastern Shore, was spanned for the first time by the Harrington Bridge. The completion of the bridge was such a significant event that President Franklin D. Roosevelt attended its dedication ceremony, sailing to Cambridge in his presidential yacht, the *Sequoia*. Prior to the completion of the bridge, a trip to Easton, about fifteen miles to the north, necessitated a whole day's outing. "When we went to Cambridge [from Easton]," recalled Bill Newhouse, "we would take our lunch."[48]

Twenty-two years later the Chesapeake Bay Bridge was completed, an event that had an even more dramatic impact on the region, ending its isolation. For centuries, Cambridge had been cut off from the cities of the mid-Atlantic seacoast. One could reach the cities only by boat, ferry, or the long circuitous overland drive. The Chesapeake Bay Bridge placed Cambridge within easy reach of students from tens of colleges and universities, reporters and photographers who worked for the biggest and most influential newspapers and magazines in the nation, and governmental officials, who now saw the Eastern Shore as their backyard. Long a remote and provincial town, Cambridge suddenly became the neighbor of Washington, D.C., Philadelphia, New York, and Baltimore.

In addition, Cambridge natives and people from nearby eastern seaboard cities and suburbs, reared in different environments, held vastly different worldviews. Many Eastern Shoresmen saw Cambridge as a hub of activity and modernity. In the 1920s Cambridge "was the undisputed queen city of the entire Eastern Shore," Philip Wingate reminisced. It had a fairground, a professional baseball park (class D), railroad and bus depots, two newspapers, a hospital, poolroom, three hotels, two movie houses, a bowling alley, two brothels, and an assortment of eating places. Steeped in local history, natives in the region knew that Cambridge was the home of two recent governors, Phillips Lee Goldsborough and Emerson Harrington, and the favored retreat of the DuPonts and other distinguished Americans.

Yet if Cambridge natives viewed their home as a center of hustle and bustle, outsiders saw Cambridge differently. Coming from communities where movie theaters, restaurants, and bowling alleys were unexceptional, they arrived in Cambridge with a predisposed disdain for its residents. The residents, whites in particular, long isolated from the outside world, did not take easily to criticism or calls for change. Perceiving themselves as progressives, they tended to take on a fortress mentality, walling themselves off from outsiders, whom they reflexively dismissed as ill informed. To a degree, some blacks shared this provincial mentality. They took pride in their local establishments and leaders and felt they lived in a relatively progressive community compared to the Deep South.[49]

Exceptions to this rule were often those who had spent time outside Cambridge and recognized the limitations of their hometown. Richardson had attended Howard University during the 1940s and traveled to Canada with her mother, where she experienced a sense of freedom that was unknown in Cambridge or Washington, D.C. Enez Grubb, who along with Richardson co-chaired the Cambridge Nonviolent Action Committee (CNAC), spent several years in San Francisco, perhaps the most cosmopolitan city in nation during the 1950s. She also regularly worked at her aunt's beach home on the New Jersey shore.[50]

Still, the construction of the Bay Bridge did not cause the civil rights movement in Cambridge. Rather, it helped create conditions under which that movement was more likely to emerge. Oblivious to the ways in which the collapse of Phillips and the construction of the Bay Bridge were setting the scene for a challenge to the racial status quo, the town's white leaders erected a sign on Route 50 at the town line boasting, "Cambridge isn't just any place, it's a place making progress." Picking up on this theme in a special news show produced in 1960, America's two most famous newscasters, Chet Huntley and David Brinkley, termed Cambridge a "model city" in terms of race relations. Whether it could retain this reputation remained to be seen.[51]

2

The Freedom Rides and the Birth of CNAC

> It has been reported that "until the outsiders came to Cambridge the colored people were satisfied." I ask, "satisfied" with what? The truth is that we have never been satisfied and unrest has been mounting for several years. . . . Something or someone was needed to stir the people to action and move them to reveal that dissatisfaction. The inspiration was brought by the first rally of the Freedom Rides.
> **Reverend John Ringold (1962)**

> They [protesters] are doing something that our people should have done 100 years ago. Some day our children will be able to say, "I wish my father could have lived as I do."
> **James Shields (1962)**

When the 1960s began, there was little evidence that Cambridge was about to embark on the most tumultuous period in its long history or that it would earn a reputation as a bastion of racial turmoil, a Bunker Hill or Gettysburg of sorts in the fight for civil rights. Hardly any discussion took place in Cambridge in 1960 or 1961 of civil rights protests in nearby Princess Anne and Salisbury or across the bay in Baltimore. Nor did the wave of massive resistance that swept across the South in the wake of the *Brown* decision inspire whites in Cambridge to establish their own branch of the Citizens' Council or the Ku Klux Klan. On the contrary, both blacks and whites appeared committed to pursuing a moderate course.[1]

The local mayoral election and the 1960 presidential election, highlighted by an inspiring visit by John F. Kennedy, suggested unity of purpose—a desire to rejuvenate Cambridge's stagnating economy, not to alter radically the racial status quo. As in other communities, Kennedy attracted large crowds of well-wishers and the curious. Attacking Eisenhower's environmental record, Kennedy pledged to help clean up the Choptank River, to the delight of many local residents who depended upon its products for a livelihood. All local Democratic politicians, who controlled nearly every office, strongly backed their nominee. For instance, describing Nixon and the Republicans as the "Party of property," Congressman Thomas Johnson declared that the choice was to "go forward or stand still." Johnson's Republican opponent sought to scare voters away from supporting the Democratic ticket by warning that "Big Labor," which was allied with Kennedy, "has moved to the shore." But these scare tactics failed miserably. Kennedy won the majority of votes in Cambridge in the general election, as did the entire Democratic ticket.[2]

In the 1960 mayoral election, Calvin Mowbray, a former president of the chamber of commerce and an officer with Consolidated Food, easily defeated Osvrey Pritchett, a plumbing supplier and a former chief of the Rescue and Fire Company. Mowbray did so by promising to build on the efforts of Cambridge's business elite, which as noted had embarked on a campaign to recruit new industries to the region. At no point did either Mowbray or his opponent suggest that racial strife would hamper economic revival. On the contrary, Mowbray, who won the vast majority of the black votes, presumed that Cambridge's progressive reputation on racial matters would play a key role in attracting new businesses to the region.[3]

The decision of several firms to locate in Cambridge as well as the optimistic spirit that swept the nation following Kennedy's inauguration added to the sense that the 1960s marked the beginning of a new era. The *Cambridge Daily Banner* reported in its end-of-year issue: "By almost any barometer, 1961 was a good year for the community. Unemployment was down. New industries produced new jobs. Retail merchants rang up record sales." Moreover, the paper continued, "the prospect of exciting growth faced the community" with an "expanded port, more industrial plants, dualization of Route 50, a city beltway." Nowhere did this year-end review mention civil rights or racial problems in Cambridge; indeed, the editors consistently contrasted their community with those of the Deep South.[4]

Further evidence of the good relations between the races came in the form of two separate appearances by African dignitaries. In June 1961, W. M. Q. Halm of Ghana spoke at Cambridge's Independent BPO Elks lodge (the black equivalent of the white Elks lodge) and attended a reception at the Waugh Church. Halm was greeted warmly by members of the black community, and the local newspaper reported favorably on his visit. Five months later, Roosevelt Burlington, the first secretary of the

Liberian embassy, spoke at a Harriet Tubman Day observance at Mace Lane High School. In attendance were Charles Cornish, Calvin Mowbray, and other black and white professionals who offered their warm welcome to the African leader. (Liberia's ambassador was supposed to appear but did not because he had to attend a function at the United Nations.) Ironically, as 1961 drew to a close, no one in Cambridge, black or white, knew that freedom rides bearing their town's name were already being organized by the Civic Interest Group of Baltimore and a loose network of other civil rights groups.[5]

The Freedom Rides

Cambridge became a primary site of the civil rights movement in part by accident and in part due to regional events beyond its control, including the refusal by restaurants in another section of Maryland to serve several African diplomats. Not long after President Kennedy took office, Adam Malik Sow, the ambassador from the Republic of Chad, one of several newly independent African nations, informed Kennedy that he had been evicted from a Maryland restaurant while en route from the United Nations in New York City to Washington, D.C. In response to this incident, and others like it involving African diplomats, the Civic Interest Group of Baltimore (CIG) and the Congress of Racial Equality (CORE) called for sit-ins or freedom rides to protest against discrimination along Route 40, which connected Baltimore to the Northeast. The goal of CIG and CORE was to pressure Governor J. Millard Tawes into calling a special session of the Maryland legislature to enact a statewide public accommodations measure. They also sought to prompt the Kennedy administration to intervene.[6]

CORE had gained national notoriety in the spring of 1961 by orchestrating freedom rides through the Deep South. In contrast, CIG, which had engaged in direct action protests against segregated establishments in Baltimore as far back as the early 1950s, was relatively unknown. Drawing primarily on black students from Morgan State College and a handful of white students from Johns Hopkins University and Goucher College, CIG had desegregated numerous businesses at the Northwood Shopping Center in Baltimore by the time that Sow was refused service.[7] Students from Philadelphia, Pennsylvania, and Washington, D.C., some of whom belonged to the National Student Movement (NSM) or the National Action Group (NAG) of the Student Nonviolent Coordinating Committee

(SNCC), shared CIG's and CORE's determination to demonstrate against racial discrimination along Route 40. In mid-July of 1961, CIG sponsored a national meeting of SNCC in Baltimore, where luminaries such as Martin Luther King, Jr., James Farmer, and Ella Baker spoke. While SNCC did not emerge from the meeting with a consensus over what type of program to undertake on a national level, the conference reinforced the desire of local activists to conduct direct action protests against segregated public accommodations.[8]

Demonstrations along Route 40 began in the summer of 1961 and continued to take place on a sporadic basis through the fall and early winter. Deeply embarrassed by the treatment of Sow and concerned about the damage that protests along Route 40 were doing to America's image abroad, the Kennedy administration pressured businesses in the region to desegregate their facilities. At the same time, Maryland's Governor Tawes agreed to promote a statewide public accommodations measure that would outlaw such discrimination. Rather than appeasing Tawes's administration by suspending the rides, CIG trained its sights on public facilities along Route 50, another main thoroughfare in the state, connecting the capital, Annapolis, to cities on the Eastern Shore.[9]

CIG's Eastern Shore rides began in Crisfield, hometown of Governor Tawes, and Salisbury, the locale of an infamous lynching in the 1930s. The protests in Salisbury prompted the town's white leaders to establish an Equal Opportunity Commission, which in turn pressured restaurants to desegregate. In Crisfield, several CIG members were arrested and charged with trespassing. CIG spokesman and Morgan State student Walter Dean declared that the demonstrators sought to awaken "the moral conscience of Maryland's citizens." Ten civil rights activists spent Christmas day in Crisfield's jail. While incarcerated, Frederick St. Clair, a bail bondsman from Cambridge and a cousin of Gloria Richardson, suggested that the group consider investigating the racial situation in Cambridge. Two of the activists, William Hansen and Reginald Robinson, agreed to do so.[10]

Robinson, who was black, had attended a business school and was a resident of Baltimore. In the late fall of 1960, he was selected as CIG's representative to SNCC. By early 1962, he had earned a reputation as one of the stalwarts of the civil rights movement, having participated in the original freedom rides and having served as one of the first volunteers in the legendary voter education campaign Robert Moses conducted in McComb, Mississippi. SNCC advisor Howard Zinn described Robinson as "slim, dark, [and] animatedly cheerful." Like Moses, Robinson gained from his experience in McComb a "strategy of action capable of sustaining a social struggle among black people who faced enormous obstacles with few resources," writes SNCC historian Clayborne Carson. This strategy emphasized developing indigenous leaders and a brashly militant style that set SNCC apart from the NAACP and the organization spearheaded by Martin Luther King, Jr., the Southern Christian Leadership Conference (SCLC).[11]

Hansen was a twenty-two-year-old white student from Xavier University in Cincinnati, Ohio. A veteran of the 1961 freedom rides, he was deeply committed to the philosophy of nonviolence. Howard Zinn, the author of the first study of SNCC and the editor of the *Baltimore Afro-American*, described him as a "new abolitionist." Hansen's first involvement in the civil rights movement came while he was still a student at Xavier, when he was evicted from his off-campus apartment after his landlord discovered that his roommate was black. Rather than comply with the landlord's order to vacate the premises, Hansen staged a "stay-in," resisting eviction much as "sit-inners" had refused to get up from their lunch-counter stools. Hansen detailed his philosophy in an essay he wrote while on an eleven-day hunger strike in an Annapolis prison. Observing that Dostoevsky and Gandhi advocated nonviolence, Hansen argued that individuals should refuse to cooperate with evil. Recent events, including World War II, Hansen emphasized, left nonviolence as the only option for addressing the world's problems. In a subsequent trial for trespassing, Hansen further displayed his unorthodox views. When the state's attorney asked him if he was Negro or white, Hansen replied that he did not know. He only knew he was part of the human race.[12]

On Saturday, January 6, 1962, following CIG-sponsored demonstrations in Easton, Maryland, Hansen and Robinson took up residence with Herbert St. Clair at 317 High Street in Cambridge. Over the course of the next few days, the St. Clairs arranged for Robinson and Hansen to meet with representatives of Cambridge's Equal Opportunity Commission and the town council. During these meetings, town officials, including Charles Cornish, sought to convince Hansen and Robinson that protests were unnecessary because Cambridge enjoyed good race relations. Drawing on information provided by the St. Clairs, Hansen and Robinson retorted that black policemen could not arrest whites without special permission. They noted that even though a plan existed to desegregate, as of

1962 no blacks had attended any of the white schools. When the council members proclaimed that Cambridge's main restaurants served both blacks and whites, Hansen and Robinson countered that in fact, only five of eighteen did so. In addition, Robinson and Hansen labeled the EOC a fraud because one of its members, a factory owner, refused to employ blacks. They also observed that Cornish could not even remember the names of the EOC's members or when last it had met.[13]

Robinson and Hansen met separately with Edythe Jolley, the black principal of the all-black Mace Lane High School. She informed them that "everything is fine" and argued there was no reason to "disturb the situation" in Cambridge. Robinson and Hansen privately recorded that "Uncle Tom" and "Aunt Jane" failed to persuade them to call off the freedom rides. Arguably this depiction of Jolley and Cornish was unfair. In the previous six months, both had met with county officials to promote a new recreation program in the Second Ward; participated in the aforementioned Harriet Tubman observation; and prodded the town council to apply for a federal grant to build public housing. Still, their assertions that everything was fine did not mesh with what other black leaders in Cambridge had been telling the two visitors.[14]

In a final attempt to convince Hansen and Robinson to cancel protests planned for the second Saturday of January, Cambridge's Equal Opportunity Commission issued a report, its first ever. The report described various steps the EOC had taken to resolve "human relations problems" peacefully in the community. For instance, the report noted that Calvin Harrington, one of the most prominent political leaders in town, had recently joined the commission. In a display of support for the EOC and opposition to the planned protests, the *Daily Banner* and *Democrat and News* published the text of the EOC's report and praised its efforts. Neither paper, however, described contentious meetings between Hansen and Robinson and the EOC and town council or mentioned the shortcomings of the commission.[15]

Nor did the local papers note that Douglas Sands, the executive secretary of Maryland's Commission on Interracial Problems and Relations, had met with Mayor Mowbray, Cornish, CIG leaders Clarence Logan and Clifton Henry, and several others. The purpose of the meeting was to negotiate a settlement similar to one agreed to by Salisbury, whereby Cambridge's sister city had established a biracial human relations commission rather than risk further demonstrations. Unlike in Salisbury, however, Cambridge's officials refused to pledge themselves to such a reform. As a result, CIG went ahead with plans to stage protests in Cambridge.[16]

On Saturday, January 13, 1962, approximately one hundred activists participated in Cambridge's first civil rights demonstrations. After congregating at Waugh Church, they marched two abreast to the downtown area and then sought to use various facilities in and around Cambridge in a desegregated manner. Many carried signs, such as one reading: "This place is segregated. We are hungry for civil rights." Among the establishments tested were Collins Drugstore, two popular white student hangouts, the Cambria, the RFC's recreation center, and the Choptank Inn. In the evening, following the sit-ins, a mass meeting was held at Waugh Church, where the demonstrators sang freedom songs and pledged to return the following week.[17]

A little over half of the protesters, whom the *Daily Banner* dubbed "freedom raiders," attended Maryland State College, one of the state's historically black colleges in Princess Anne, or were members of CIG. The other half lived in Cambridge. While a majority of participants were black, a number were young whites who shared the CIG, SNCC, and CORE vision of creating an interracial movement and society. In a confidential report to SNCC headquarters, Reginald Robinson and William Hansen described the scene:

> The streets of Cambridge were lined with a great many jeering whites. Negroes also crowded the streets. . . . A number of incidents happened all over the downtown area. Picketers were shoved and jostled quite frequently. The most serious incident happened at the Choptank Inn. Bill [Hansen] and another demonstrator were the only two who got inside the restaurant. On the outside . . . a crowd of about 150 very hostile whites gathered. Approximately fifty near hysterical people were on the inside. . . . The mob on the inside converged on Bill and started beating him. He was thrown bodily out of the door. He got up and entered the restaurant again. This time he was knocked down again, and kicked out of the door. When he tried to enter a third time, he was again knocked down. At this juncture he was arrested for disorderly conduct, by a state policemen who had been standing nearby watching the entire proceeding.[18]

Even more than Robinson and Hansen, who had been battle-toughened by their involvement in protests in the Deep South, freedom riders from Baltimore were shocked by the violence they encountered. While they had experienced years of resistance in their struggle to desegregate establishments in Baltimore, Cambridge seemed like a "little Georgia," to borrow the words of Cliff Durand, a John Hopkins University student. "Probably the most rabid Negro-haters in Maryland reside in the Eastern Shore," explained Walter Dean to his fellow Morgan State students in the college newspaper. "The deeply-rooted hatred burst its bounds and thrust its ugly head" in response to the first sit-ins, "proving that the Shore is the citadel of race-hate," Dean added. Echoing the judgment H. L. Mencken had reached following two infamous lynchings during the 1930s, Durand stated that Cambridge was simply a "different world."[19]

Steeped in the belief that their town had a history of progressive race relations, Cambridge's leaders blamed everybody but themselves for the turmoil. Mayor Mowbray railed at "outside agitators" for stirring up trouble. The *Cambridge Daily Banner* and *Democrat and News* described Hansen as a "professional integrationist" who had no knowledge of the town's progressive racial record. The newspapers repeated the EOC's list of Cambridge's "accomplishments" and warned that the protesters "jeopardized . . . four decades of biracial progress." The Reverend Richard C. Hubbard, of Grace Methodist Church, complained that the freedom riders "sent children to do a man's work." Police Chief Brice Kinnamon protested that "youngsters were used to picket beer joints." Cambridge's Ministerial Association, which included ten whites and four blacks, proclaimed that while they considered racial discrimination to be "morally wrong" and upheld the "right of protest," they disapproved of the timing and method of these protests. The ministers also pleaded with CIG to call off demonstrations planned for the following weekend. Nowhere did local elites acknowledge that Hansen and Robinson had met with the EOC or that the two had effectively rebutted the city council's claims. Clarence Logan, of CIG, responded to the ministers' plea by decrying the "un-Christian" attitudes of those who tolerated racism and by making clear that on January 20 demonstrations would take place.[20]

The warm reception that the riders received in the black community suggested that race relations were not as good as community leaders often presumed. It cast doubt on the claim that the protests were caused (rather than stimulated) by outsiders. Approximately three hundred men and women attended a mass meeting at Waugh Church on the evening of the first rides. An enthralled Robinson reported: "These people had their mind on the prize." On the Monday following the first rides, scores of students from the all-black Mace Lane High School walked out of their afternoon classes to attend the riders' court hearings. Even though high school officials suspended three of the students, fourteen black students demonstrated with Hansen and Robinson at Dizzyland and Collins Drugstore. Similarly, in spite of a warning issued by administrators, a sizable contingent of Maryland State College students joined these demonstrations. After "testing" various restaurants, the protesters and many adult supporters convened for a mass meeting at the Bethel AME Church.[21]

The following day, at 5:00 P.M., about three hundred men and women gathered at St. Luke's AME Church, where they established the Cambridge Nonviolent Action Committee, CNAC for short, pronounced "C-nack." With Reggie Robinson presiding, the assembly expressed support for the protests and desire for further actions. Two young adults, Frederick St. Clair and Enez Grubb, both Cambridge natives, were elected co-chairs of CNAC. Gretchen Cephas, Marcie Banks, Dr. J. E. Fascett, and Herbert St. Clair assumed the roles of adult advisors.[22]

On Saturday, January 20, CIG conducted its second freedom ride in Cambridge. In organizing the rides, CIG drew on a broad network of student and adult activists from Baltimore and other eastern seaboard communities. Students and nonstudents who belonged to CIG, local chapters of CORE, SNCC, and the Northern Student Movement flocked to Cambridge, in part because of its relative proximity and because of their desire to make a personal statement against racial discrimination. Penny Patch, for instance, a freshman at Swarthmore College, journeyed to Cambridge along with busloads of other students, most of them white, from Swarthmore, Haverford, and Bryn Mawr Colleges. She was recruited to take part in the protests by black students from several predominantly black schools in the region, such as Lincoln College and Howard University. The force of the movement "was electrifying," Patch recalled. "I can remember the . . . sense that we were doing something important, and we were doing it together, black and white." Patch and other volunteers returned to college on the Monday morning following the rides and an overnight spell in the Cambridge jail. For some, like Patch, going to Cambridge marked the beginning of a full-time commitment to the movement. For others, Cambridge proved one of their only experiences with direct action protest.[23]

Violence erupted again on January 20 at the Choptank Inn, one of the targets of the freedom rides. After Hansen entered the establishment, a white mob kicked him into unconsciousness. When he regained his wits, the mob shoved him through a glass door, knocking him unconscious a second time. Then police arrested him for trespassing. Gifford Pinchot, the grandson of the famous progressive conservationist, was also assaulted by the white mob and arrested by police.[24]

Unlike in the Deep South, police and state troopers, although slow to act, ultimately intervened and arrested some of the white assailants. To the absolute befuddlement of the state's attorney, the magistrate, and the alleged assailants, however, Hansen and Pinchot refused to testify, thus compelling the state to drop its charges. Since he did not understand Hansen's goal of transforming the hearts of his assailants, State Attorney C. Burnham Mace questioned Hansen's motives. In spite of "previous experience and in the face of direct advice as to what he [Hansen] might encounter," Mace remarked, Hansen entered the Choptank Inn. This "leads one to wonder if peaceful integration . . . is any part of his real aim."[25]

While the rides had little impact on the town's commercial facilities—none desegregated—they had a considerable impact on local blacks. A moribund branch of the NAACP, headed by the Reverend Theasdar M. Murray, Reverend John Ringold, Mrs. Clementine Griffin, and Dr. Edwin Fascett, was revived. More moderate than CNAC, its leaders tended to be more middle class and older than those of CNAC. Like the NAACP on the national level, the NAACP in Cambridge favored using legal channels as opposed to direct action protest to effect change. Temperamentally, the local NAACP leaders were more conservative than those of CNAC or SNCC, especially Hansen and Robinson. Its members felt less comfortable offending white moderates, whom they saw as potential allies. The local NAACP refrained from criticizing Cornish, Edythe Jolley, and Helen Waters, three of the town's black leaders, while CNAC tended to air disagreements with these gradualists. As already suggested, most of the black ministers in Cambridge, some of whom were members of the NAACP, opposed the freedom rides, calling instead for "calmness and Christian tolerance."[26]

Nonetheless, CIG leaders were so impressed by the "size and momentum" of the local movement and the vigor Cambridge natives displayed, factional differences and all, that they chose not to bus in outsiders for a third freedom ride during the first week of February. Instead, the CIG leaders turned their attention to other communities on the Eastern Shore. Hansen and Robinson spent much of the late winter and early spring of 1962 organizing and/or participating in demonstrations elsewhere. They regularly traveled to Princess Anne, Easton, and Salisbury. They joined NAACP president Roy Wilkins in a pilgrimage in Annapolis to pressure the state legislature to enact a statewide public accommodations law. Along with CIG and several NAG members they staged a sit-in at the Justice Department in Washington, D.C., to protest the mistreatment of several of their colleagues in Louisiana and the inaction of the federal government. Even if CIG had chosen to conduct more freedom rides in Cambridge, it would have been difficult because of an unusually ferocious March snowstorm. As Hansen put it, "If you leave your house you might not find your way back for a week." Certainly, freedom riders in the Deep South did not have to contend with such a deterrent.[27]

Mobilizing Community Resources

Although the local civil rights movement appeared to have sprung out of thin air, in fact it had built on several long-term developments, nearly all of which resulted from the close-knit character of Cambridge's black community. To use the jargon of social scientists, the civil rights movement in Cambridge mobilized resources accumulated during the pre–civil rights years. As noted, blacks in Cambridge knew one another by sight and knew who lived, worked, and worshiped where. They lived in close proximity to one another in about ten to fifteen city blocks, and many were interrelated. Lemuel Chester, one of the young civil rights leaders, recalled: "We were family . . . we were community." Such personal interconnections made the organization of protests easier than in more impersonal urban areas. Even many southern cities, such as Birmingham and Atlanta, had experienced a mass influx of newcomers during the middle decades of the twentieth century and thus were not as tightly bound together as Cambridge was.[28]

The intimacy of the black experience in Cambridge was reinforced by the fact that blacks interacted at school, in church, and in black places of business along Pine Street. Even on occasions when blacks and whites shared a common space, blacks were still not treated equally. They were physically separated from whites in movie theaters and received separate and inferior treatment in downtown drugstores. For example, Enez Grubb recalled being served out of a paper cup at Collins Drugstore while the white patrons drank their ice cream sodas out of fancy glasses.[29]

Black churches played an important role too, particularly by establishing a foundation upon which the civil rights movement could build. African-American churches in Cambridge fostered a sense of community identity, pride, and dignity as well as interpersonal contacts, all necessary prerequisites to community activism. The very existence of African-American churches stood as a constant reminder of the decision that blacks had made to separate themselves from those who failed to live up to their egalitarian rhetoric and theology. Members of the AME Church, for instance, knew that Richard Allen had founded the church in protest against white bigotry. Furthermore, they knew that the AME Church had adopted a socially activist mission, one dedicated to the betterment of the black community. Black churches created the space where black women could develop both self-confidence and political experience (broadly defined), otherwise off-limits to them; and they drew upon these experiences during the civil rights years. As Sunday school teachers, members of the choir, and unofficial caretakers for the elderly, sick, and bereaved, black women gained important organizational skills and respect. In addition, churches themselves offered blacks a physical place to assemble.

At the same time, most of CNAC's members felt that black churches had serious limitations or shortcomings. Black churches in Cambridge tended to favor a gradualist doctrine, at least in terms of secular matters. Rather than risk antagonizing white moderates, church leaders had historically accommodated themselves to what they perceived as the realities of segregation. As indicated, the arrival of the freedom rides did not automatically alter this position. Gloria Richardson and others recall that Cambridge's preachers felt uneasy with direct action protest. They did not want to risk the "goodwill" of white moderates. In addition, a number of church leaders distanced themselves from the budding civil rights movement because their livelihood depended upon whites. At times, Cambridge's most prominent black churches closed their doors to CNAC or sought to dampen its efforts. For instance, on one occasion, Reverend T. Murray, who was not a member of CNAC, tried to take over a mass meeting. William Hansen recalled that in response, an older woman who was a member of the church "got up and told him to shut up and sit down." He did. Black churches also limited the effectiveness or reach of the civil rights movement because blacks belonged to different denominations and not all blacks were churchgoers (a good number were considered "sinners" by the church hierarchy).[30]

Wanting to mobilize a mass movement not limited by denominational divisions and rivalries or restricted to churchgoers, CNAC sought to transcend the black church. When CNAC held meetings in churches, loudspeaker systems were set up outside to reach overflow crowds and reach out to the "sinners" who felt unwelcome in the churches. CNAC even used an underground network of informants to watch preachers to make sure that they were not making secret deals with the white establishment.[31] At the same time, CNAC drew on church traditions and assets to strengthen the movement. At mass meetings and during marches activists sang tunes they had learned in church or that had gospel origins. Quite often women who participated in church choirs took the lead in singing these freedom songs. "Everyone sang," recalled Penny Patch, and "the songs bound us together and made us strong." During one of the first freedom rides, a large mob of whites surrounded the black and white demonstrators. The mob "gathered around us, screaming, waving baseball bats," and threw things at demonstrators trying to walk in a peaceful circle around a restaurant that catered to whites only. "I was scared," Patch stated. "But I also drew enormous strength from the song we sang."[32]

Even though Cambridge was not home to a college campus, as were many other sites of the civil rights movement—Greensboro, North Carolina; Albany, Georgia; Montgomery, Alabama—and thus could not depend on students and faculty to sustain a movement, Cambridge did benefit from its proximity to numerous colleges in the region, as earlier noted. Black students from Maryland State College regularly participated in protests in Cambridge. One Maryland State student, John Wilson, spent about a year in Cambridge before focusing his efforts on building a movement in Princess Anne. Wilson ultimately became one of the leaders of SNCC and a city councilman in Washington, D.C. On the eve of the first freedom rides, Lawrence Cundiff, head of the Student Appeal for Equality Committee (SAEC) at Maryland State and a participant in one of SNCC's founding meetings, pledged his support for the rides. Maryland State's student body president James Phipps initially helped Cundiff organize student support for the demonstrations. While school administrators blocked Hansen and Robinson from addressing the student body of Maryland State, they did not otherwise prevent Cundiff from rallying student support behind the actions in Cambridge. (Helen Waters's father was a dean at Maryland State College. He shared her accommodationist approach to attaining racial reforms.)[33]

The Cambridge Nonviolent Action Committee depended on community institutions and connections to organize protests, to provide lessons from the past, and to pressure community members to support to the movement. The "grapevine," which operated via common hangouts like barber shops, beauty salons, and pool halls as well as by telephone, was used for advertising upcoming actions. One activist described the grapevine as "remarkably fast and accurate." Black elders helped tutor younger activists on the history of the struggle. As one student recalled, "older people told you folk tales from slavery." Still other adults acted as spies, following blacks who acted as informants for whites. When young mothers participated in demonstrations, they turned to their elderly relatives to watch their children. In a community in which individuals did not know one another neither the grapevine nor the spying or unofficial babysitting arrangements would have worked well.[34]

The tight-knit nature of the black community also made it easier to stress the communitarian goals of the movement. Conducting a survey of the needs and attitudes of Cambridge's blacks, three Swarthmore students were impressed by the "inclusiveness and unity of the 2nd Ward." When in response to one of the survey questions an eighth grade student asked what socialism was, and was informed that it meant people sharing, the eighth grader responded: "That's like up on Park Lane. When someone does not have, everybody gives. And if you have, everybody comes around to help himself."[35]

Cambridge's relatively large black business class, although not wealthy, served as another important resource. For some, like the St. Clairs, economic independence made political activism possible (although not necessary). A degree of economic independence allowed other blacks to support the movement in subtle ways. Dr. Fascett, the community's only black doctor, lent financial support to CNAC and, because of his stature in the black community, attracted others to the movement and reinforced the sense that they were doing the right thing. Other black business people privately provided funds for bail and other costs of the movement. Black-controlled institutions, like the Elks, provided a further resource that the movement utilized. When several black churches closed their doors in response to CNAC's increasingly militant tactics, CNAC used the Elks' auditorium. When they were thrown in jail, demonstrators could turn to Cambridge's own black bail bondsmen for help. (Bail also came from the NAACP, particularly its Baltimore branch.)[36]

The existence of a large number of black veterans and the knowledge that blacks had distinguished themselves as soldiers served as another building block of the movement in Cambridge. Montro Curtis Askins, a Cambridge native, was a member of the elite Tuskegee airmen who, like Jackie Robinson, Jesse Owens, and other black entertainers, helped break down stereotypes about black inferiority. His brother, Kermit Quitman Askins, spent most of World War II overseas, including a stint in Japan after the war ended. Upon Montro's return, he took his nieces and nephews to V-J Day parades in Cambridge, where black veterans like himself had the opportunity to demonstrate pride in their service and accomplishments. Numerous younger activists had fathers and uncles who had served in World War II, the Korean War, or both. Yet pride was often mixed with anger because of the community's failure to change. One black veteran recalled: "There was a lot of resentment on my part. I had served in World War II overseas and when we came home we had difficulty getting GI loans. I knew white vets were building homes with nothing down," he emphasized, and "black vets couldn't get a loan at any bank." Exceptionally high unemployment, the collapse of the Phillips Packing Company, continuing caste barriers, and shoddy housing in the Second Ward added to the black veterans' anger and sense of betrayal.[37]

Somewhat paradoxically, the close-knit nature of the black community in Cambridge had the potential to mute protest. It was more difficult for those who favored radical change to censure those who did not because they all shared close and at times familial ties. Publicly criticizing Cornish and Jolley, for instance, was difficult for those who regularly interacted with them in church and on the streets. Not surprisingly, it was Hansen and Robinson, not natives of Cambridge, who tended to term Cornish an "Uncle Tom."[38]

As in several other communities, young blacks stood at the forefront of the rebellion against the racial status quo. Donna Richardson, Gloria Richardson's daughter, mobilized high school students in support of the first freedom rides. Other youths, like Lemuel Chester, Dinez White, and Dwight Cromwell, were unwilling to accommodate themselves to the slow pace of change. Lists of those arrested during the initial freedom rides displayed the willingness of youths to take the lead. As a group, black youths defied parental fears, hoping that their elders would follow them. In a few instances, white youths participated alongside black youths in protesting against racial inequality. Edward Dickerson, a young white native from Cambridge, was evicted from his home and threatened with being committed to a mental institution for taking part in a sit-in. CNAC requested legal advice from the NAACP to see what protection it could offer Dickerson from such threats, and the NAACP responded that Dickerson's parents could not lock him up.[39]

The town's white leaders routinely railed at CNAC for enlisting the support of juveniles. In reference to one of the freedom rides, the *Daily Banner* declared: "The saddest of Saturday's events" was the fact that the young were being "brainwashed" into participating in actions that their parents did not favor. The fault with this analysis was that black youths did not need to be bribed or tricked into participating. On the contrary, they were often much more willing to engage in direct action protest than were their parents.[40]

The leadership provided by Cambridge's most prominent black family, the St. Clairs, proved crucial. As noted, the St. Clairs' relative wealth and the fact that they operated businesses that depended largely on black customers freed them from white economic pressure. In contrast, town councilman Charles Cornish and school board representative Helen Waters ran businesses that catered to whites and depended on white patronage, a bus service and beauty parlor, respectively. Still, the St. Clairs did not have to step forward and assume a leadership role. Their decision to do so grew out of their desire to be treated as equal human beings and their sense of responsibility to give something back to the black community. Paradoxically, the St. Clairs may have gained additional support in the early 1960s because none of them held political office at the time, and they thus could not be blamed for any of the contemporary troubles. Some may even have romanticized Maynadier St. Clair's reign and reasoned that a return of the St. Clairs to political power would lead to better times.[41]

Frederick and Herbert St. Clair, Jr., were two of the first St. Clair family members to assume a leadership role. As indicated earlier, Frederick St. Clair, while providing bond to civil rights activists in Crisfield, initially suggested that the freedom riders investigate conditions in Cambridge. Herbert St. Clair, Jr., Lemuel Chester recalled, "opened his home, his wallet, his love" to the budding movement. Activists used his home day and night as a place to meet, eat, sleep, and rest. Herbert became an adult supervisor to CNAC upon its formation. Along with Enez Grubb, Frederick was elected one of CNAC's co-chairs. Even after he resigned as co-chair because he felt more comfortable working behind the scenes, Frederick remained deeply involved in the movement. As Dwight Cromwell observed: "He came from a family that has always been involved in social change. He gave his whole life for the movement."[42]

Gloria Richardson and CNAC

In January 1962, when the freedom riders arrived in Cambridge, Gloria Richardson was busy working ten- to twelve-hour days in her family's drugstore. Born in Baltimore, Maryland, in 1922, she moved to Cambridge with her parents in 1931. Her mother was Mabel St. Clair, the daughter of Maynadier and Mamie St. Clair. Her father, Virginia native John Edward Hayes, opened a drugstore in the Second Ward. Through most of Gloria's teenage years they lived in her grandparents' house. From the St. Clair side of the family, in particular, Richardson gained an insider's view and appreciation of politics. She also gained from the St. Clairs and from her father and mother a belief that she could be anything.[43]

In the fall of 1938 she enrolled at Howard University, majoring in sociology. Her teachers included Rayford Logan, E. Franklin Frazier, Sterling Brown, Mordecai Johnson, and Highland Lewis—all giants of black scholarship. They reinforced several lessons she had learned from her grandfather. As Richardson put it, they taught that "you were as good as anybody," that blacks had a long history of achievement, and—especially from Frazier—that the black bourgeoisie or middle class had a duty to serve the black community. Her teachers also taught her to think critically and, in the words of Richardson's biographer Annette Brock, "how to analyze racism, and the dynamics of social action."[44]

During her college years, Richardson participated in a smattering of civil rights protests. While the Howard University environs offered blacks greater freedom than did Cambridge, Washington, D.C., was still a segregated city. As Richardson recalled, black people could not even try on gloves at the department stores, although they were expected to wear gloves while downtown. On several occasions during the late 1930s and early 1940s, Howard students participated in demonstrations against racial discrimination, early versions of the sit-ins, particularly at the stores and restaurants in the Howard neighborhood. Richardson did not play a leadership role in these demonstrations. Yet she did take part, risking punishment from the administration. Others who took part included Pauli Murray, who went on to become one of the most prominent black women in the country, and Edward Brooke, who became the first black senator from Massachusetts.[45]

After graduation, Richardson returned to Cambridge. There she was unable to secure employment as a social worker because of the color bar.

She married Harry Richardson, a schoolteacher, and bore two children, Donna and Tamara. Her husband was much less political and more conservative than she; he even termed some of her views communist. Largely for personal, not political reasons, however, their marriage fell apart. Shortly after their divorce, Richardson and her mother traveled to Canada, where as Richardson recalled, for the first time in her life she was treated by whites as a "normal" person, rather than as a black person.[46]

Richardson was drawn into the movement by her cousin Frederick St. Clair, who because of the demands of his work could not devote his time to the movement, and even more so by her elder daughter, Donna. As we have seen, Donna played an active role in the sit-ins from the start. After about two months of protesting, however, Gloria recognized that her daughter and many other youths were growing disillusioned, even morose, because of the lack of progress. This convinced Richardson that she had to become more actively involved. In the late spring of 1962, she agreed to become the adult supervisor of CNAC. Shortly thereafter, she and Frederick St. Clair's wife Yolanda attended a conference of SNCC in Atlanta. At the conference, CNAC applied to become the only adult-led affiliate of SNCC and was so authorized. Ironically, even though Richardson was about twenty years older than many of SNCC's members, they did not view her as an older mentor. Rather, perhaps because of her militancy, perhaps because of her beauty and vigor, they saw Richardson as a contemporary, as a fellow foot soldier in the crusade for racial equality. As white activist Dorothy Zellner recalled, Richardson personified fearlessness and defiance, two traits that SNCC members held in high regard.[47]

While Richardson rejected the accommodationist tactics of her grandfather, in many other ways she followed in his footsteps. For one thing, Richardson recalled, Maynadier St. Clair had been a "race man." He believed that it was the responsibility of blacks who were better off to give back to their community. She did too. She applied the organizational techniques she had learned from her grandfather as well. During his fifty years as a councilman, St. Clair had relied heavily on a cadre of lieutenants, each of whom was responsible for his neighborhood. (As far as I can tell he had no female lieutenants.) Similarly, Richardson and CNAC developed a network of grassroots activists throughout the Second Ward and she relied on them for input. At meetings, these board members or officers would make suggestions regarding the goals and tactics the movement should adopt. For instance, at a meeting on October 2, 1962, during a discussion of a proposed voter education drive, Sally Garrison called for door-to-door canvassing of the Second Ward. Betty Jews endorsed the idea as well as the call for reaching out to blacks at various halls, such at the where the Elks met. CNAC agreed to implement these suggestions.[48]

Most important, Richardson built CNAC into one of the few civil rights organizations in the country with strong support from poor or working-class blacks. She did so, in part, by shunning the conciliatory or "Tom-ish" black leaders of Cambridge, such as councilman Charles Cornish, Mace Lane High School Principal Edythe Jolley, and Helen Waters, a member of the school board. Richardson included a welfare recipient and a factory worker on CNAC's executive committee. While her critics claimed that she recruited uneducated men and women to the executive committee so that she could dominate it, Sandra Millner has shown that Richardson did so because she believed lower-class blacks, though lacking formal education, were street smart and had the intelligence to steer the movement in a constructive direction. Unlike many other black leaders, Richardson also recognized that by integrating working-class blacks into leadership positions, she would be better able to broaden the base of the movement.[49]

In addition to reaching out consciously to working-class blacks, CNAC probably included more women (proportionately) in positions of leadership than did local civil rights groups elsewhere, especially those led by the SCLC or NAACP. Even before Richardson assumed a leadership role, CNAC had a number of female officers, including Enez Grubb, who was one of the original co-chairs. Before and after Richardson became actively involved, there were just as many women on CNAC's board or slate of officers as there were men. Even if Richardson did not consciously recruit women to the movement, arguably they felt more comfortable assuming leadership roles than did women in communities where the local movements were headed by men. Notably absent from CNAC's board were ministers, who of course would have been men. In so far as women are more fully integrated into the community and are in better positions to reach out to all classes of blacks than are black men (particularly preachers), the high proportion of women who were involved in CNAC contributed to its ability to build a mass movement.[50]

Richardson also won the support of a broad spectrum of blacks through the sheer strength of her personality, a trait her supporters and detractors both highlighted. Lemuel Chester described her as "tenacious" and "determined." She "could have stayed within the confines of her upper-middle-class type of life," Chester added. Instead, she acted like "all the rest of us." Not long after the movement emerged in Cambridge, whites sought to buy Richardson's silence, offering her a professional position in Ocean City, Maryland. Seeing the offer for what it was, she turned it down. Reflecting on her unselfishness, Chester argued that Richardson deserved to "get a monument." To date, Cambridge has not acted on this recommendation.[51]

White Retrenchment

If the local white elite had reacted more constructively to the initial freedom rides, as did leaders in Salisbury, Maryland, the history of Cambridge might have turned out differently. But they did not. (In recognition of its efforts on the racial front, Salisbury's Biracial Commission won the coveted Sidney Hollander Foundation Award in 1961.) As late as January 1963, Mayor Mowbray refused to ask the town council to pass some sort of public accommodation law, even though several other Eastern Shore communities already had one. Nor did the city make progress in several other crucial areas. In spite of the well-documented need for more and better housing in the Second Ward, a plan to apply to the federal government for public housing stalled because of a squabble between the county commissioners, who were controlled by Malkus, and the city government. The school board refused to budge on its desegregation plan. Rather than acknowledge its flaws or problems of race relations in general, School Superintendent James G. Busick blamed the turmoil in the community solely on outside agitators. He persistently contended that the schools were open if blacks would only apply.[52]

In fact, in the fall of 1962, Richardson's daughter Donna applied to and was enrolled in Cambridge High School. She was joined by several other blacks, becoming the school's first black students. The *Daily Banner* and Busick hailed their admission as proof of Cambridge's progressive position. Less than two weeks after enrolling, however, Donna and the other blacks withdrew because of the open hostility they encountered from white students, teachers, and staff, including physical harassment. Richardson contended that other blacks did not apply because they feared economic reprisals for doing so, a reasonable concern given that the vast majority of blacks were employed by white-owned firms. No one in the white community, however, lent credence to these charges. Cambridge High School Principal Otis Trise denied Richardson's charges, declaring that the teachers had done a great job of "maintaining classroom discipline."

Yet the *Daily Banner*'s argument—that the students should have stood up like Jackie Robinson—suggested that they were not truly welcomed. "The failure of the three youngsters to meet this challenge," the *Daily Banner* proclaimed, "points up one hard truth which the civil rights workers are not willing to accept. The courts can force integration in certain areas . . . but it is up to the individuals to win the respect of their contemporaries."[53]

While white moderates blamed Richardson, CNAC, and outsiders for the turmoil, their reaction to the unsuccessful attempt to desegregate Cambridge's schools displayed their failure to provide true leadership. Rather than championing the principle of creating a color-blind society and placing the onus on whites to sacrifice, the *Daily Banner* and others placed the burden on blacks to stand up for their rights. One explanation for the local white elite's negative response to the freedom rides and to the unsuccessful attempt to desegregate the schools in Cambridge lay in the particular political history of Cambridge. Town officials did not see themselves as bigoted because they knew that blacks in Cambridge enjoyed the vote and representation on the town council and school board. Furthermore, black officials, steeped in the accommodationist tradition, assured white officials that Cambridge enjoyed good race relations. These officials also reinforced the notion that outside agitators caused the trouble in the first place. Unaccustomed to seeing blacks demand change, in part because Richardson's own grandfather had followed an accommodationist approach, local leaders also proved unprepared to react to Richardson's and CNAC's new assertive tack. Living in all-white sections of town and belonging to all-white institutions, white leaders did not realize the extent to which Cornish, Jolley, and Waters no longer spoke for much of the black community.

In addition, the rights revolution was expanding expectations and definitions of rights. While much of the mainstream civil rights movement was willing to call upon blacks to make extreme sacrifices in order to desegregate society—from withstanding mob violence, as had the Little Rock Nine and James Meredith, to enduring brutal attacks without striking back, as had the sit-inners and freedom riders—Richardson's reaction to the mistreatment of her daughter hinted at an alternative vision, one that would gain prominence over the course of the decade within the civil rights movement. Most simply stated, she questioned the argument that blacks should have to win the respect of whites in the first place. As Julius Lester observed in 1966 in "The Angry Children of Malcolm X": "Was this [demand that blacks endure violence and mistreatment] not another form of the bowing and scraping their grandparents had to do to get what they wanted? Were they [the mainstream movement who followed King's strategy] not acting once again as the white man wanted and expected them to? And why should they [African Americans] have to be brutalized, physically and spiritually, for what every other American had at birth?" In general, Richardson would retain her faith in the ultimate goal of creating an integrated society. However, her response to her daughter's attempt to integrate the local school served as an omen of her subsequent militancy and unwillingness to accommodate the demands of white moderates for the sake of unity.[54]

Ironically, if blacks in Cambridge had never had any political rights or representation, whites might have had less of a reason to believe that their town had a good racial record, and they might have reacted more constructively to black demands. Such was the case in Salisbury and Crisfield, although not in many communities in the Deep South. Even if the local elite had pushed for a more rapid desegregation of the schools and public accommodations, they would have had to overcome Cambridge's severe economic problems. The black unemployment rate remained abysmal, above 20 percent, more than twice as high as that for local whites and four times the national average. Although most of the town's factories were officially integrated, blacks could often obtain only menial jobs such as custodianships. To make matters worse, two large employers, Cambridge Wire and Cloth and Airpax Electronics, both major defense contractors, employed only whites, a fact that particularly angered black veterans. Apparently management and white workers made tacit agreements whereby management pledged not to hire blacks and the workers promised to keep unions out. The housing situation was even worse. Only 18.8 percent of all blacks in Cambridge had sound plumbing, compared to more than 80 percent of the white population. The median value of homes owned by blacks was half that of homes owned by whites, and only slightly more than a quarter of all Cambridge blacks owned a home at all, compared to more than 55 percent of white families.[55]

Several of Cambridge's poor put the meaning of these conditions in human terms. Unemployed Korean War veteran James Sloan said: "Here, if you are a colored person and go looking for a job, they tell you they only want skilled workers. If you have the particular skill, the vacancy suddenly 'has been filled.'" Henry James added: "Things for us can't get any worse. We have nothing to lose and maybe something to gain by backing them [the civil rights movement]. I don't have anything but time and my life to give to the movement. I'm willing to give both if necessary."[56]

A statewide battle over civil rights legislation angered blacks further. In 1962 Governor Tawes called a special session of the Maryland state legislature to consider a public accommodation law that would outlaw racial discrimination in inns, hotels, and restaurants. Opponents of the bill, including the entire Eastern Shore contingent led by State Senator Frederick Malkus, watered down the law by applying a loophole that allowed individual counties to exempt themselves from the measure. Initially the bill went down in defeat by two votes. Ultimately, Tawes gained its passage and signed it. At this point, representatives from Dorchester County led a drive to repeal the bill by referendum. They did so even though the law did not apply to their home county because of the loophole.[57]

On a day-to-day level, racial tensions were exacerbated by the actions of two prominent community institutions, the police department and the local fire company. Although integrated, the police followed an unofficial policy that restricted black officers to the Second Ward and prohibited them from arresting whites, though whites could arrest blacks. During the freedom rides, as we saw, the local police often allowed whites to beat civil rights activists wantonly and then arrested the activists for disturbing the peace. Blacks often received more severe sentences for the same crimes than did whites or, due to the absence of black attorneys, had to depend on white attorneys to defend them, including Malkus and Emerson Harrington, both open segregationists.[58]

Freedom riders targeted as objects of protest the segregated skating rink and swimming pool operated by RFC. Despite the fact that it received tax dollars from both black and white citizens, the fire department rebuffed all attempts to desegregate either facility. Hence, blacks swam only in the polluted Choptank River, in which one or two people drowned nearly every season. As events heated up, the racial composition of the fire company became even more important. During the first weeks of the freedom rides, the fire company threatened to deny ambulance service to blacks. Following an outbreak of violence and fires in 1963, Mayor Mowbray had to force the RFC to enter the Second Ward by threatening to replace it with a paid force. In addition, the Rescue and Fire Company included some of Cambridge's most outspoken critics of CNAC. Two of its leaders were Brice Kinnamon, the police chief, who enjoyed a very poor reputation in the black community, and Osvrey Pritchett, Mayor

Mowbray's opponent in 1960 and later the "law and order" or white back-lash candidate in 1964.[59]

Project Eastern Shore

The months between the freedom rides of January 1962 and the protests that erupted in the spring of 1963 appeared relatively calm. Yet, under-neath the surface, the black community was becoming increasingly aware of the obstacles it faced in achieving equality and increasingly capable of sustaining a broad-based and militant challenge to the racial status quo. Much of the credit for this development goes to CNAC and CIG, in par-ticular to an initiative they launched in the summer of 1962 known as Project Eastern Shore. This began in earnest in the summer of 1962 with the arrival of two new full-time field workers, Bill Henry and Tom Ken-nedy. Henry, a native of Baltimore and a sophomore at Maryland State College, was the son of the Reverend J. Wayman Henry of Allen AME Church in Baltimore and the brother or Clifton Henry, one of the leaders of the CIG. Kennedy, a nineteen-year-old Bostonian—no relation to John F. Kennedy—was a student at Swarthmore College and a member of the Northern Student Movement, one of many proto–New Left groups in the early 1960s.[60]

Through "workshops, classes, mass meetings, speakers," Project East-ern Shore was aimed at raising political awareness in the black community and broadening the base of the civil rights movement through a voter education drive. The NAACP, for instance, both locally and regionally, backed the voter registration drive with little, if any, criticism, and blacks, who had traditionally stayed away from the polls, became more interested in electoral politics.[61]

While most interpretations of the civil rights movement focus on Mar-tin Luther King, Jr., and the confrontations that gained national atten-tion, the operation of Project Eastern Shore reminds us of the many re-gional efforts to register black voters simultaneously across the country. Rather than prodding the federal government to enact civil rights re-forms, these regional efforts sought to empower blacks as citizens, in the broadest sense of the term. Mississippi or Freedom Summer was simply the most famous of these regional efforts. A lesser known voter registra-tion drive took place in Fayette County, Tennessee, where SNCC execu-tive secretary James Forman got his first taste of a locally based civil rights struggle. Septima Clark, Bernice Robinson, and others operated citizen-ship schools in the Carolinas, which sought to raise the political con-sciousness of blacks. In the wake of the famous march from Selma to Montgomery, Alabama, SNCC initiated a similar drive in the black belt of Alabama.[62]

Of course, one crucial difference existed between the voter education drive on the Eastern Shore of Maryland and similar drives in the Deep South. While voter education was initially perceived as less confronta-tional than direct action, and thus was promoted by the Kennedy Admin-istration and other liberal forces as the preferred form of civil rights activ-ism, in the Deep South whites resisted it as much as they resisted sit-ins and freedom rides. Robert Moses and his colleagues quickly discovered in McComb County, Mississippi, that whites were just as likely to resort to violence in repressing attempts to register blacks as they were to crush with violence demonstrations against segregated establishments. In con-trast, in Cambridge, whites did not react violently to the voter registration drive. White moderates publicly endorsed voter registration as a con-structive alternative to the freedom rides. Whereas the *Daily Banner* did everything it could to discredit outsiders who organized or participated in the sit-ins of January 1962, it painted the Project Eastern Shore field workers in a favorable light, noting that Kennedy was no "stranger" to the Eastern Shore and that Henry came from a deeply religious family.[63]

Perhaps whites in Cambridge reacted this way because they had learned that the black vote did not necessarily translate into black power. Unlike whites in the Mississippi Delta, they did not have to worry about becoming the political minority. Yet it would be wrong to conclude that all whites responded favorably to CNAC's voter education drive for this reason. Having grown up in a society where blacks voted, they did not share the Deep South's aversion to the concept of blacks voting, period. Their sense of what it was to be white or black was not tied to white enfranchisement and black disenfranchisement. Unlike many white southerners who could not imagine a black political official, no one in Cambridge could remember the day when there had not been a black member of the town council. Moreover, the white community's experi-ence with black voting had not led them to fear black participation in the political process. On the contrary, it allowed them to see Cambridge and themselves as progressive.

While Project Eastern Shore moved away from direct action protests, on occasion confrontations between civil rights activists and whites took place. On July 26, 1962, for instance, Gloria Richardson, Enez Grubb, Bill Henry, Tom Kennedy, and Arnold Goldwag, a member of Brooklyn CORE who had joined Henry and Kennedy, went to the White Owl Inn to determine whether the restaurant had hired a black scrubwoman. Rather than discuss the scrubwoman's situation, White Owl's owner, Early Hoge, informed the group that the restaurant was closed. Hoge then called the police. Richardson left to speak with Betty Jews, a CNAC member who was in her car outside the restaurant. At this point, several white men entered the White Owl Inn and were served by Hoge. Shortly thereafter, officer Randall Dayton and another policeman, both white, arrived. According to a complaint filed by the NAACP, Dayton then shoved Kennedy across the room. No arrests were made; nor did the city act upon the NAACP complaint against Officer Dayton.[64]

In the fall of 1962, Henry and Kennedy returned to school. They left with the hope of participating in an expanded round of the project the following summer. To this end, they helped write a formal proposal and submitted it to SNCC's headquarters. The proposal called for sending approximately fifteen volunteers to spread out across the Eastern Shore in the summer of 1963. These volunteers, both black and white, the plan stated, would assume a variety of duties, including adult education and student tutorials. Volunteer educators would teach the three Rs, "Negro Culture," and "Negro History." Those penciled in as potential volunteers included Mimi Feingold, Vernon Gizzard, and Carl Wittman, all of whom became active in movement activities of one form or another during the 1960s.[65] Before anyone could pursue this expanded plan for another round of Project Eastern Shore, however, the movement entered a new phase in Cambridge, one in which direct action protest again took center stage.

Fig. 1. Private Farrell Wootten of the 115th Infantry, Maryland National Guard, stationed on Race Street, Cambridge, Maryland, 18 June 1963. *Baltimore News-American* collection, Special Collections, University of Maryland Libraries. By permission of the Hearst Corporation.

Fig. 2. Gloria Richardson of Cambridge Nonviolent Action Committee (CNAC) leading a Cambridge civil rights march beside Reginald Robinson of the Student Nonviolent Coordinating Committee (SNCC) and Philip Savage of the NAACP (*far right*), 15 June 1963. *Baltimore News-American* collection, Special Collections, University of Maryland Libraries. By permission of the Hearst Corporation.

Fig. 3. Enez Grubb of CNAC (in plaid dress) leading demonstrators on Pine Street with chants of "C'mon over here with the right folks," 11 June 1963. *Baltimore News-American* collection, Special Collections, University of Maryland Libraries. By permission of the Hearst Corporation.

Fig. 4. Flag-waving demonstrators gathering on Pine Street before marching on the courthouse, 12 June 1963. *Baltimore News-American* collection, Special Collections, University of Maryland Libraries. By permission of the Hearst Corporation.

Fig. 5. After the signing of an agreement with Attorney General Robert F. Kennedy in Washington, D.C., civil rights activists sing freedom songs at a mass rally in Bethel AME Church in Cambridge, 23 July 1963. Among the rally leaders are Gloria Richardson (*at the podium*), Phil Savage (*to her left*), and Reginald Robinson and Stanley Branche (*at her right*). By permission of AP Wide World Photos.

Fig. 6. White businessmen staging counterprotests on Race Street in reaction to the freedom rides, 2 February 1962. *Baltimore News-American* collection, Special Collections, University of Maryland Libraries. By permission of the Hearst Corporation.

Fig. 7. Robert Fehsenfeld, owner of Dizzyland, breaking an egg on the forehead of civil rights demonstrator Edward Dickerson, 8 July 1963. *Baltimore News-American* collection, Special Collections, University of Maryland Libraries. By permission of the Hearst Corporation.

Fig. 8. Two unidentified white men roughing up a news photographer in Cambridge on the night of 18 July 1963. By permission of AP Wide World Photos.

Fig. 9. Attorney General Robert F. Kennedy announcing an agreement to end racial problems in Cambridge, 23 July 1963. (*Left to right*) Gloria Richardson, Kennedy, and Mayor Calvin Mowbray. © Bettmann/CORBIS.

Fig. 10. Governor George Wallace of Alabama addressing a rally at the Rescue and Fire Company arena, 11 May 1963. *Baltimore News-American* collection, Special Collections, University of Maryland Libraries. By permission of AP Wide World Photos.

Fig. 11. Black leaders meeting in Chester, Pennsylvania, to form Associated Community Teams (ACT), an independent radical civil rights organization. (*Left to right*) Lawrence Landry, Chicago school boycott leader; Gloria Richardson; comedian Dick Gregory; Malcolm X; and Stanley Branche, Chesterton, Pa., NAACP. 14 March 1964. © Bettmann/CORBIS.

Fig. 12. SNCC leader H. Rap Brown speaking to a crowd in Cambridge, urging militant action, 24 July 1967. Later that night gunshots rang out and a fire claimed more than twenty buildings in the all-black Second Ward. © Bettmann/CORBIS.

Fig. 13. Maryland national guardsmen escorting a fire truck into the heart of the Second Ward, where two square blocks had burned to the ground on the night of 24–25 July 1967. AP Wide World Photos.

Fig. 14. The aftermath of the "Brown riot" and fire, 25 July 1967. *Baltimore News-American* collection, Special Collections, University of Maryland Libraries. By permission of the Hearst Corporation.

3

A Cauldron of Hate

It seemed impossible to me that this was America—the land of the free.
It [Cambridge] reminded me of driving into German towns in World
War II.

Bill Jones, aide to George Wallace

After bursting onto the national scene in 1960, the direct action wing of
the civil rights movement appeared to stall in the winter of 1962–63. Police Chief Laurie Pritchett deftly outmaneuvered Martin Luther King, Jr.,
in Albany, Georgia, leaving many pundits wondering if his strategy of
nonviolence had reached its natural limits. SNCC activists in McComb,
Mississippi, similarly, found themselves with little to show for their efforts, due in this case to the absolute power of the state. Organizational
rivalries among the NAACP, SCLC, SNCC, and CORE threatened to
hamper the movement further. As 1963 dawned, President Kennedy had
yet to propose new civil rights legislation, while his brother, Attorney
General Robert F. Kennedy, had authorized FBI director J. Edgar Hoover
to increase the bureau's surveillance of Martin Luther King, Jr. Hoover in
turn leaked information to foes of the civil rights movement, aiming to
undermine King's stature. Moreover, white supremacists remained defiant. For instance, on January 23, 1963, George C. Wallace was sworn in as
the new governor of Alabama. In his inaugural address he vowed: "Segregation now, segregation tomorrow, segregation forever." At the time he
also made his first overtures to the North. Within a year he would be
making plans to run for the Democratic presidential nomination.[1]

The situation in Cambridge tended to parallel the national scene.
Project Eastern Shore had not unseated Malkus; sit-ins and freedom rides
failed to convince the proprietors of the Rescue and Fire Company's
arena, Dorsett Theater, Choptank Inn, or Dizzyland, a local hangout for
white students, to desegregate. Cambridge's schools remained all white;

blacks still suffered from high unemployment and deplorable housing conditions. Nonetheless, Cambridge's black officials, Charles Cornish and Helen Waters, continued to praise the town's progressive racial record, and white leaders gladly cited them to support the claim that outside agitators had caused the community's racial turmoil. The *Daily Banner* sharply contrasted outside agitators "who claim to speak for the black community" to the "handful of our colored citizens who have . . . brought progress to this community without wrecking racial relations in the process." The newspaper went on to argue that "no evidence" existed to "show that the extremists," as opposed to the elected leaders of the Second Ward "command any kind of popular following."[2]

Yet in Cambridge, as in many other communities, the notion that the civil rights movement had passed proved illusory. Put differently, the winter of 1962–63 was the proverbial calm before the storm. By the summer of 1963, hardly a day passed without new civil rights demonstrations erupting in one community or another. By then, as President Kennedy observed, "The fires of frustration and discord [were] burning in every city, North and South." The nation had not witnessed such social upheaval in years.[3]

The standard interpretation of the civil rights years contends that the protests organized by Martin Luther King, Jr., and SCLC in Birmingham, Alabama, unleashed this massive wave of protests. Harvard Sitkoff writes: "Further racial disorder . . . swept across much of the rest of the nation as a result of the impact of Birmingham on black America." Yet the protests that erupted in Cambridge were not inspired by those in Birmingham. On the contrary, a new phase of demonstrations initiated by CNAC began shortly before SCLC launched Project C (for Confrontation), rather than in response to those in Birmingham.[4]

Direct Action Protest Renewed

The immediate causes of the new phase of protests in Cambridge were several needless actions by members of the white community. In late March of 1963, the Dorsett Theater, one of the targets of civil rights demonstrations in 1962, altered its seating policy, limiting blacks to sitting in the back half of the balcony—previously they had had access to the entire balcony. CNAC condemned this "step backward," which, it observed, contrasted sharply with the ideal of brotherhood recently expressed at Lenten services. Exactly why the theater decided to change its policy remains unclear, although members of CNAC believed the shift resulted from the desire of the theater owners to punish blacks for the earlier demonstrations. On the last Monday in March, Gloria Richardson, Enez Grubb, and Sally Garrison, representing CNAC, and Clarence Logan of CIG met with Mayor Mowbray and the town council to discuss the Dorsett Theater's action and the lack of progress in desegregating the schools and certain workplaces. At the meeting, CNAC juxtaposed the progress that had been made in Salisbury to the "foot dragging" that had taken place in Cambridge. The group also issued a set of demands, namely, complete school desegregation, equal opportunities in labor and industry, complete desegregation of all places of public amusement, and improvements in housing. Noting that it enjoyed the support of CIG, CNAC warned that it would not stand by idly any longer. "We have not the time for further delaying tactics; our children are growing up and we wish to leave them more than hope."[5]

According to CNAC, Mowbray and the council "rebuffed the group with vague statements, indignation and an occasional joke." The town council argued it had "nothing to do with the schools" and denied that unfair employment practices existed. It did not address the situation at the Dorsett Theater. Prior to the meeting, Richardson and Grubb had met with leaders of CIG and students from Swarthmore, Beaver College of Pennsylvania, and Maryland State College to discuss renewing direct action protests. The council's reaction to their concerns convinced CNAC to resume them "immediately."[6]

On Friday, March 29, about fifty men and women, including students from Swarthmore and other regional colleges, marched downtown and either staged sit-ins or picketed outside the Dorsett Theater or the Rescue and Fire Company's arena. They were met by crowds of jeering young whites. No violence erupted, but authorities arrested seventeen demonstrators, including Gloria Richardson, for trespassing and disturbing the peace. On Saturday, March 30, protesters again engaged in direct action protests. They held a "sit-down" at Collins Drugstore and protested outside the RFC's arena, the Dorsett Theater, city hall, the county courthouse, the town jail, and the offices of the State Board of Education and State Employment. Coincidentally, the Academy Award–winning film *To Kill a Mockingbird*, based on Harper Lee's best-selling novel about racism in a southern city, was the feature film at the Dorsett Theater during the first week of April. Direct action protests continued on a regular basis throughout April, tapering off toward the end of the month, partly due to a depletion of bail funds and partly due to the arrival of examination time at nearby colleges and universities.[7]

Like their counterparts in Birmingham, the protesters in Cambridge first gathered at black churches (initially at the Mount Sinai Baptist Church), where they sang freedom songs and listened to sermons or speeches by ministers and lay leaders. "Crack Dorchester County and you got the state," declared one speaker. Following prayer, they would march downtown, singing and chanting freedom songs and slogans. Often they knelt down for prayer and then, assuming no one was arrested, returned to church for another meeting. Even more so than in SCLC actions in Birmingham, many of the protesters, when arrested, chose jail over bail. "It was the goal of CNAC," Richardson explained, "to show, through the medium of direct action, the desperate need to eliminate discrimination." Local high school students and students from Swarthmore, Morgan State, and other regional colleges and universities constituted the bulk of the demonstrators. Richardson's home and her family drugstore served as CNAC's headquarters, buzzing with activity at all hours of the day. Because of threats against her life, Richardson often remained behind the scenes. Enez Grubb recalled that the campaign resembled a military engagement. Sleeping and living together, movement activists developed bonds similar to those developed by soldiers in the field. In addition to staging demonstrations, CNAC orchestrated a "full-scale" boycott of the downtown area.[8]

In a span of seven weeks, eighty men and women were arrested, including Richardson. About half of those arrested were students, including Penny Patch and Vernon Grizzard of Swarthmore and Carol Rogoff of Beaver College; about half of those arrested were black, including Lester Green, who was affiliated with Fellowship House of Philadelphia, and Judy Richardson, a member of SNCC. On more than one occasion, several family members were incarcerated at the same time. The Enals family, of Cambridge, for instance, repeatedly had different family members thrown in jail at the same time. In so far as authorities arrested and incarcerated protesters with the goal of deterring others from joining the demonstrations, they did not achieve this objective. As Clarence Logan informed one reporter, the arrests "haven't altered our plans" to stage additional protests.[9]

As in Birmingham, the town's leaders asserted that they would not negotiate while under threat of violence and reiterated that the demonstrations jeopardized years of racial progress.[10] William Downs, the one-time black leader of the 1937 strike against the Phillips Packing Company and Cornish's opponent in the 1958 town council race, countered: "Hell, I have never been satisfied." On the contrary, Downs exclaimed, he had been "fighting the race war" since the thirties. Gloria Richardson's mother, Mabel Booth, added: "I have never seen this place stirred up like this. It has always been quiet. But I'm glad. It was only quiet then because the white man was having his way about things."[11]

This stage of the movement climaxed with the so-called "penny trials." On May 7, 1963, fifty-four civil rights activists—including Gloria Richardson, who had been arrested with her mother during a sit-in—were tried together in Dorchester County Circuit Court by Judge W. Laird Henry, Jr., one of the most distinguished and prominent whites in the community. Henry's father had been a judge and a congressman. His great great grandfather, John Henry, had been a member of the Continental Congress and Maryland's first U.S. senator. In many ways, Henry embodied the views of Cambridge's historical elite and the Phillips Packing Company, which he represented as legal counsel. Henry had attained his judgeship shortly after he helped devise the legal strategy that the Phillips Packing Company utilized to thwart the 1937 strike.[12]

After the defendants agreed to waive their right to individual jury trials, Henry heard a brief summary of the evidence and then found forty-seven of the defendants guilty of one count of disorderly conduct and seven of the defendants guilty of two counts of disorderly conduct. After dismissing all of the remaining charges, Henry fined each defendant "one penny" and then suspended their sentences. (The youngest individual convicted was sixteen-year-old Marc Steiner of Baltimore. Years later Steiner became a prominent talk show host on public radio.) In the midst of the proceedings, Henry reprimanded the activists for their deplorable behavior. "Your time," Judge Henry propounded, "would be more profitably spent in your books than in . . . making nuisances of yourselves." After lecturing the college youths, Henry turned to Richardson, calling her a disgrace to her family's good name. Cambridge is trying hard "to do what is good for you and your people," he admonished. Perhaps Henry reasoned that Richardson would respond to his paternalistic rebuke much in the same way as her grandfather traditionally had, by accommodating herself to the demands of the white elite. After all, Richardson's grandfather had sided with the Phillips Packing Company during the 1937 strike, and Charles Cornish collaborated with Cambridge's business leaders to recruit new industries to the town in the early 1960s. "Do you know of any other community in this area making greater strides in integration than Cambridge?" Henry inquired, fully expecting her reply to be no. Instead, Richardson retorted, "You are not going to like this but I think far greater progress is being made in Salisbury." Richardson knew that Henry took great pride in Cambridge's reputation as a progressive community. Hence, she knew her answer that Salisbury had a better record—despite being a city with a poor reputation in racial matters—would sting. Yet, she was unwilling to accommodate Henry by presenting a favorable view of the racial situation in Cambridge.[13]

While the penny trials gained Cambridge coverage in the *New York Times*, they failed to restore peace and order in the community. Courtland Cox, a Howard University SNCC leader who joined the protest on occasion, perceptively observed that seeing Richardson reject the rebukes of Henry startled the white elite. If Richardson, a solid member of the black middle class, was no longer willing to follow their lead, what protection did the community have from the impetuousness of working- and lower-class blacks? For years the white elite had depended on the black middle class to act as a bulwark against rash actions. By refusing to play this role, Richardson threatened to usher in a wave of instability and uncertainty.[14]

In fact, as the *Democrat and News* observed, local blacks grew increasingly defiant in the wake of the penny trials. For instance, on May 14, some 250 blacks staged a nighttime march. Congregating on Pine and Elm streets in the heart of the Second Ward, they marched downtown. Well after midnight they continued to chant and sing songs, in spite of threats of arrest and police orders to disperse. When arrests were made, protesters went limp, forcing authorities to carry them off to jail.[15]

Nor did Henry's one-penny sentence satisfy working- and lower-class whites, who felt the protesters deserved a stiffer penalty. Long before the trial, rumors abounded that Henry and Richardson were distant relatives. The minimal sentence lent credence to these rumors; many reasoned that Henry's familial ties to Richardson accounted for the one-penny fines. In addition, the white working class harbored long-standing resentment of Henry because of his elite background and ties to the Phillips Packing Company. Perhaps, as students of the white working class have suggested, their authoritarian outlook also led them to dismiss Henry's view that a light sentence coupled with a verbal reprimand would accomplish more than a lengthy jail sentence or a harsh fine.[16]

Civil War on Race Street

In mid-May of 1963, riots nearly erupted following attempts to integrate the Dorsett Theater, the recreational center, and Dizzyland.[17] Rioting was averted when Judge Henry again intervened, this time via the newly formed Committee for Interracial Understanding (CIU). Made up of some of the town's most powerful figures, including one of the "four horsemen," the CIU replaced the Equal Opportunity Commission, which CNAC had long considered a farce because it included officials with racist records and had accomplished little since the freedom riders had arrived in January 1962. Under Henry's direction, the CIU sought to convince CNAC to agree to a temporary moratorium on sit-ins (though not the boycott) in exchange for meaningful negotiations with white proprietors and state and local authorities. Partly out of respect for Henry and partly because the CIU legitimized the movement's demands by terming them "reasonable," CNAC expressed willingness to cooperate. The CIU's efforts, however, backfired when only a handful of white restaurant owners attended negotiating sessions. To make matters worse, those who did attend announced that they would desegregate only if the majority of restaurants did so as well, something the owners knew would not occur.[18]

Underlying the restaurateurs' defiance lay years of class antagonism. Most of the restaurant owners were or catered to working- and lower-class whites. Many of the owners and customers lived in the same neighborhoods, attended the same schools, went to the same churches, and belonged to the same community organizations. As among blacks in Cambridge, family ties knit these whites together. And as indicated, these people saw Henry as one of the remaining symbols of Phillips company power and relished the opportunity to get even with him by thumbing their noses at his committee. The fact that many of the members of Henry's committee frequented upscale social establishments, like the Yacht Club, further motivated the restaurant owners and their clients to rebuff the CIU. Several restaurant owners denied being racists, contending that they had to remain segregated or go out of business due to the prejudices of their customers. Embedded in this response was a common complaint that white elites did not have to deal with the consequences of desegregation. Most people assumed that clubs could remain segregated because they were private establishments. Defenders of segregated education often complained that northern liberals demanded integration and then sent their own children to private schools. Similarly, residential desegregation did not affect the neighborhoods of the white upper class, since few blacks could afford to live in upscale homes. A similar pattern of resentment arose over attempts to provide blacks greater access to jobs, usually in blue collar or unskilled white collar fields.[19]

While rifts grew among whites, the protests unified blacks in Cambridge. Not only did Cambridge's black churches and ministers and the local NAACP support the demonstrations, but Charles Cornish publicly berated his fellow council members for refusing to support a public accommodations ordinance similar to those enacted by other Eastern Shore communities. The fact that no one on the town council even seconded Cornish's motion to adopt such an ordinance prompted Cornish to condemn his colleagues' action, or lack thereof, as a vote of no confidence in his "moderate leadership."[20]

All across the region, civil rights groups rallied around the movement in Cambridge. As noted, students from Morgan State, Beaver College, and Maryland State College participated in the demonstrations. The Baltimore branch of the NAACP, one of the most prominent branches in the nation, bestowed awards on Richardson and her mother for their "courage and leadership in the integration campaign." Philip Savage, a onetime CIG leader and an executive secretary of the NAACP in 1963, and Stanley Branche, head of the tristate region of the NAACP, participated frequently in the protests in Cambridge. At times Savage was even more vociferous in his defense of CNAC's actions than were representatives of SNCC. For instance, in mid-June, after the National Guard intervened, Savage told five hundred demonstrators that they should continue to march, notwithstanding the governor's orders to desist from such public demonstrations.[21]

Tensions reached new heights when Cambridge authorities arrested two local black youths, Dwight Cromwell and Dinez White, and charged them with disorderly conduct. Like Richardson, Cromwell came from a family with a history of social activism. His grandmother, Brownie Waters Cromwell, was one of the town's oldest members of the local branch of the NAACP. Even though their actual offense was praying outside a bowling alley, which owner William Le Compte admitted was done in an orderly manner, the two were thrown in jail without bail. Their case came before Judge E. McMaster Duer, whose name was synonymous with racial repression on the Eastern Shore; he had presided over a trial in the thirties that had resulted in a lynching. After a hasty hearing, he sentenced White and Cromwell to an *indefinite* term in the state institution for juvenile delinquents. Prior to receiving her sentence, Dinez White wrote a "Letter from a Jail Cell." Written long before Martin Luther King's famous "Letter from a Birmingham Jail" was published, White's letter struck many of the same chords. In the face of repression and arrest, White urged her fellow activists to persevere. "They think they have you scared because they are sending us away," she wrote. "Please fight for freedom and let us know that we are not going away in vain."[22]

Not long after White penned this piece, the situation temporarily allayed by Henry's committee warmed up again as several developments converged to produce a riot that lasted three days. The arrest and rapid sentencing of White and Cromwell angered the black community more than any other act of white intransigence. "It is becoming more and more difficult to contain violence here in the Second Ward," warned Richardson in the wake of their arrest. Their prosecution, Richardson stated, "makes us wonder if we are really dealing with Christian people or heathens." The release of the two youths became one of the paramount demands of CNAC, one that authorities would have to meet before CNAC would agree to a moratorium on protests and the economic boycott. Prior to their arrest, Herbert St. Clair expressed his doubts about the philosophy of nonviolence as espoused by King. "We are not going to initiate violence," said St. Clair. "But if we are attacked, we are not going to turn the other cheek." After the arrest of the two youths, many blacks displayed their break from King's views by carrying guns and defending themselves from whites.[23]

On the same day that Duer sentenced White and Cromwell, the Maryland Commission on Interracial Problems and Relations, which had rushed to the region hoping to reach an accord, issued a report concluding that there was virtually no middle ground in Cambridge upon which to build. In general, the commission blamed small businessmen and poor whites for much of the trouble and criticized Superintendent of Education James Busick for his intransigence. Almost simultaneously, Judge Henry disbanded the Committee on Interracial Understanding, because, in his words, no progress was in sight.[24]

On the national scene at nearly the same time, Governor George Wallace defied President Kennedy's attempts to desegregate the University of Alabama. Mass demonstrations in Jackson, Mississippi, culminated with the assassination of NAACP leader Medgar Evers. Perhaps influenced by these national events, protesters in Cambridge grew increasingly frustrated. On the evening of June 11 a large crowd of blacks gathered on a vacant lot in the Second Ward for CNAC's first outdoor mass meeting. Fifteen at a time, waves of protesters marched downtown, decrying the sentencing of White and Cromwell. There they encountered a crowd of about 150 to 200 whites. When blacks marched back to the Second Ward, many whites followed, and some skirmishes between black and whites occurred. Whereas through much of the spring CNAC had sought to get as many blacks as possible into the streets, now for the first time they pleaded with protesters to go back home.[25]

On June 12 tensions remained high. Clemon Cephas and NAACP leaders Reverend Charles Edmonds and T. S. Murray led more than a hundred blacks and whites in a march on the downtown jail. Cephas had been struck in the head the previous evening when a white counter-demonstrator threw a rock at him. Waving American flags and singing "I'm gonna sit at the white man's table one of these days" and "I'm gonna bowl at the bowling alley one of these days," the protesters displayed a new level of commitment and unity. Hard-helmeted police and state troopers sought to keep the civil rights activists and white counter-demonstrators separated. After returning to the Second Ward, the civil rights activists listened to speeches, including one by Richardson, in which she pleaded with them to remain nonviolent.[26]

Close to five hundred men and women marched downtown on the evening of June 13. Anticipating violence, many of demonstrators carried weapons. Many whites were equally defiant. Approximately four hundred whites gathered for a counterprotest outside the county jail, where they demanded the release of "Whispering Bill Todd," a local waterman who had been arrested for drunken and disorderly conduct and breaking through a police line. (In fact, Todd had already been released by authorities.)[27]

No violence occurred on the thirteenth, but all hell broke loose on the night of the fourteenth. Fires erupted at several white-owned businesses in the Second Ward. Guns were fired, apparently by both blacks and whites. Jerome Shenton, the thirty-seven-year-old owner of one of the businesses that had been set afire, was hit by one of the shots. Local police who entered the Second Ward were met with a barrage of bricks and bottles. State police accompanied by canine units and armed with riot sticks rushed into the area to restore order.[28]

In response to the first outbreak of violence, Governor Tawes convened an emergency meeting in Annapolis to which he invited Richardson, Reginald Robinson, Mayor Mowbray, and the city council. Tawes tried to convince those present to accept a last-minute compromise: the council would promise to speed up the pace of school desegregation, build public housing, enact a public accommodations ordinance, and establish a biracial commission. In exchange, CNAC would agree to a one-year moratorium on demonstrations. Noting that an earlier moratorium had failed to produce tangible gains, that the governor lacked the power to ensure implementation of the agreement, and that their only leverage rested on their ability to protest, CNAC rejected the offer.[29]

As a result, Tawes saw no choice but to comply with an earlier request made by Mayor Mowbray to call out the National Guard and to declare martial law. On June 14, five hundred guardsmen rushed into town; up to fifteen hundred more readied themselves for action. The Guard proceeded to encamp themselves on Race Street, which, as we have seen, literally divided the white and black sections of Cambridge. From the start, CNAC welcomed the National Guard, because state troopers had "proven as intolerable and prejudiced as local police." CNAC contended that if the Guard had not been brought into Cambridge, local blacks would have been forced to defend themselves. Already, blacks had displayed their willingness to carry guns both in and outside their homes. Sometimes at the height of the protests, Richardson recalled, there would be shootouts in the streets. Richardson explained that during the spring of 1963, men in the black community, "when they got home from work, would change clothes and go and lay in the yards and in the fields, around the perimeter of the second ward, with guns." While CNAC remained officially committed to nonviolence, it did not dissuade black men from arming themselves.[30]

Middle- and working-class whites had a much different response to the arrival of the National Guard. They strongly disapproved of the decision to station the Guard in Cambridge. Store and restaurant owners complained that the Guard's prohibition on the sale of liquor jeopardized their livelihood. In spite of the fact that most of the guardsmen came from the region and they were commanded by General George Gelston, a Maryland native, many whites viewed the troops as "an army of occupation." One reason they felt this way was that they were unaccustomed to seeing law enforcement authorities act in a color blind fashion.[31]

Perhaps the most vociferous critic of the Guard was William B. Yates, a local white attorney with political aspirations. Yates fumed at the indignity he suffered at the hands of the Guard, alleging that armed soldiers had searched his car without a warrant. Yates added that the Guard treated blacks and whites disparately, noting that two white girls had been improperly detained by the National Guard after they inadvertently drove downtown after curfew. Even though a subsequent newspaper story cast doubt on Yates's allegations, many whites agreed with the gist of his complaints. On July 16, upward of 150 whites gathered at the RFC's arena to protest against the Guard's reluctance to punish CNAC leaders and protesters who had defied the curfew. County Commissioner M. Baker Robbins warned of violence if the Guard "didn't change its ways." Siding with the white working class, the usually moderate *Daily Banner* chimed in: "Negroes Walk over the National Guard."[32]

The Agreement

A flurry of activity followed the mid-June riots. The town council offered to pass an amendment to the city charter that would make discrimination illegal in the town's hotels, inns, and restaurants. CNAC rejected this offer on the basis that such an amendment could be put up to a referendum by the city's voters and, in any case, would not go into effect until November 1964. Instead, CNAC called upon officials to rescind the county's exemption from the statewide public accommodation bill or to pass a local public accommodations ordinance that would not be subject to a referendum vote. This local legislators and Mayor Mowbray refused to do.[33]

During the same time span, CNAC's leaders were busy meeting with Assistant Attorney General Burke Marshall, Governor Tawes, and other state and federal officials. As a result of these meetings, Maryland's State Board of Education pledged to pressure the local school board to scrap its gradual desegregation plan in favor of one that would completely desegregate the schools in the fall of 1963, and the Kennedy Administration prodded the federally funded local employment bureau to hire a black interviewer. In addition, Marshall hinted that the federal government would channel money to several local establishments (such as Airpax, a minor defense contractor), which in turn would open up new jobs. Even though tensions remained high, the National Guard left town at noon on July 8.[34]

Seeking to keep the pressure on local leaders, CNAC initiated a new round of demonstrations, including sit-ins at Dizzyland. In response, Dizzyland owner Robert Fehsenfeld knocked to the ground Eric Dickerson, a white native of Cambridge and a sympathizer with the local civil rights movement. Cracking a raw egg over Dickerson's head gained Fehsenfeld and Cambridge front-page coverage in the *New York Times* and other newspapers. While a sizable number of the protesters from outside Cambridge were white, Dickerson was the only local white to engage in direct action protest against local establishments. The following day, CNAC returned to Dizzyland and several other segregated establishments. A white mob attacked the demonstrators. On the night of the ninth, close to two hundred black and white civil rights activists participated in a nighttime mass march to the courthouse, where some of that day's protesters were being held. They encountered a crowd of about seventy-five angry whites. When police arrested twenty-seven-year-old white waterman John Thomas for punching Swarthmore graduate Michael Manove, the white counter-demonstrators jeered, "Let him go" and "Arrest the niggers." Remarkably, no more violence took place, although tensions remained extremely high even after the demonstrators returned home to the Second Ward.[35]

On July 12, a white mob once again attacked demonstrators at Dizzyland. A *New York Times* reporter described the scene: "About 200 Negroes rushed to the aid of six white and Negro demonstrators who were being beaten up in the restaurant by white patrons. . . . The police made no attempt to enter the restaurant until the Negro crowd rushed across the street and tried to break the door down. The door had been locked from the inside. As the Negroes swarmed toward the restaurant several of them . . . sent up as a cry: 'They're getting them. My God, They're getting them.' As the Negroes tried to break down the door, white spectators moved up and for nearly 10 minutes the intersection was filled by a milling, punching mob."

That same evening more than 250 civil rights demonstrators staged a "freedom walk" to the courthouse, where they encountered a white mob of about 700, who were there to demand the release of a white man arrested during that afternoon's melee. Whites pelted the civil rights demonstrators with rocks and eggs. As darkness fell, violence erupted once again. A carload of whites drove through the Second Ward and exchanged shotgun fire with black residents. White-owned businesses located in the Second Ward were set on fire; stones were thrown through the window of Helen Waters's home, most likely by militant blacks. George Collins, a writer for the *Afro-American*, wrote: "For what seemed like an eternity the Second Ward was a replica of the Old West as men and boys of all ages roamed the streets, stood in the shadows, and leaned out of windows with their weapons in full view." By dawn more than twelve people had been shot. It was only by an "act of God," Collins added, that no one was killed. With protests having subsided in Birmingham, Alabama, and Jackson, Mississippi, Cambridge now commanded front-page coverage in several national newspapers. In response to these developments, the governor ordered the National Guard to return to Cambridge, where they would stay for nearly a year, the longest peacetime occupation of a community in the history of the United States, with exception of military occupation of former Confederate states during Reconstruction.[36]

Even before this new round of violence, the Kennedy Administration had expanded its mediation efforts. On July 9, Gloria Richardson attended a White House function with leaders of three hundred women's organizations. Before joining the group, she met privately with Kennedy administrator Maceo Hubbard, a longtime civil rights lawyer and the top black official in the Justice Department. At the same time, black and white leaders of Cambridge were conferring with other parties: General George Gelston, commander of the National Guard in Cambridge; State Attorney Thomas Finnan; and members of the Maryland Human Relations Commission, which had been founded in 1951 by Governor Theodore McKeldin, a moderate Republican with a strong civil rights record. While Richardson shuttled back and forth between Cambridge and the nation's capital, NAACP activist Stanley Branche, SNCC leader Reginald Robinson, and CORE's Dwight Campbell were arrested following a sit-in at Collins Drugstore. On the night of their arrest, close to five hundred demonstrators amassed in the Second Ward and threatened to march if those arrested were not released. Fearing another riot, General Gelston freed them from prison. In spite of this act of goodwill, Savage remained defiant. "If we have to die in the streets, at least it can be said we died honorably," he declared. Not surprisingly, whites lambasted the Guard for releasing Robinson and Campbell.[37]

As already indicated, on July 13 at a national press conference, President Kennedy criticized the civil rights movement in Cambridge for having lost sight of the goal of its protests. His admonishment of the movement in Cambridge contrasted sharply with his endorsement of the upcoming March on Washington. Local white officials sought to use the president's remarks to prove that they were acting in good faith but that CNAC was not. Nonetheless, less than two weeks later, Robert F. Kennedy met with Richardson and state and local officials. After nine grueling hours of negotiations, he emerged from his office and announced that representatives of the black community, the city, the State of Maryland, and the Justice Department had signed an agreement whereby CNAC would suspend protests in exchange for "material and tangible" reforms.[38]

SNCC Chairman John Lewis, who participated in the negotiations, recalled the scene. Richardson, Lewis observed, was very cynical at the time. She distrusted the Kennedy Administration and felt that the meeting was largely a ritual aimed at enhancing the image of the Kennedys. Seeking to break through Richardson's serious and reserved demeanor, Robert F. Kennedy teased, "Do you know how to smile?" She did offer a smile, Lewis recalled, "but it was a weak one." The turning point in the negotiations came after Kennedy reviewed a study of the Cambridge situation that CNAC had compiled early that summer, with the help of several Swarthmore students. The study presented an overview of the history of the community and a detailed description of its economy, political traditions, and racial problems. Drawing on a door-to-door questionnaire answered by nearly every resident of the Second Ward, the study contained a wealth of data on the needs and views of Cambridge's black residents.[39]

While much of the nation, including the Kennedys, tended to see integration as the main goal of the civil rights movement, the study made clear that something much larger was at stake. Most concretely, the study established that in Cambridge, jobs and housing mattered more than desegregation. More abstractly, in concert with Richardson's steadfast negotiations, the study demonstrated that the African-American community wanted respect and a real shift of power in Cambridge. Both Lewis and Richardson recalled that the study had a tremendous impact on Kennedy. Its thoroughness convinced him of CNAC's resolve and made him realize that the situation in Cambridge was much worse than he suspected. Richardson even suggested that RFK's examination of the situation in Cambridge sparked his concern with poverty across the nation. As Lewis observed, after reading the survey and meeting with Richardson, RFK drew him aside and remarked that these "young people of SNCC have educated me. You changed me. Now I understand."[40]

The agreement met most if not all of the concrete demands CNAC had made in early 1962, demands the town council had refused to address or been unable to implement as late as May 1963. Most important, Cambridge authorities agreed to establish a locally based human relations commission similar to the one that had been established in Salisbury, which would consist of both black and white representatives, including individuals acceptable to CNAC. In addition, they pledged to speed up the desegregation of schools and construction of public housing and to amend the city charter to make racial discrimination in public accommodations illegal. Last, the agreement included a pledge to implement an innovative federally funded manpower or job training program, devised in part by Morgan State economist Dr. Melvin Humphrey and to be administered by the college.[41]

In the past, CNAC had refused to suspend protests in exchange for the pledge to amend the town charter. This time, however, when the said amendment was accompanied by other reforms and had backing of the federal government, CNAC agreed to halt demonstrations. Yet, even if it was not clear at the time of the announcement of the agreement, CNAC and Cambridge's authorities viewed the significance of charter amendment differently. For CNAC, the promise to amend the town charter was only a part of a much broader agreement to combat racial discrimination. For local authorities (and for many liberals, nationwide), it was perceived as the centerpiece of the pact.[42]

Regardless of differences over the relative importance of different parts of the deal, the agreement represented the most direct involvement of the Kennedy Administration in the affairs of a single community relating to racial matters. Prior to October 1962, President Kennedy had avoided intervening in local affairs and making strong pronouncements on racial matters for risk of losing the southern support necessary to accomplish his other initiatives, foreign and domestic. Beginning with the crisis at the University of Mississippi in October 1962, JFK showed signs of growing concern with racial matters. However, not until the spring of 1963, in reaction to the wave of demonstrations that swept across the nation from Birmingham to Cambridge, did he adopt a more proactive stance, which was symbolized by a televised address in which he called for civil rights legislation. With the Cambridge agreement, the Kennedy Administration went even further, moving beyond words and proposals. Historians of the movement and of the Kennedy Administration have made scant mention of it, but the Cambridge agreement committed the federal government to promoting racial reforms to a far greater degree than did any other accord promoted by the administration. Indeed, the Cambridge agreement exceeded similar pacts reached in Birmingham and Jackson, where the federal government was able to settle unrest without committing to concrete reforms.[43]

Exactly why the Kennedy Administration intervened so concretely in the affairs of Cambridge will never be known, although several factors clearly played a role. Fear of renewed violence in Cambridge influenced the administration. But violence or the threat of violence alone cannot explain the administration's actions; it did not intervene in many other communities that experienced sustained violence and protests, from St. Augustine, Florida, to Danville, Virginia. The proximity of Cambridge to Washington, D.C., reinforced the administration's decision to do something. Richardson's negotiating skills and her resolve not to accommodate the Kennedys or others by accepting abstract promises in exchange for peace impacted the degree to which the administration became involved. Once Robert F. Kennedy, not his surrogates, became involved, it became more difficult for the administration to extricate itself from the situation without some type of agreement. In addition, unlike in many other communities, the agreement in Cambridge enjoyed the backing of white leaders with a moderate reputation, the backing of the business community, and the support of the state government. Last, there were fewer political risks to forging an agreement in Maryland than in Deep South states that had already displayed willingness to bolt from the Democratic Party in opposition to civil rights reforms.

Somewhat along the same lines, the turmoil in Cambridge in the spring and summer of 1963 encouraged many other Eastern Shore communities to institute racial reforms. For instance, even before RFK negotiated the Cambridge agreement, Ocean City's mayor announced that practically all Ocean City restaurants had agreed to serve customers regardless of their race and that the city had established a biracial commission to "combat racial problems at the resort." One city commissioner, D. Bishop, explained that Ocean City's reforms were directly related to "what has happened in Cambridge" and the business community's desire to avert similar strife. Other Eastern Shore communities that had been targets of CIG protests in 1962 similarly hastened the pace of reform lest they end up like Cambridge.[44]

Back in Cambridge, the National Guard readied for its departure. Mayor Mowbray expressed his hope that "the entire community now can pull together." The *Daily Banner*, expressing the belief that the agreement would bring an end to the civil rights protests, termed the pact a "victory for Cambridge," adding that those who did not like the compromise had a "clear responsibility to suggest an alternative solution." Sharing a desire to move beyond protests in the streets, blacks gathered for a mass meeting, where they heard Philip Savage praise Richardson. "Nobody in this community should ever forget Gloria Richardson," Savage declared. "You all know you owe her a debt of gratitude." With tears in her eyes, Richardson humbly stood to the side as the crowd gave her a standing ovation.[45] Obviously, many conservative whites in Cambridge did not share Savage's sentiments. On the contrary, they saw her as a troublemaker and malcontent. Ironically, before the year was over, many moderates and liberals, white and black, in Cambridge and elsewhere, would question Savage's characterization of Richardson as well.

4

Good-bye to Gradualism

By the time we got to town, Cambridge's blacks had stopped extolling
the virtues of passive resistance. Guns were carried as a matter of course
and it was understood that they would be used.
Cleveland Sellers, SNCC

The period 1963–64 has often been described as the golden age of the
civil rights movement. Beginning with the dramatic protests of Martin
Luther King, Jr., and SCLC in Birmingham, Alabama, and ending with
Freedom Summer, this period of the black freedom struggle prompted
President Kennedy to propose sweeping civil rights legislation, and it riv-
eted the nation's attention on the symbolic last bastion of white supremacy, Mississippi. In between were the March on Washington and
King's "I Have a Dream" address, one of the more majestic moments in
the history of the United States. To most casual observers, the civil rights
movement appeared remarkably unified in purpose and strategy during
this period. Integration was the goal and nonviolence the method. A cor-
ollary to this observation was the belief that the movement owed its success to its essential unity.

While most scholarly studies of the civil rights years have shown that
significant disagreements lay beneath public appearances of unity, these
same studies also suggest that black nationalism, which carried with it an
explicit rejection of integration and nonviolence, did not take hold until
1965 or 1966. This is so, in part, because the mass media tended to over-
state the breadth and depth of the commitment to nonviolence prior to
1965 and exaggerated the extent of violence afterward. Historians also
tend to portray this period as a low point for conservatism, especially old-
fashioned white supremacists. From the desegregation of the University
of Alabama to the signing of the Civil Rights Act by Lyndon Johnson,
white supremacists suffered one defeat after another. Johnson's landslide

victory over Barry Goldwater in 1964 and the Republicans' devastating losses in congressional races further signaled conservatism's malaise.[1]

Yet appearances were deceiving. Goldwater's ability to win votes in the traditionally Democratic South and Wallace's limited electoral success in the North during the primaries suggested that a new right was in the making. Building on Wallace's populist style, the new right would seek to characterize itself as the people's party and to portray liberals as representatives of the elite. This new right would jettison the blatant racist language of white supremacy. Yet through code phrases like "law and order" and "right of association," and through attacks on the dangers of a strong federal government, it would win broad-based support for many of the objectives of the Goldwater campaign of 1964.

One could have predicted these national developments by paying close attention to Cambridge. Not only did activists in Cambridge sour on nonviolence and adopt a more radical posture than the mainstream movement before black power became a national cause; Cambridge also witnessed the emergence of a new right in the form of a law and order ticket in advance of Goldwater's defeat. Put differently, the liberal or moderate center collapsed in Cambridge in 1963 and 1964. At the time, this led many to describe Cambridge as unique or unusual and helps explain the marginalization of Cambridge by scholars. Yet looking backward with the advantage of historical hindsight, we can see that the developments in Cambridge presaged several broader trends.

The Referendum

In the wake of the signing of the RFK-brokered agreement, a new and powerful political force emerged in Cambridge. The immediate goal of this political movement was to repeal the part of the agreement that made racial discrimination in public accommodations in Cambridge illegal. The organization that orchestrated this campaign was the Dorchester Business and Citizens Association or DBCA. Even before the agreement had been negotiated, a number of businessmen had joined together to defend their right of association, which they feared would be jeopardized by local, state, or national actions. Prior to negotiation of the agreement, the DBCA counted only about a dozen members. Afterward its membership expanded exponentially. By the end of July 1963, it officially had four hundred members; some suggested it had closer to a thousand adherents. Beginning almost immediately after the agreement was signed, the DBCA easily accumulated the number of signatures necessary to challenge the public accommodations measure via a referendum. It simultaneously registered additional voters, who were expected to oppose the new anti-discriminatory measure.[2]

The DBCA was not simply an anti–civil rights organization. Rather, it was rooted in long-standing divisions within the white community. The DBCA's leader, William Wise, owned an oil distribution business that competed with the Phillips Packing Company. An active participant in local Democratic politics, Wise belonged to the Harrington faction of the party, the main rival to the Winterbottom faction that had controlled most political offices during the heyday of the Phillips Packing Company. In the early 1960s, Wise was elected to the central committee of the Democratic Party in Dorchester County. He was also prominent in the Elks Club, a fraternal organization to which several other conservative politicians belonged as well. Other DBCA leaders included Thomas Merryweather, a beer distributor and Dorchester County's representative in the state legislature, and Leslie Handley, a trial magistrate and former head of Cambridge's American Legion. Like Wise, both Merryweather and Handley were allied with Frederick Malkus, Cambridge's conservative state senator who had bested the Winterbottom machine in the early 1950s.[3]

Many DBCA members belonged to the Rescue and Fire Company. The DBCA used the RFC's arena to hold meetings and as a place to register new voters. RFC members helped the DBCA add five hundred whites to the voting rolls within a matter of weeks. The RFC's board of directors endorsed the DBCA's initiative and notified RFC members about this stance. Among the DBCA members who took a lead in circulating a petition for the repeal of the charter amendment were Samuel Le Compte, the operator of the Rescue and Fire Company's recreation center; Alonzo Anderson, the brother-in-law of Dizzyland owner Robert Fehsenfeld; and Mrs. Franklin Collins, wife of the owner of Collins Drugstore; all three had seen their businesses targeted by the freedom riders.[4]

Although all its members were white, the DBCA rejected an invitation to affiliate with the southern-based White Citizenship Council or the KKK. Insisting that the DBCA was not a white supremacist organization, Wise argued that the DBCA sought to implement programs aimed at improving the "economic welfare and conditions" of all citizens of the county. For example, while the DBCA opposed federally funded public housing, it offered an alternative plan that it claimed would better meet the housing needs of the community. This plan, modeled after a plan in place in Indianapolis, called for establishing a loan fund administered by the city and county, which the DBCA claimed would enable working- and lower-class residents to become homeowners. Wise explained that the DBCA alternative, by allowing potential homeowners to earn down payments for their homes by building new homes, would increase housing values rather than erode them in the Second Ward. He also called for the creation of a vocational school to enhance the skills of all Cambridge citizens. In regard to the public accommodations measure, Wise neither blatantly defended segregation nor derided blacks as second class citizens. Rather, he insisted that all private businesses had the right to "refuse service to anyone." Why anyone would "want to go where they are not wanted," exclaimed Wise, made no sense.[5]

As the campaign for the referendum heated up, Wise accused the town's white elite of playing dirty politics. According to Wise, powerful whites promised political appointments to people who broke with the DBCA and threatened the same individuals with loss of their jobs or with other difficulties if they did not.[6] In fact, the white elite reacted quickly and vigorously to the DBCA's efforts. Cambridge's established leaders founded the Cambridge First Committee headed by Arnold Deane, owner of the *Cambridge Daily Banner*; William Hart, president of the local Chamber of Commerce; J. Edward Walter, postmaster of Cambridge; and Levi Phillips, Jr. The committee emphasized that passage of the referendum would threaten the "economic welfare of the city." (Levi Phillips, Jr., was one of the original members of the DBCA. He quit the organization when it initiated its referendum campaign.) To bolster this position, Mayor Mowbray sent a personal letter to every signee warning that a vote for repeal jeopardized Cambridge's reputation as a progressive community. More practically, the *Daily Banner* printed a form that allowed residents to rescind their names from the petition calling for repeal of the amendment. (The legality of such recision was questionable.)[7]

As I have noted, generally the DBCA framed its effort in nonracist terms, arguing that the amendment violated property rights and the right of association. According to Wise, one should not have to be called a segregationist just because one believed in protecting constitutional rights. As the election neared, however, the DBCA and its supporters invoked racist feelings to solidify their base. "If God Almighty had intended this [black and white together], he would have made us all one color," exclaimed one DBCA supporter. Citing the "George Report," which had been developed at the behest of Alabama governor John Patterson, another DBCA partisan noted that blacks had "less intelligence and brain power than white persons" and higher rates of illegitimacy and crime. Nineteen-year-old Ruth Ann Pritchett, who had become somewhat of a cause celebre among local white conservatives following her arrest for allegedly violating the curfew, rhetorically inquired: "Do you think that I want to go into a restaurant and eat with a Negro or go to a motel and sleep in the next room or in the same bed where a Negro has slept? . . . There is one other thing," Pritchett exclaimed. "I hope that the Negroes never try to step in and take South Dorchester over, because that is when the real trouble begins. We don't want to integrate and We Won't Integrate."[8]

The Cambridge First Committee countered the DBCA's appeals to racial prejudice with appeals to patriotism. "BUDDY, YOUR BUSINESS GREW OUT OF A FOXHOLE," declared one Cambridge First broadside. Blacks and whites had cooperated during the war to preserve American freedom, the advertisement continued. "Isn't it about time we decided if the Negro is good enough to die in our foxholes, he's good enough to eat in our restaurants?" The Cambridge First Committee conveniently forgot that the military had been segregated until the Korean War and that the local American Legion branch remained segregated.[9]

Richardson's Bombshell

In contrast to what happened in the white community, the signing of the agreement initially unified the black community in Cambridge. Living up to its promise, CNAC refrained from organizing sit-ins. When the National Guard lifted restrictions on hours of operation for white-owned businesses adjacent to the Second Ward, CNAC did not resume protests. Charles Cornish declared that the agreement laid the groundwork for the community's recovery and pledged to defeat the referendum. The Cambridge Human Relations Committee, which included CNAC members Herbert St. Clair, Emerson Stafford, and Elaine Adams, urged the DBCA not to file its petitions. After the petitions were filed, the local branch of the NAACP made clear that it would urge blacks to vote against the amendment's repeal.[10]

Yet, as with the civil rights movement in general, this unity between different factions within the black community, and between blacks and white moderates, was fragile. In spite of the *Daily Banner*'s efforts on be-

half of the agreement, CNAC promoted a boycott of the newspaper because of its allegedly biased (anti-CNAC) reportage. The organization
distributed its own newspaper, the *Cambridge Free Press*. CNAC's paper
included commentary suggesting that CNAC was lukewarm, at best, toward focusing its energy on defeating the DBCA's initiative. Rather than
urge each voter to vote against the referendum, the *Cambridge Free Press*
recommended that "each citizen must make up his own mind as to
whether to vote or not." Richardson added that personally she did not feel
that "we should have to vote on what is our right." Such statements, however, went unnoticed by white moderates because they did not read the
Cambridge Free Press.[11]

If Cambridge's white moderates had enjoyed a better understanding of
CNAC and the rifts within the black community, they would have been
better prepared for Richardson's and CNAC's ultimate response to the
referendum. Throughout the early 1960s, Richardson and CNAC shared
an uneasy relationship with moderate blacks and whites in Cambridge and
with the mainstream civil rights movement nationwide. When protests
first erupted in Cambridge, local activists there, as in many other communities, invited Martin Luther King, Jr., to their hometown, believing his
presence would help them. At the time, King or his aides pleaded that he
was too busy and demanded an appearance fee that CNAC could not afford. Later on, as the movement gained strength and notoriety, King offered to come to Cambridge for free. By then, however, CNAC determined that it did not need King's help and rejected his offer. Some, like
Richardson, even contended that King would hurt the movement and
considered him too egotistical and too committed to the philosophy of
nonviolence. While a contingent of CNAC members participated in the
March on Washington—Richardson herself was honored at the Lincoln
Memorial as one of the "women of the movement"—CNAC and Richardson felt that the march should have been more militant.[12]

As the referendum vote approached, local and national developments
drove CNAC farther apart from moderate whites and blacks. More blacks
enrolled in previously all-white schools at the beginning of the 1963–64
school year than in the past—twenty-nine in all—but Richardson expressed dismay with Superintendent Busick for refusing to register an additional thirteen black youths on the grounds that the school system received their transfer requests "too late." CNAC reiterated its stance that
blacks should not have to request transfers in the first place. The fact that
the local newspaper and other representatives of the white elite supported

CNAC becomes more radical

Busick's decision increased Richardson's and CNAC's distrust of them. To make matters worse, about two weeks before the special election, a bomb exploded in a black church in Birmingham killing four black girls. This heinous act of terrorism shattered the optimistic mood that had existed within much of the movement through most of the summer months. Several days after the bombing, CNAC announced it would hold a memorial march. The National Guard, which CNAC had seen as one of the most progressive white-run institutions, denied CNAC permission to conduct the march. While CNAC leaders chose not to defy this order, the bombing increased their unwillingness to accommodate moderate whites and blacks for the sake of unity.[13]

On September 27, Richardson held a press conference where she urged blacks to boycott the special election. Constitutional rights cannot be given or taken away at the polls, she explained. "A first-class citizen does not beg for freedom. A first-class citizen does not plead to the white power structure to give him something that the whites have no power to give or take away. Human rights are human rights, not white rights." In addition, Richardson observed, even if the amendment were upheld, the DBCA would probably challenge it in court. Following the press conference, CNAC officially called upon blacks to boycott the upcoming election.[14]

In spite of earlier signs that CNAC and Richardson were lukewarm toward the idea of getting out the vote to uphold the public accommodations measure, the decision by Richardson and CNAC to call for a boycott of the special election shocked black and white moderates in Cambridge and liberals nationwide. After the press conference, Reverend T. Murray, president of the local chapter of the NAACP, and most of Cambridge's other black ministers, denied CNAC access to their churches. The NAACP's national office sent to Cambridge two field secretaries, both of whom had participated in CNAC demonstrations in the spring, to urge blacks to vote. Regional NAACP officer Philip Savage lambasted Richardson as the "most fickle woman that you can imagine" and asserted that she had known the accommodations measure would be subjected to a referendum when she signed the agreement. Savage later claimed that Richardson had threatened his life in the days before the election. Many years later, Richardson accused Savage of working as an undercover informant for the FBI. Echoing the sentiments of Savage and Reverend Murray, Charles Cornish and Mayor Mowbray suggested that personal glory rather than principle motivated Richardson.[15]

R's
views on
voting

While she never downplayed the importance of the right to vote, Richardson believed that liberals had overestimated its significance to the broader goals of the black freedom struggle. Rather than serving as the ultimate goal of the movement, Richardson reasoned that the vote constituted a means to an end. Racial equality entailed human dignity, and if the vote was used in a way that demeaned one's dignity, then she felt blacks should not exercise it. Her particular situation, as the granddaughter of the most prominent black elected official in a community where blacks had voted for decades, added to her understanding of this subject. She saw firsthand that her grandfather had attained reforms by accommodating himself to whites who controlled the community. Yet he was never accepted as an equal, nor was he able to challenge basic caste barriers that prohibited blacks from becoming first class citizens. Moreover, unlike her grandfather, Richardson proved unwilling to accommodate herself to the wishes of moderates, black and white, for the sake of unity itself. Like a growing number of black activists, she believed that confrontation could produce better results.[16]

In addition, Richardson felt that overemphasizing electoral politics diverted attention from the gravest problem faced by blacks: pervasive economic inequality. The door-to-door study CNAC volunteers made in the summer of 1963 revealed that only 6 percent of Cambridge blacks considered equal access to public accommodations their top priority, while 42 percent named unemployment and 26 percent listed housing. Jobs and housing were the main concerns of blacks in Cambridge, Richardson insisted; only by forging a movement that revolved around the demand for human rights would such concerns rise to primacy.[17]

Even though black moderates criticized Richardson for adopting this position, she knew that she did not stand alone. In addition to CNAC's support, which was unanimous, numerous activists on different occasions had expressed similar sentiments. As early as the first sit-ins, SNCC leader James Lawson insisted that legal equality was not the primary goal. Diane Nash, one of the leaders of the sit-ins in Nashville, recalled that she found segregation degrading because it was a humiliating institution that treated her as a second class citizen. It was not so much that she wanted to drink a cup a coffee at the local Woolworth's; rather, she sought to topple an institution that denigrated her as a human being. Without a doubt, the more radical wing of SNCC, especially those associated with the Nonviolent Action Group at Howard University, sought much more than integrated lunch counters. They proved receptive to the black nationalist views of

Malcolm X and listened astutely to the advice of an assortment of other radicals who offered a vision significantly different from that presented by the national officers of the NAACP and to a lesser extent by King, which emphasized attaining legal equality and national civil rights legislation. Even the March on Washington took as its official goal "Jobs and Freedom," although the public saw integration as the primary goal of the demonstration, partly because of King's address and partly because of the media's coverage.[18] *differing goals ...*

CNAC, Richardson, and this loose collection of more radical thinkers held similar views on nonviolence as well. While CNAC and Richardson officially continued to endorse nonviolence, they saw it as a tactic, not as a way of life or a philosophical imperative. At the least, CNAC and Richardson tolerated armed self-defense of the black community. And at times they hinted at a view that would gain adherents in the latter part of the 1960s: that nonviolence as preached by King had the potential to reinforce the inferior status of African Americans because it compelled blacks to adopt a submissive rather than an assertive posture.[19]

By portraying the movement as an outgrowth of the *Brown* decision and the Montgomery bus boycotts, and by focusing on King's campaigns to win national civil rights legislation, contemporary liberals and orthodox histories of the civil rights movement have presumed that the primary objective of the movement was legal equality or civil rights, no matter the costs. Yet the fact that alternative views existed, namely those expressed by Richardson and a loose collection of independent radicals, suggests that the movement was much more diverse than was presumed. Since many *diverse mvt ...* Americans tended at the time (and still tend) to conceive of the movement in narrow, even myopic terms, as an embodiment of the views of Martin Luther King, Jr., they fail to see the ways in which Richardson represented, rather than misrepresented, the principles of many activists. To reiterate, Richardson did not reject the political process and the struggle for blacks in the South to win the vote or to desegregate public accommodations. Nor did she endorse armed struggle. But she felt that the fight for these rights was part of a broader struggle to attain full equality, which included jobs, housing, and the acceptance by society that blacks, as humans, enjoyed the same rights—to public accommodations, self-defense, the vote—as whites and should not have to accommodate themselves to the whims of the white majority to attain these things.

While a few national commentators agreed with Richardson, most decried her for her hardheadedness and inflexibility. In particular, they argued that Richardson's unwillingness to compromise proved that her real goal was power. In making this argument, Richardson's critics failed to acknowledge that CNAC endorsed her position; that other black leaders, from Malcolm X to Robert Williams and Adam Clayton Powell, had expressed similar views; and that, as we shall see, a good many blacks in Cambridge displayed their agreement with her views on election day.[20]

Some argue that Richardson's stance was shaped by her gender, with Sandra Millner and Belinda Robnet contending that Richardson had a "womanist" philosophy. According to this interpretation, Richardson and other female civil rights activists, because they were women, held a different, more egalitarian view of the objectives of the movement than did men. This included an emphasis on jobs and housing as opposed to desegregating public accommodations. Because they were more deeply embedded in the community and held fewer leadership positions, Robnet suggests that women in the movement placed greater emphasis on means than on just ends.[21]

Even though Richardson herself contends that being a woman had little to do with her position at the time, Robnet's argument has much validity. Clearly the predominant attitudes about the proper role of women framed the reactions of others and the way people viewed her. While many Americans accepted and at times heralded the reserved activism of women like Rosa Parks, they had much greater difficulty digesting Richardson's forthrightness. Indeed, they had few points of comparison. In several instances, the press described Richardson as a modern Joan of Arc. Such comparisons were aimed not at flattering Richardson but rather at suggesting that she would suffer a similar fate if she did not mend her ways. The language journalists and politicians used to describe Richardson revealed the sexual lens through which they viewed her. President Kennedy allegedly called her a "dragon lady." Reporters described her as a "live wire," "irrational," "temperamental," and "insecure," all terms commonly associated with personally troubled, middle-aged women. In fact, while Richardson had her share of trying personal experiences prior to the early 1960s, she described the years in question as the most fulfilling, personally, in her life. Ironically, as Millner aptly notes, one way liberals accounted for Richardson's break from much of the civil rights orthodoxy, from her support of self-defense to refusal to exercise the franchise, was to claim that since she was a woman, she did not know better.[22]

Yet such a claim, given Richardson's background and the close ties that CNAC enjoyed with the community, displayed the ignorance of the pundits. From the beginning of the movement in Cambridge, Richardson allied herself with working- and lower-class blacks. She shunned her privileges as a member of the black elite in favor of a broad-based movement. Her decision to do so grew out of her insistence that her goal was human rights, not civil rights narrowly defined. As a child and later at Howard University, she had parents and male teachers who encouraged her to be whatever she wanted to be. Her father wanted her to become a pharmacist, traditionally a male profession. She chose instead to pursue a degree in sociology and social work, a field many activist women entered. The fact that she was drawn into the movement by her children was another thing she held in common with other women who became active during the civil rights years.[23]

Building on Robnet's insight, it is interesting to note that those who criticized Richardson most harshly were largely men. Even those who had supported CNAC's direct action protests, most notably Stanley Branche and Philip Savage, ended up lambasting her in public for her position on the special election. In contrast, CNAC, which as we have seen contained a disproportionate number of female officers compared to civil rights organizations in other cities, supported Richardson's stance without an iota of public dissent.[24]

For the sake of unity within the black community and as a sign of good faith to white moderates, Richardson and CNAC could have supported the charter amendment. Other black leaders, such as King, and other civil rights organizations, most notably the NAACP, certainly compromised on occasion so as to maintain alliances with sympathetic moderates. Perhaps Richardson misled local whites and moderate blacks into believing that she would support the amendment. More likely, whites misled themselves into believing that integration was the primary goal of the movement. Either way, we need to see that Richardson made a tactical decision of the kind that movement leaders made all the time, analogous to King's decision to forge ahead with protests in Birmingham and SNCC's decision to recruit whites to Freedom Summer. All these tactical decisions carried the risk of alienating an important block of supporters. In retrospect, one can fault Richardson for the tactical decision she made. But given her objective of promoting human rights and gaining jobs and housing, she felt it was the right decision at the time.[25]

A Polarized Community

On the date of the special election, Cambridge voters turned out in record numbers. The referendum to repeal the public accommodations measure passed by 1,994 votes to 1,720 or 53.6 percent to 46.7 percent. The referendum passed in every white ward of the city, gaining more than 80 percent of the vote in the blue collar wards and passing by a narrower margin in the more middle-class wards. Eighty-five percent of registered whites voted, the highest turnout in Cambridge history. The high turnout of many new, largely working-class voters essentially canceled out the votes of white moderates, who historically went to the polls. Even though nearly 95 percent of the voters in the black Second Ward opposed the referendum, only about 50 percent of eligible blacks voted. This represented a slightly higher turnout than normal but a much lower turnout than moderates had hoped to see. If a much higher percentage of blacks had voted, the referendum might have failed. Still, the key to the result was the fact that whites outnumbered blacks two to one.[26]

The most important long-term consequence of the special election was not that public accommodations remained segregated, because the federal Civil Rights Act enacted the following year compelled their desegregation. Rather, the most significant impact of the process was on the white community. Victory at the polls emboldened those who had sponsored the referendum. After years of submitting to the will of the white elite, working-class whites began to assert themselves. Probably Richardson's greatest miscalculation was underestimating the degree to which working-class whites might use the racial struggle of the 1960s to seize political power. Raised during the reign of the Phillips Packing Company, she failed to recognize the precariousness of the white elite's position. Richardson reasoned that those who had held the reins of power should remain the objects of her attention. Yet, it was not clear that the traditional elite—weakened by the demise of the Phillips Packing Company and dispirited by the course of events of the early 1960s—had the power or the will to affect change further. J. Edward Walter's lament reflected the mood among many in this traditional elite in the wake of the vote. "As it stands right now," declared Walter, "the town is gone. I don't see how we are going to survive."[27]

In spite of this sense of gloom, some moderates made a perfunctory attempt to reassert their role after the loss at the polls. The Reverend Allen Wheatley, head of the Human Relations Committee, sought to rally the community around the goal of economic growth and racial harmony. At year's end, Wheatley claimed that there was "a better atmosphere altogether" between blacks and whites in Cambridge than before the strife began. Wanting to remain optimistic, the *Daily Banner* echoed Wheatley's assessment. "Progress being made by Cambridge as reported by the Human Relations Committee is remarkable when it is viewed in light of events last summer. It shows the community has a basic strength and its citizens a degree of common sense."[28]

Believing that white moderates deserved their backing for having supported the charter amendment and opposing the referendum, a number of black moderates, including Cornish, Edythe Jolley, and Hansel Greene, endorsed Wheatley's efforts. The local NAACP invited Daisy Bates, a famed leader in the school desegregation crisis in Little Rock, Arkansas, to speak at its annual meeting. Emphasizing the need for "togetherness," Bates called on the "more moderate elements . . .[to] assert themselves" so as to achieve better "working relations" between blacks and whites.[29]

Yet such calls for moderation fell largely on deaf ears. While Richardson expressed her willingness to meet with the Human Relations Committee, neither she nor CNAC expressed any intention of retreating to a gradualist stance. The November 7 acquittal of a fifty-eight-year-old white man, accused of assault and battery against an eight-year-old black girl, strengthened Richardson's resolve. In response to the decision, Richardson exclaimed, the "bigotry of the white citizens" has even "infected our judicial system." In spite of the Human Relations Committee's objections, she called for a boycott of all white merchants. Many young blacks joined Richardson in questioning the wisdom of black moderates who seemed to seek togetherness for the sake of togetherness. Octavene Saunders, a young black woman who would be elected to the town council nearly twenty years later, rhetorically inquired: "What kind of understanding are you suggesting? For the Negro to be satisfied with whatever the white people say is okay? Or would you rather the Negroes bow and scrape as our forefathers did?"[30]

In the winter of 1963–64, CNAC invited several prominent black leaders to Cambridge, all of whom endorsed its radical stance. Speaking to a crowd of between four and five hundred, New York Congressman Adam Clayton Powell, Jr., one of the nation's foremost symbols of independent black activism, heralded Richardson as "one of the greatest women in America today." Powell urged Cambridge blacks to demonstrate and picket until they received their equality and declared that Richardson "had more guts than any man in town." Fannie Lou Hamer, soon to gain fame through her leadership in the Mississippi Freedom Democratic Party, similarly encouraged Cambridge's blacks to rally around Richardson's dynamic leadership. In a separate appearance, Minister Lonnie 3X, better known as Louis Farrakhan, lambasted whites for having "robbed the Negro deaf, dumb, and blind."[31]

As already suggested, while CNAC retained nonviolence as part of its name and remained publicly committed to ending segregation, the organization increasingly took on a black nationalist posture. Its leaders clearly saw themselves as more closely allied with a network of activists that included Malcolm X, the National Action Group of SNCC, and certain renegade chapters of CORE and the NAACP than with the mainstream movement represented by King, the SCLC, and the national leadership of the NAACP. A trip Richardson took to Detroit at the end of 1963 symbolized her journey into this unofficial network of activists. Even before she went to Detroit, she had grown close to NAG. With the trip, she became an unofficial ally of Malcolm X. Ironically, she went to Detroit to participate in workshops sponsored by SCLC. Finding the workshop discussions far removed from the concerns of blacks in Cambridge, however, she ventured over to the church of the radical black minister Albert Cleage. There she met Malcolm X and heard him deliver his famous "Message to the Grassroots" speech. Already lukewarm toward nonviolence, she was enthralled by Malcolm's talk of revolution and his derision of the integrationist wing of the movement. She recalled, "That was the first time I had heard him, except over television and I had the feeling, *wow!*—you know, this could be a really great man if he could break himself from the Nation of Islam thing."[32]

Malcolm's suspension from the Nation of Islam and his search for allies following his break with Elijah Muhammad made an alliance between Richardson and Malcolm X the next logical step. In mid-March 1964, Richardson attended a meeting in Chester, Pennsylvania, with Malcolm X, Stanley Branche, Julius Hobson of CORE, Brooklyn and Chicago school boycott leaders Milton Galimson and Lawrence Landry, and Jesse Gray, Harlem's rent strike stalwart. Shortly thereafter, Richardson helped cofound Associated Community Teams (ACT), the immediate predecessor of the Organization of Afro American Unity (OAAU), Malcolm X's alternative to the Nation of Islam and the big five (the NAACP, SCLC, the National Urban League, SNCC, and CORE). As Benjamin Muse wrote, ACT and the OAAU evolved "out of the impatience with the Big Five's leadership's preoccupation with pending civil rights bills and its [the Big Five's] anxiety to please the white community." An FBI report named Richardson as part of the OAAU's "brain trust." While the FBI attempted, unsuccessfully, to confirm this report, it could have observed that in many ways Richardson's views dovetailed with those expressed by the OAAU's manifesto.[33] Whether Richardson and Malcolm X would have grown closer had he not been assassinated we cannot know. The FBI's J. Edgar Hoover clearly feared that Malcolm X might pull together a network of independent radicals, including Richardson and Robert Williams, the exiled NAACP activist who advocated armed revolution. Hoover kept close tabs on ACT and OAAU so as to prevent such an occurrence.[34]

In an essay published in the left-wing journal *Freedomways*, Richardson spelled out her views more fully. Warning that the nonviolent battle for equality "could turn into a civil war" if the nation did not deliver, Richardson demanded "freedom—all of it, *here* and *now!*" Four years later, in the wake of a series of urban uprisings, she suggested that she favored such a civil war. But in 1964, at the time she wrote the *Freedomways* article, she still hoped to avoid bloodshed in the street. Nonetheless, as we have seen, she was unwilling to temper her demands so as to diffuse the situation.[35]

While Richardson and CNAC staked out an increasingly radical position, those who had rallied around the DBCA's referendum asserted themselves ever more aggressively. Following its victory at the polls, the DBCA put out feelers to affiliate with other groups. "Unless we affiliate," Wise explained, "our rights [will] gradually be whittled away." To this end, the DBCA planned a series of meetings at volunteer firehouses on the Eastern Shore. As winter gave way to spring, the DBCA began to cast an eye on local elections and on forging ties with conservatives nationwide. One of the DBCA's primary targets was pending federal civil rights legislation, which Wise termed a "very vicious bill." Indeed, the DBCA hinted that it would spearhead an effort to hold a national referendum on proposed federal civil rights legislation.[36]

At the same time, the DBCA articulated its position more fully than in the past. A spokesman reiterated that DBCA did not favor segregation but emphasized that whites had a duty to defend their constitutional rights from the encroachments of an ever-expanding state. Presaging the rise of the new right, Wise cast the DBCA as part of a broader "silent majority" caught between "minority groups who demand everything now and some segregation groups [who] say never." In regard to the particular reforms favored by white and black moderates in Cambridge (and liberals nation-wide), the DBCA proffered its own separate course. When asked why he did not join the Human Relations Committee, William Wise answered that he did not see how it "will accomplish anything." Whereas the Human Relations Committee and Mayor Mowbray promoted urban renewal as a key to the city's revitalization, Wise and the DBCA labeled the plan "forced integration." When white moderates bemoaned the damage that the public accommodations vote had done to the town's reputation, Wise heralded Cambridge as "America's Fortress of Freedom."[37]

During the same period, white politicians associated with the DBCA attempted to punish blacks for their activism, making clear that racial harmony was not their paramount goal. The County Commission blocked efforts to distribute free food to the poor, who were disproportionately black. Claiming the media had distorted events in Cambridge the previous year, state legislator Richard Matthews introduced a bill to limit the freedom of the press in covering civil rights disturbances. Along with the Eastern Shore's other representatives in the state assembly and senate, Matthews fought against a statewide public accommodation law. Matthews and Malkus also spearheaded the opposition to proposals to reduce (proportionately) the number of representatives that Dorchester County and other rural areas held in the state legislature. For them, the battle against desegregation and reapportionment were intricately linked. They felt this way, in part, because the need to reapportion votes in the state legislature stemmed from the Warren Court decision that established the principle of one person, one vote. Of course, it was the Warren Court that had declared segregation illegal in the first place.[38]

Moderates sought to counter the polarization of the community by drawing on outside help. Maryland senator Daniel Brewster sponsored a special lunchtime meeting in Washington, D.C., to reopen dialogue. Baltimore Colt star wide receiver Raymond Berry joined the Human Relations Committee as an unsalaried administrator. Some hoped that his star status and friendship with several black Baltimore Colt players would help him win support among both blacks and whites in Cambridge. Yet these efforts failed too, because many local whites resented outside interference regardless of the outsider's credentials and because they felt that the moderates were too willing to appease black radicals. As Malkus's ally County Commissioner Robbins put it, "I don't want violence . . . but I'm not willing to sell my birthright away to avoid it."[39]

The growing strength of the new right in Cambridge became even more evident in May 1964 when the DBCA invited Alabama governor George Wallace to deliver a major address at the RFC's arena. The previous fall Wallace had journeyed to Baltimore to announce his intention to seek the Democratic nomination. Afterward, he participated in a debate on civil rights at Goucher College. During the debate, Wallace shared the stage with Dorchester County's state senator, Frederick Malkus, who, like Wallace, decried pending civil rights legislation as un-American and referred to Martin Luther King, Jr., as a communist. (Wallace and Malkus were opposed by Harry Reasnor, a prominent white broadcaster.)[40]

Out of this debate, Wallace and his aides developed contacts with the DBCA and prominent Democrats in Cambridge. After faring surprisingly well in the Democratic presidential primaries in Indiana and Wisconsin, Wallace decided to enter Maryland's race. No sooner had he announced his intention to enter the Maryland primary than the DBCA invited Wallace to come to Cambridge, offering the RFC's arena as an ideal site for him to speak. As the date of his appearance approached, Wallace's aides warned that the atmosphere in Cambridge was explosive. Fearing for his safety and not wanting to spark a riot, Wallace considered canceling the address, but ultimately he determined that he could not renege lest he appear weak.[41]

On the morning of May 11, an Associated Press story on the views of DBCA president William Wise appeared in newspapers across the country. In the story, Wise hinted at the message that Wallace would deliver later that night. Wise insisted that he was not "anti-Negro." Displaying a letter he had allegedly received from a member of a white supremacist group, Wise proclaimed: "This fellow isn't trying to solve any problem. He's just trying to create hate." Wise contended that unlike the said white supremacist, the DBCA was a democratic movement; he said he had no patience with those who opposed integration but offered no alternative. That he opposed liberal economic and social programs, such as urban renewal, did not mean he favored maintaining the status quo. Instead, he told the AP, the DBCA had developed its own plans to improve the economic and social conditions of all of Cambridge's citizens, all of which plans relied on private enterprise rather than the federal government. At the same time, Wise reiterated his opposition to pending federal civil rights legislation, arguing that it violated the right of association.[42]

Wallace arrived in Cambridge just before nightfall. Between fifteen hundred and three thousand men and women, all whites, packed the Rescue and Fire Company's arena. Wallace stripped his speech of blatant racist remarks, emphasizing instead his antistatist and pro-constitutional views. "I have spoken all the way from New Hampshire to Alabama," he said. "I believe there are in this country hundreds of thousands who say stand firm and keep working." Pending civil rights legislation, Wallace warned, endangered long-held American beliefs. Most important, it threatened the right of association. Americans must protect their individual liberties from the encroachment of the federal government. Local communities had to fight to protect their autonomy before the federal government's power grew too great. To sharpen these points, Wallace criticized the recent Supreme Court decision that banned prayer in the classroom and the section of the pending civil rights bill that stripped defendants of their right to a jury of their peers. He often faced hecklers, but he faced none inside the RFC's hall, partly because whites who disagreed with him chose not to attend the event. On the contrary, the all-white crowd interrupted his fifty-minute speech more than forty times with hardy applause and cheers. And when Wallace called on the audience's support on election day, people responded with chants of "We'll win! We'll win!"[43]

As earlier noted, upon learning of Wallace's pending appearance, CNAC organized a counter-rally outside the fire company's arena. Activists from all over the eastern seaboard, including Stokely Carmichael, Cleveland Sellers, and H. Rap Brown, responded to CNAC's call. Wallace was so concerned about the danger counter-demonstrators posed that he left Cambridge immediately upon completing his address.[44] And indeed, a confrontation ensued when four hundred black and white civil rights activists squared off against an equally large National Guard contingent. Armed with rifles, bayonets attached, the guardsmen waited to see how the demonstrators would respond to their commander's order to disperse. In his autobiography, *The River of No Return*, Cleveland Sellers recalled: "It was a crucial moment, the kind that can make or break a movement. We all understood that Gloria was the only one who could decide its outcome. If she had told us to return to the [Elks] lodge," he wrote, "we would have done so, even though we would not have wanted to." In a similar situation, he observed, Martin Luther King, Jr., turned protesters around, away from a confrontation with armed troops in Selma. In contrast, Sellers wrote, Richardson declared: "I'm going through." No sooner had she stepped forward than the Guard placed her under arrest and whisked her away. Other demonstrators, Sellers continued, immediately took her place and went limp in the street. Frustrated, Colonel Tawes, who commanded the troops, ordered the Guard to don their gas masks and spray the demonstrators indiscriminately. As noted in the introduction, when a black child died that night, some blacks in Cambridge accused the government of intentionally gassing blacks to death.[45]

In addition to displaying the racial polarization of the community, the counter-demonstration helped cement Gloria Richardson's reputation as an exemplary leader, especially among young black activists. Among those gassed, Courtland Cox remembered, was Stokely Carmichael. Colleagues had to rush him to the hospital due to the severity of the gassing. Carmichael vowed never to submit to being gassed again.[46]

Not surprisingly, Wallace's speech and the riot that followed gained Cambridge national attention, reinforcing its new reputation as a racially strife-torn community. A week later Wallace won 44.5 percent of the statewide vote in the presidential primary, just barely losing to Senator Daniel Brewster, President Lyndon Johnson's stand-in. Wallace won sixteen of Maryland's twenty-three counties, including all those on the Eastern Shore. Even though 95 percent of the voters in the all-black Second Ward of Cambridge voted against him, Wallace defeated Brewster by a four-to-one margin in Dorchester County. Notably, CNAC did not advise blacks to boycott this vote, yet commentators failed to mention this in their descriptions of the movement in Cambridge or of Gloria Richardson.

In the wake of Wallace's appearance several more clashes took place. On a couple of occasions the National Guard resorted to tear gas to restore order. At the end of May, the Guard first disallowed and then, under threat of wider protests, allowed black comedian and activist Dick Gregory to hold a "benefit" performance in Cambridge. Gregory got around the National Guard's prohibition against public demonstrations by casting his appearance as a form of entertainment. During his "performance," Gregory dared authorities to stop his "show," adding "if we can't have entertainment, then no one can," a not too thinly veiled threat to resume sit-ins at a local movie theater.[47]

The decision to allow Gregory to speak gratified CNAC and its supporters, but it infuriated local whites. Aroused by Wallace's primary showing, they charged that General Gelston repeatedly bent over backward to placate black militants.[48] Police Chief Brice Kinnamon complained that the Guard could stop the demonstrations at any time simply by arresting all the ringleaders. Outraged by Richardson's release following the anti-Wallace demonstrations and by the Guard's failure to arrest black protesters who violated the ban against demonstrating, city officials decried Gelston as "incompetent" and insisted on his "speedy removal." In a telegram to Governor Tawes, one disgruntled citizen sarcastically inquired: "Is Queen Gloria governor or are you?" DBCA president William Wise warned of white violence unless Gelston demonstrated firmer control of the situation. Mayor Mowbray, usually a voice of moderation, chimed in that the press pictured people in Cambridge "as bigots and reactionaries" yet failed to acknowledge that the radicals "stopped industrial development," that "Richardson is trying to usurp the duties of elected officials," and that outsiders, not locals, caused the problem in the first place. Even Edward Dickerson, the white Cambridge native who had participated in the freedom rides, broke with CNAC. Based on the growing radicalization of CNAC and other civil rights groups, he suggested that communists had infiltrated the movement. The local movement had "lost sight of its primary objectives," Dickerson asserted, adding that he hoped that the white people of Cambridge would "forgive and forget" his previous actions.[49]

Meanwhile, the race for mayor and town council heated up. The mayoral race pitted Charles Walls against Osvrey Pritchett. Walls, a former Phillips Packing Company official, represented the interests of the white elite. Like Mowbray before him, Walls insisted that enlightened leadership and civility stood as the keys to progress. Pritchett, who had lost by a wide margin to Mowbray in 1960, was a former chief of the Rescue and Fire Company and business partner of Baker Robbins, a conservative member of the County Commission and a key member of the Harrington faction of the Democratic Party. In contrast to Walls, Pritchett pledged a "return to law and order." Pritchett also declared his opposition to the civil rights program that was "being shoved down people's throats" by local moderates, such as the charter amendment, and criticized "federal and state politicians" for intervening in local affairs. Like William Wise, Pritchett cast "private enterprise" as the key to Cambridge's progress.[50]

As election day neared, political divisions widened more than usual. Although they did not use the language of old-fashioned white supremacists, Pritchett's forces made clear that he represented white voters. For

Table 4.1. A comparison of Cambridge's 1960 and 1964 mayoral
elections

Ward	1960		1964	
	Mowbray	*Pritchett*	*Walls*	*Pritchett*
1st	729	296	350	520
2nd	249	73	685	25
3rd	32	36	184	235
4th	356	298	75	658
5th	254	274	157	457
Total	1,620	977	1,461	1,895

instance, one Pritchett advertisement observed that during the primary
Walls had won a majority of votes in only one ward—the black Second
Ward. In contrast, the advertisement declared, Pritchett enjoyed the
overwhelming support of all four white wards. The advertisement then
posed a question: "Do You Want to Be Represented by a Minority
Group?" Likewise, the day before the election, Pritchett's supporters declared that their candidate would "carry out the mandate of the majority
of the people."[51] Other DBCA candidates for local offices took a similar
stance.[52]

Four years earlier Pritchett had lost to Calvin Mowbray by a margin of
nearly two to one. This time Pritchett won in a landslide. Even though
only 25 out of 710 voters in the Second Ward supported him, Pritchett
captured more than 75 percent of the total vote. Robert Anderson and
Thomas Hooper defeated incumbents R. Virgil Spedden and William
Wright, respectively, in town council races. Both Spedden and Wright
had supported the charter amendment banning racial discrimination in
public accommodations. In only one ward did the incumbent stave off a
DBCA challenger. (Two of the seats were not up for election until 1966.)
Voter turnout was high, especially in the white working-class wards. Even
more than in the vote on public accommodation, the final results displayed the polarization of the community and the declining power of
white moderates. In the Fourth Ward, for example, Pritchett won by a
margin of nearly ten to one, having received less than 50 percent of the
vote there in 1960. Similarly, in the Third Ward he garnered nearly two
hundred more votes in 1964 than he had in 1960. Town council candidate
Robert Anderson won by almost a two-to-one margin, and Thomas

Hooper outpolled the incumbent, William Wright, by a decisive margin, 355 to 261 votes.[53]

"For the second time in less than a year the voters of Cambridge have expressed themselves decisively," the *Daily Banner* lamented in a post-election editorial. Evidence of "a white backlash" in the First, Fourth, and Fifth wards coincided with evidence of "black backlash" in the Second Ward. (Quite how the vote represented back "backlash," given the ward's support for Walls, remains unclear.) Voter turnout in the working-class Fifth Ward was exceptionally high, nearly 85 percent. Three of the four successful candidates enjoyed the support of the DBCA. Fearing that the election represented a turn away from Cambridge's history of moderation, the *Daily Banner* reminded the city's elected officials that they represented "all the citizens" and that the town's recent history had demonstrated the "value of unity" as opposed to the dangers of turmoil. Based on the rhetoric of the campaign and the events of the preceding year, however, it did not appear that the community would heed the *Daily Banner*'s words of wisdom.[54]

5

The Paradox of Change

You made me serve them. I didn't wanna do it. I didn't wanna do it.
Businessman's lament (to the tune of "Tin Pan Alley," 1964)

The mid-1960s present students of American history with a conundrum, particularly in racial matters. Passage of the Civil Rights Act of 1964 and the Voting Rights Act of 1965 exemplified the tremendous progress that had taken place on the racial front in a remarkably short period of time. A wide assortment of civil rights leaders celebrated these accomplishments, prompting many pundits to predict that the days of racial protests had passed. Yet, in the immediate aftermath of the enactment of the Voting Rights Act, America experienced a wave of racial rioting that displayed the tremendous frustration and anger within much of the African-American community. Tapping into this anger, SNCC, CORE, and other black organizations spoke in increasingly militant terms, demanding "black power." At least implicitly, by doing so they were arguing that the achievements of the movement to date were wholly inadequate. What explains the concurrent enactment of reforms and emergence of a militant black power movement? Was it simply a matter of too little, too late? Or are there more sophisticated explanations for the turmoil of the mid-1960s?

The events in Cambridge suggest that black militancy did not grow simply because reforms came too slowly or because of the persistence of economic deprivation. Between 1963 and 1967, Cambridge experienced a period of improving economic conditions and the dismantling of age-old de jure caste barriers. In addition, blacks in Cambridge gained additional political power, allowing them to have greater impact on the community than they had had in the past. These advances left many whites believing that the days of protest should have passed and questioning the motivation of those who continued to demand more. What most whites in Cambridge did not understand was that the process whereby blacks achieved legal, political, and economic gains often reinforced and/or made clearer the depth and persistence of racism and racially based inequality. With increased political and economic rights, blacks became painfully aware of what they had not yet achieved in terms of fundamental social equality. The growing awareness of continued disparities in turn fueled black anger and demands for even more fundamental change. In the process of fighting for civil rights, many blacks gained a greater sense of self-worth and dignity. In struggle, as Clayborne Carson has suggested, blacks attained a new sense of themselves. No longer would they "Shuffle Along," as Howard University students sang. Transforming white attitudes and practices and overcoming social and economic disparities that had accumulated over generations, however, proved a far more difficult task than enacting legal reforms.[1]

Still, as we shall see, not all forces led to an inevitable showdown or to renewed violence in Cambridge. Racial polarization existed side by side with signs of a return to normalcy. Men and women associated with white backlash decried appeasing black radicals but also worked with them concomitantly to garner federal funds for a variety of projects. CNAC's leaders maintained their militant rhetoric while simultaneously shifting their focus away from direct action toward achieving reforms through traditional legal and political channels. While the events of the latter years of the 1960s made it appear as if confrontation was inevitable, a degree of contingency or choice existed, and if slightly different actions had been taken, things might have turned out quite differently.

A Return to Normalcy

In the spring of 1964, Governor Tawes created a special committee to investigate the situation in Cambridge. Heading it was one of the most prominent citizens of the Eastern Shore, Clarence Miles. After meeting with representatives of the city, CNAC, DBCA, and others, the "Miles Committee," as it was known, concluded that all parties "appear anxious to restore their community to a more normal and peaceful way of life." As a result of its findings, the Miles Committee recommended that the National Guard withdraw, a recommendation the governor agreed to implement just prior to Osvrey Pritchett's assumption of his mayoral duties. In the same period, the town council selected Charles Cornish as its leader, making him one of the first blacks to attain such a high political position in the nation.[2]

Days before Cornish assumed his new duties, civil rights activists in Cambridge tested the new federal civil rights law (the Civil Rights Act of 1964) by demanding service at previously segregated public establishments. They did so largely without incident, which suggested that by removing from local hands the decision about whether private businesses had to serve blacks, the law had made it easier for whites to accommodate themselves to desegregation. The peaceful outcome of these tests also finalized the decision to remove the Guard from Cambridge. In the months that followed, no new calls for the Guard were issued. Reflecting on the town's compliance with the Civil Rights Act and on Cornish's election, Stanley Wise, SNCC's field representative in Cambridge, stated: "If developments in Cambridge follow their present course, perhaps we can go back [to college] soon."[3]

Nearly all whites offered a similar explanation for this somewhat surprising turn of events, one consistent with views they had expressed in the past. Most whites reasoned that the disturbances of the past two years had primarily been the work of outsiders, exacerbated by reports in the national press, the actions of hidden subversive groups, and General Gelston. Most Cambridge whites described Gloria Richardson as a local malcontent motivated by personal ambition and jealousy, and they insisted that Gelston had abetted the demonstrations so that he could gain publicity and recognition. While admitting that some problems existed, most whites maintained that Cambridge had a good record of race relations and had been on its way toward implementing significant reforms when the freedom "raiders" first arrived. If only outsiders had left Cambridge alone, they lamented, the community would have taken care of its own problems. The fact that peace returned upon Gelston's and Richardson's departure convinced them that they had been right all along.

In September 1964, Richardson married Frank Dandridge, a black photographer whom she had met during the turbulence in 1963. Shortly before their wedding, she moved with her husband-to-be and younger daughter, Tamara, to New York City, Dandridge's home. She continued to live in New York City even after divorcing Dandridge. While she remained in contact with movement activists and family members in Cambridge, she displayed few regrets about relocating. Her move resulted in new professional opportunities in the field of social work. In addition, as many activists found, the movement had taken an emotional toll and the move to New York provided her with a respite from the day-to-day turmoil that had dominated her life for several years.[4]

Richardson's departure left the movement in Cambridge with a significant void. Emotionally exhausted like Richardson, Enez Grubb left for several years. A group of younger activists tried to fill Richardson's shoes, including Dwight Cromwell, one of the juveniles arrested and detained indefinitely in 1963; Grubb's cousin, Lemuel Chester; and Elaine Adams. But none of them had the charisma, economic independence, or political savvy to do so effectively. Similarly, the field representatives SNCC sent to replace William Hansen and Reginald Robinson lacked their organizing skills; John Batiste, who took over in late 1964, had few distinguishing qualities.[5]

Yet, other factors also helped Cambridge's return to a "more normal and peaceful way of life," to borrow the words of the Miles Committee. With the exception of protests that erupted in Selma, Alabama, in early 1965, the southern civil rights movement largely subsided after the summer of 1964. This was not simply because "outside agitators" departed. Many civil rights activists, especially those affiliated with SNCC, were exhausted, both physically and emotionally. They felt that they had won many of their objectives and catalyzed indigenous movements capable of carrying on the struggle. In addition, SNCC and CORE went through a period of introspection aimed at determining their future course. Personality and ideological disputes divided the movement and dissipated its energies. Likewise in Cambridge by the fall of 1964, as noted, members of CNAC were tired and found themselves divided by ideological differences. Even if Richardson had remained in Cambridge or been replaced by more capable leaders, the local movement probably would have hit a lull, although through the sheer strength of her personality she might have been able to sustain it more successfully than did her successors.[6]

Furthermore, in spite of the law-and-order rhetoric of the mayoral campaign of 1964 and the portents of a period of massive resistance, Cambridge's new white leaders steered a fairly moderate course. They did so in part because they did not want to provoke the federal government into intervening further in local affairs, which sustained defiance of the Civil Rights Act would have entailed. As a result, they did not mount a campaign of resistance after President Johnson signed the Civil Rights Act into law. Similarly, nationwide, neither the political standard-bearers of white supremacy nor the representatives of the new right focused on repealing the law once Congress passed it.[7]

To an extent the bill's enactment proved a cathartic event. Earlier in the decade when Robert Fehsenfeld and other local proprietors had physically rebuffed attempts by freedom riders to desegregate their businesses, they claimed they were not racists. Even if they wanted to desegregate, they explained, they could not do so because their all-white clientele would take their business elsewhere. Passage of the Civil Rights Act of 1964 freed owners from making this choice. White patrons could not blame them for the desegregation of their establishments, nor could patrons take their business to openly segregated establishments, since none existed. One proprietor admitted that the law allowed him to breathe a sigh of relief because it brought an end to the ordeal of appearing racist or going out of business. The Cambridge *Daily Banner* observed: "However we may view the federal civil rights act, it does get Cambridge restaurants and other public places off the hook they have dangled on for two years. By acceding to a federal law, in which state and local officials played no direct part," the editorial continued, "the restaurants are able to drop segregation barriers without incurring the wrath of most of their patrons."[8]

An additional explanation for the decision to comply with the Civil Rights Act, ironically, lay in the recognition that law had serious limitations. While most studies of American history describe the Civil Rights Act as one of the seminal achievements of the post–World War II era, many people quickly discerned that it did not alter their day-to-day lives dramatically. The law could not compel individuals to change their attitudes. It had little immediate impact on folkways as opposed to stateways. "Does the Negro really think, by the passing of the Civil Rights bill that people will actually want to associate with them?" asked one white. "This sociability is something no law can force in the next two hundred years."[9] Nor did the act alter the historical legacy of years of legal racial discrimination. It did not undo the years of employment and educational discrimination that left whites, in general, with a reservoir of advantages. Nor did the law affect residential segregation, which underlay unequal educational opportunities and an assortment of other inequalities. And nor did the Civil Rights Act directly affect the private sphere, the area of life that the noted social philosopher Hannah Arendt iconoclastically termed the most important arena of segregation. (For example, the rate of intermarriage barely changed.)

Of course over time, the law did impact folkways as well as stateways. By outlawing racial discrimination in public places, the Civil Rights Act altered the public etiquette of race relations. Seeing blacks and whites in the same public spaces became normal rather than abnormal. The sanction of the law also undercut one of the more important justifications for discrimination: that it was the "American way." Still, this shift in folkways came slowly, and many whites who fought to maintain segregation may not have understood the ways in which stateways would come to affect folkways.

Indeed, while most whites in Cambridge complied with the desegregation of public spaces, they fought to maintain institutions that reflected and reinforced their private spaces, or the spheres that shaped their sense of racial identity and caste privilege. For example, in the year following the passage of the Civil Rights Act, working- and lower-class whites rallied around the all-white status of the Rescue and Fire Company and its facilities. As described, the RFC constructed an indoor skating arena in 1955 and an outdoor pool in 1958. RFC members took great pride in these facilities, largely oblivious to the fact that they could and would soon become sources of great conflict with civil rights activists. Both facilities were open to the public on a segregated basis until 1962, when, as a means to fend off protests staged by the freedom riders and CNAC, the RFC established the Arena Pool Club. Although officially open to blacks, the club, like the RFC itself, had no black members.[10]

In the months following passage of the Civil Rights Act of 1964, the directors of the RFC presumed that the new law did not apply to them because of the pool's club status and its color-blind bylaws. However, an interracial group of civil rights activists who thought differently decided to seek admission to the pool on July 4, 1965. One of them, the Reverend Joseph W. Williams, later explained that he sought entry because he saw the swimming pool club as a constructive alternative to the immoral places where blacks tended to hang out, such as pool halls and bars. After the cashier handed one of the "testers" a ticket, a pool attendant quickly took it away on the grounds that he was not a member. When Thomas Holt, a Howard University student, attempted to apply for membership, he was informed that the pool was private property. The attendant also threatened Holt with arrest if he did not depart immediately. To intimidate the group further, the attendant informed them that Police Chief Brice Kinnamon, who was one of the pool club founders, was present. The testers retreated temporarily, only to return a couple of hours later to be arrested. After holding them without bail for two days, town authorities released the protesters and charged them with trespassing and disorderly conduct.[11]

On August 15, Reverend Williams and several of the other arrestees filed suit in federal court on the grounds that the RFC, the mayor, and the

City of Cambridge had violated the Civil Rights Act of 1964. At the heart of their case, detailed by Baltimore-based attorneys Marvin Braiterman and Elisabeth Levy Bothe and supported by an *amicus curiae* brief submitted by the United States Justice Department, was the contention that even though the pool purported to operate as a private establishment, in reality it was a public facility. Government funding had made construction of the pool possible and allowed the RFC to remain fiscally sound. The RFC and city, represented by Charles Edmondson, soon to be district attorney, countered that the pool was a private entity and that it did not bar blacks from membership. To refute the claim that the RFC had established a club to circumvent the law, Kinnamon testified that the club had begun operations two years before the Civil Rights Act was passed. Kinnamon also testified that no "Negroes" were members because none had ever applied for membership.[12]

Drawing carefully on the minutes and financial records of the RFC and the City of Cambridge, as well as the testimony of key officials, the plaintiffs' lawyers revealed numerous weaknesses in the RFC's case. While the city and county did not contribute directly to the construction of the arena or pool, records showed that public funds and favors paved the way for the building of both facilities. The city paid for the grading and filling in of land on the grounds where the pool was dug and for city-furnished prison labor to build the pool. In addition, the RFC shared space with the city government in a city-owned and -operated building, at no expense to the fire company, and the city helped pay for the RFC's equipment and personnel. The plaintiffs also established that in the late 1950s several blacks had applied for membership to the RFC but had been rejected on the grounds that membership was closed. Yet several whites who applied at the same time were admitted as members. The plaintiffs bolstered their case further by citing statements recorded in the RFC's minutes in opposition to renting facilities to organizations that might not be all white. Most notably, in the late 1950s and early 1960s, the RFC denied the Red Cross permission to use its pool for swim lessons because of the possibility that the Red Cross might teach integrated classes.[13]

After dismissing the RFC's motion for summary judgment, the District Court of the District of Maryland ruled in favor of the plaintiffs. In clear and unambiguous language, Judge Northrup rejected every one of the defendant's claims, declaring that the pool and arena were "public accommodations" and that the RFC discriminated against blacks in violation of the Civil Rights Act of 1964.[14]

While the court's decision represented a victory for the civil rights forces in Cambridge, it concurrently augmented the trend toward the normalization of race relations. In contrast to earlier in the decade, civil rights forces in Cambridge found themselves fighting for equality in the courts rather than in the streets. Legal expertise, rather than direct action protests, produced the victory. Hence, even though civil rights activists won the battle, those who sought law and order succeeded as well. Put differently, in the long run, the "rights revolution" of the mid-1960s tended to diminish the power of public or direct action protest and of those groups that sought social change in the streets, while strengthening the power of those who had legal expertise, such as the NAACP.[15]

Somewhat similarly, the manner in which the RFC defended itself reflected a retreat from an open defense of segregation and caste privileges. While the RFC avoided blatantly racist language, membership overlapped considerably with that of the DBCA, and it was common knowledge that RFC was an all-white organization and opposed desegregating public accommodations. Yet, rather than defending the all-white status of the pool club in racist language and pronouncing itself a proponent of white supremacy, RFC's spokesman argued that the RFC pool could remain segregated because it was a private club. Kinnamon even produced evidence of occasions when black groups had gained use of the RFC's arena. By doing so, the RFC's leaders implicitly conceded that the government had the right to outlaw segregation in public accommodations or in the public sphere but not in the private one. Along the same lines, the RFC conceded that public establishments had to abide by the Civil Rights Act of 1964, reasoning, however, that the act did not apply to a private club. Just a year earlier the RFC had played a leading role in opposing the local public accommodations measure and had rallied around the law-and-order banner. Ironically, this same law-and-order rhetoric limited the RFC's ability to protest against the extension of the Civil Rights Act to its own "private" facility, except in the courts.[16]

Even though the RFC did not openly defend its practice in white supremacist language, the court battle, especially the evidence obtained from private transcripts of the RFC's meetings, displayed its members' deeply felt racist beliefs and the commitment of many whites to maintaining the color line in the private sphere. The case confirmed for all to see the multiple interconnections between the all-white fire company and city officials. Even if Cambridge's single black representative had wanted to pressure the RFC to desegregate, the case suggested that he would not have had the power to override the will of the white majority. Until 1965, Cambridge's blacks implicitly recognized this by simply accommodating themselves to the wishes of the majority. How blacks would ever gain access to the back rooms where political decisions, such as the funding of the RFC, were made, was not even broached during the trial.

In the 1980s, Enez Grubb and her cousin George Meekins applied for membership to the RFC itself. After a lengthy legal battle, they were finally accepted as members. Grubb vividly recalled her first impression of the RFC's meeting room. "I felt as if many evil things had taken place there," she stated. Without elaborating, she left the impression that the RFC still operated as a bastion of white supremacy. While Grubb's impression cannot be verified, the closed nature of the RFC doubtless fostered continuing mistrust between the white and black communities before and after the courts compelled opening of the pool.[17]

The War on Poverty

As mentioned, following the 1964 election, the town council selected Charles Cornish as its president. Cornish owed his election in part to the fact that the old elite, not the DBCA/Harrington faction, still controlled three of the five town council seats. Cornish's seat and that of Leon Majors were not up for reelection in 1964. Cecil Webster, of the First Ward, defeated the DBCA's candidate in the primary. As town council president, Cornish pursued a moderate agenda. Most important, under his lead the council applied to the federal government for a slew of antipoverty funds aimed at addressing some of the economic pressures that underlay the protests of the early 1960s. In spite of pledging to return the community to the control of its citizens, Mayor Pritchett largely supported these applications. So too did the two DBCA candidates elected in 1964. Paradoxically, these federal programs, or at least the process of winning them, concurrently normalized race relations and sowed the seeds for further turmoil.

Even before the first freedom rides, Cambridge had applied for and received $213,000 from the Area Redevelopment Administration (ARA) for the construction of sewage lines and stations. Largely the brainchild of Illinois senator Paul Douglass, the ARA sought to reinvigorate depressed areas. While the bulk of ARA funds went to Appalachia and various inner city areas, Cambridge was the second community in the nation to receive one of its grants. In 1962, the ARA awarded Cambridge an additional

$450,000 to help construct a deep sea port. Airpax Electronics, a defense contractor located in Cambridge, also won $659,000 to allow it to rebuild one of its plants, which had been destroyed by a fire.[18] Expenditures on structural improvements like sewers and the port allowed Cambridge to recruit new industries and to keep others from leaving. One government press release bragged that the ARA helped "reduce its average unemployment from 14.4 percent . . . in 1959 to 8.5 percent in the fourth quarter of 1963" and to increase weekly earnings, especially of minority workers, and the tax rolls. By 1967, partly due to ARA funding, the unemployment rate had declined to less than 4 percent.[19]

Ironically, the ARA's success in bolstering the economy of Cambridge whetted the community's appetite for more federal funds and programs, particularly those that affected the everyday lives of its poorer residents. Large capital projects did not provide blacks with the skills necessary to take advantage of some of the new jobs; nor did they alleviate people's need for better housing and recreation. The aforementioned sewers, for instance, were constructed to help commercial and industrial establishments, not to enhance the homes of Cambridge's poorer, disproportionately black residents, many of whom continued to suffer from substandard plumbing. Such concerns, however, lay at the core of Johnson's "War on Poverty," and Cornish and Pritchett aggressively pursued some of these funds. Cambridge and the surrounding region received about $4.7 million in federal funds, not counting ARA and Manpower Development and Training Act (MDTA) expenditures, between 1963 and 1967. This included more than $500,000 for a Community Action Project, a Neighborhood Youth Corps, Head Start, and summer and adult education, and over $3 million from the Department of Housing and Urban Development (HUD) for urban renewal and public housing. By some estimates, Dorchester County received more federal funds per capita than any other jurisdiction in Maryland during the 1960s.[20]

At the heart of the War on Poverty were the community action projects (CAPs). These were intended to empower the poor by involving them in decisions over how to use federal funds. At the same time, CAPs strengthened the federal government's hand in the community by allowing national officials to select who would run them. The Cambridge CAP, which was officially named the Dorchester County Community Development Program, was headed by J. Edward Walter, the postmaster general and president of the Cambridge First Committee that had fought to enact the public accommodations amendment in 1963. Walter and the CAP's fifteen-member board of directors, nine of whom were black, largely represented the moderate black and white elite of the community. Specifically, the Dorchester County Community Development Program aimed at obtaining more employment opportunities for the poor in Cambridge. It applied for and won state funds that allowed 450 men and women to take job-training courses in fields such as nursing, auto mechanics, and electrical appliance repair. Working in conjunction with other state and local agencies, Cambridge's community action project also won federal funding for remedial education courses for youths, illiterate adults, and migrant workers in the agricultural industry on the Eastern Shore.[21]

Two better-known federal programs, at the time and since, were Head Start and the National Youth Corps. Cambridge opened its first Head Start program in the summer of 1965, enrolling 218 youngsters, 204 of whom were black. The program employed twenty teachers and thirty-eight aides, the majority of whom were black. Under the direction of Viola Connegys, Cambridge's Head Start program won the praise of outside evaluators, one of whom stated that it "exemplified how far men of good conscience have progressed since the summer of 1963." While only about half as many children attended Head Start programs in 1966, federal funds allowed almost as many black youths to attend a summer school program to prepare them for middle and high school.[22]

Between 65 and 130 blacks and whites participated in National Youth Corps programs in 1965, 1966, and 1967. Most of them worked at the local state hospital, where they learned a variety of jobs. Dr. Harold English said that the program sought to open "new vistas" to its participants. All of those who completed the program would be offered permanent employment, promised CAP director Jennings Brinsfield. Most of the jobs paid poorly, but they offered an alternative to working in the packing plants, which employed fewer people than in the past, Brinsfield added.[23]

Even though the programs won accolades from several prominent figures, they faced persistent uncertainty. The fiscal demands of the Vietnam War, a growing national backlash against the liberal programs of the Great Society, and the long-standing antistatist and provincial outlook of the Harrington faction of the Democratic Party left the recipients of these funds on edge. While the local National Youth Corps and Head Start programs received full funding in 1967, the summer remedial education program did not. To state matters differently, the Great Society sought to ameliorate racial tensions by decreasing poverty and displaying the goodwill of the state, but continued uncertainty over the programs decreased the effectiveness of the Great Society in achieving either end. The programs may initially have co-opted some black activists, turning them away from the streets into neo-welfare case workers; for example, Freedom Summer veteran Steve Fraser moved to Cambridge in 1965 expecting a hotbed of radicalism, but instead found CNAC and SNCC field representatives preoccupied with applying for federal grants. In time, however, the necessity of continually having to reapply for funding reradicalized some people, turning them back to the streets to reawaken the state about the needs of the community. At the same time, the token nature of training for menial jobs served as a reminder of the segmentation of the labor market along racial lines and the persistence of racism, the Civil Rights Act notwithstanding. In addition, since the community action projects were neither administered nor designed by the newly elected law-and-order government, they failed to endear an important local constituent to their maintenance.[24]

Battles to obtain funds for housing—either directly or indirectly funded (via FHA loans)—were a necessary part of the drive to improve race relations in Cambridge.[25] Before the freedom rides, the city council had won the right from the state legislature to apply to the Public Housing Authority for federal funds to build housing. Yet plans for building public housing stalled for a variety of reasons. The county commissioners refused to sign off on public housing because they did want to get stuck having to pay for the public services that new housing demanded—from roads and sidewalks to schools and water lines. After the state's attorney and federal officials ruled that the city did not need county approval, plans for public housing remained in limbo, in part because the town council continued to insist that it needed clearance from county officials. These delays angered the black community. CNAC argued that nefarious motives, not red tape, accounted for the inaction. More specifically, CNAC contended that several influential figures, including a member of the County Commission and the principal of one of the all-white junior high schools, owned numerous dwellings in the Second Ward. These landowners, CNAC reasoned, feared that the construction of public housing would undercut their ability to charge high rents on their properties. Analyses by both federal and state investigators later substantiated these claims.[26]

Regardless of the reasons for the delay, Cambridge's authorities did not commit to building public housing until the agreement was signed in the summer of 1963. Work on the projects did not begin for another six months. While moderate whites pointed to the ultimate construction of public housing projects, named after former mayor Calvin Mowbray, as proof of the progressive racial record of the community, blacks saw the difficulties and obstacles of getting them built as evidence of the depth of racism in Cambridge. Rather than celebrate the completion of units in 1966, they demanded more.[27]

The process of desegregating the region's schools similarly aggravated racial tensions. As earlier noted, following the *Brown* decision the county implemented a plan to desegregate its schools gradually. Yet for nearly a decade the "freedom of choice plan," which allowed black children to apply for admission to white schools, led to little desegregation. School Superintendent James Busick exacerbated ill feelings by routinely denying Gloria Richardson's charges that blacks did not apply to white schools out of fear of reprisals. As he informed members of the statewide human relations committee, "the good people of Cambridge would not conceivably stoop" to such actions. Busick and State Senator Malkus defended the freedom of choice plan by noting that Helen Waters, the black member of the school board, endorsed it. Busick added that "organized agitators . . . ignored every accomplishment of the Dorchester schools."[28]

Under pressure from the federal government, the pace of desegregation quickened in the mid-1960s. In the fall of 1965, 187 blacks enrolled at previously all-white schools, up from 78 in 1964. In the fall of 1966, 323 blacks, or 17 percent of the African-American school population, attended white schools. Busick proudly pointed to these figures to defend the county's approach, adding that "no application for any grade has been turned down" and that "any child can go to any school he desires." While white moderates privately prodded Busick to speed up the process, they publicly took his side by noting that the U.S. Office of Education had signed off on the county's plan.[29]

CNAC never denied Busick's claim that all black applicants had been admitted. However, it continued to criticize the freedom of choice plan. No whites "chose" to attend black schools, CNAC observed, and "white" and "black" schools continued to be funded at vastly different levels. Nevertheless, Busick stuck to the freedom of choice plan although redistricting, which would have sped up the desegregation process and decreased the transportation burden for many rural blacks, made more sense. Blacks in rural areas were bused as far as forty miles to an all-black high school, passing South Dorchester High on the way, so that the county could avoid assigning students based on geography rather than race. Enez Grubb recalled, "My classrooms were . . . in a little storage area where books were stored. . . . We got the discarded textbooks. . . . Students . . . had to spend long hours on the bus. Some had to get up at 4:30 in the morning and walk for four and five miles to catch the bus. . . . And what makes it so sinful was that they had to ride past [white] schools . . . to come to segregated schools in Cambridge."[30]

Busick's opposition to establishing a vocational technology school, when such an institution might have helped blacks obtain the training they needed to gain better paying jobs, was a source of additional tension. Busick claimed he opposed vocational education on economic and ideological grounds, asserting that the county could not afford vocational schools and that limited funds could be better spent educating students in traditional subjects. Yet, others felt that Busick opposed vocational education for a different reason, namely that such a school would have to be desegregated from the start. The DBCA, meanwhile, presented a tortured position on vocational education and refused to support federally funded public housing. While calling vocational education a top priority, the all-white organization opposed the only specific plan put forth by the board of education, on the grounds that the proposed school would be run by an outsider. Similarly, rather than endorse the construction of federally funded public housing units, the DBCA continued to promote its alternative plan of establishing a loan fund administered by the city and county, which the DBCA claimed would enable more blacks to own homes and would decrease the vulnerability of poor blacks to the exploitative actions of wealthy whites. Without federal support for such a program, this alternative never had a chance of materializing, leading many to conclude that it was simply a ruse.[31]

The Rebirth of the Labor Movement

The civil rights protests of the early 1960s and the War on Poverty of the mid-1960s coincided with the unexpected reemergence of a vibrant labor movement in Cambridge. Inspired and supported by civil rights forces, the United Packinghouse Workers successfully organized several plants in and around the town. Given Cambridge's history of anti-unionism, one might have expected that this labor drive would have contributed significantly to the instability of the community. And there is little doubt that initially it did. However, over time, the acceptance of organized labor by the remnants of the Phillips Packing Company institutionalized labor relations and contributed to the normalization of the social order.

The revitalized labor movement in Cambridge originated in a decision made by the United Packinghouse Workers (UPWA). In the mid-1950s, the UPWA decided to initiate a nationwide organizing campaign among cannery workers. It did so largely because of an internal study that revealed the existence of 288,000 canning workers, mostly unorganized—one of the single largest blocs of nonunion industrial workers in the nation. Even though the industry appeared decentralized, a union study showed that eight companies, including Campbell Foods, Heinz, Hunt Foods, and Stokely Van-Kamp, controlled 35 percent of the business. The study further revealed that the eastern seaboard contained some of the greatest concentrations of unorganized canning workers, including those at the Phillips Packing Company, which had adamantly resisted organization to date. Its workers, the union's study added, "seem very anxious to cooperate with us" and provide "a very good opportunity to really set the pace for organizing the area."[32]

Several factors stalled the organizing campaign at Phillips, including the company's purchase by Consolidated Foods and an aborted Teamsters effort to organize the plant. Campaigns at a number of sizable canning and sugar plants in Baltimore diverted the attention of UPWA's field representatives as well. Assignment of field representative Vernon Thomas to the region in 1962, however, lent the drive a fresh start.[33]

Thomas, a black man in a union that had a good reputation among minorities and civil rights groups, arrived on the Eastern Shore not long after freedom riders had catalyzed civil rights protests.[34] His first victory came on March 1, 1963, in Chesterton, some fifty miles north of Cambridge, when the UPWA won the right to represent more than five hundred workers at a Campbell Soup poultry plant, the majority of whom were black. Following the victory in Chesterton, Thomas moved to Cambridge.[35]

By building on UPWA contacts in the area, Thomas established good relations with CNAC. During the peak of protests in the spring of 1963 he spoke at CNAC rallies, where he endorsed the campaign to desegregate public accommodations and the schools. He joined a contingent of CNAC and UPWA members who marched at the Great March on Washington. At the same time, Thomas's colleague Ruth S. Haynes, another Maryland UPWA field representative, championed his efforts among Baltimore civil rights activists.[36]

The public and open identification with and endorsement of the civil rights movement in Cambridge on the part of Thomas and the UPWA reflected the union's unique position. While most liberals steered away from endorsing the local movement because of its militancy, Thomas did not. Civil rights activists in Cambridge welcomed Thomas's backing and reciprocated by praising the UPWA in general and offering aid in various endeavors. During this period, "All the Way with UPWA" became the battle cry of workers in the plant and of CNAC protesters in the streets.[37]

A lengthy study issued by CNAC in the summer of 1963, just before the UPWA won the right to represent workers at the Coastal Foods plant, praised the Packinghouse Workers as one of the few unions in the nation in which "the local unions are integrated and predominantly Negro in membership and leadership." The same study also cast the unionization of Cambridge's workers as one of the primary means for improving their economic status, adding that workers in the few factories that were represented by unions on the Eastern Shore were paid more than those who were unorganized.[38]

Moving beyond words, CNAC's members rushed to Trappe, Maryland, to join volunteers associated with the Student Nonviolent Coordinating Committee and CORE and displayed their mettle by maintaining the picket lines against various forms of intimidation, such as snarling dogs. UPWA officials commended them for convincing the migratory workers not to cross the picket line.[39]

Another sign of the interconnections between CNAC and UPWA came in the form of personnel. Leroy Banks spearheaded the organizing campaign inside the Coastal Foods Plant and was subsequently elected to head the local. His wife, Marva Banks, served as CNAC's first treasurer. Other families helped organize workers inside the plant and marched with CNAC in the streets. For instance, Enez Grubb's relatives on her mother's side, the Staffords, had a long history of labor activism. Grubb's own father had quit working for the Phillips Packing Company during World War II because the company union treated German prisoners of war who worked in the plants better than it treated native blacks. George Cephas had been killed during the 1937 uprising. Gilbert Cephas became a leader in the local union. Still other civil rights and student activists found work with the UPWA.[40]

In the spring of 1964, District Six of the UPWA invited Gloria Richardson to attend its twentieth anniversary convention in New York City. Delegates greeted Richardson with harmonies of "We Shall Overcome" and other anthems of the freedom movement. After the UPWA honored Richardson for her contributions to the labor movement, she delivered a passionate pro-labor address. Proclaiming that a revived labor movement was one of the keys to uplifting workers, especially African Americans, she pledged her continued cooperation with the union.[41]

The UPWA followed up its drive at Coastal Foods, which it won without even having to stage a strike, with two more successful organizing campaigns at Maryland Tuna (Bumble Bee) and Chung King, a producer of Chinese foods. A favorable ruling from the National Labor Relations Board, which issued a cease and desist order prohibiting Coastal Foods from hiring only members of the Dorchester County Workers Organization (DORCO), the longtime company union the Phillips Packing Company had established in the 1930s, guaranteed the UPWA's victory.[42]

While the white elite did not openly condemn CNAC or Richardson for allying with the UPWA, clearly the labor drive concerned them. As they saw it, unions posed a threat to higher profits and to their ability to attract new industries to Cambridge. The "four horsemen," the same four business leaders who had spearheaded the Cambridge redevelopment effort, paternalistically reasoned that African-American workers would be the primary beneficiaries of the recruitment of new businesses, and they contended that Cambridge's history of anti-unionism stood as one of its main drawing cards, distinguishing it from many other eastern seaboard and mid-Atlantic cities where labor was well represented. In addition, Cambridge's old elite saw trade unions as another example of outside intervention in local affairs. The UPWA drive aggravated relations between moderate whites and supporters of CNAC, reinforcing the moderates' sense of betrayal while adding to the sense of independence and empowerment among CNAC supporters. White workers tended to support the UPWA. Yet, as we shall see, the segmentation of the labor market along racial lines made the UPWA's campaign to organize the packing plants less important to them than it was to black workers.[43]

At the same time, one reason the UPWA succeeded in the 1960s when previous organizing drives had failed was that the managers of Coastal Foods, Maryland Tuna, and Chung King were not as anti-union in their views as were the owners of the Phillips Packing Company. Coastal Foods (today Sara Lee) was a subsidiary of a large Chicago-based firm that had learned to work with labor. Most of the managers of these new firms were not natives of the Eastern Shore and thus did not share the region's extreme anti-union sentiment. While Cambridge's non-union record had attracted these firms to the town, the company's managers reasoned that it made better sense to recognize the UPWA than to face continual work stoppages, once the decision to locate in Cambridge had already taken place.[44]

The impact of the UPWA's campaign on lower- and working-class whites is difficult to gauge. While precise figures on the number of black and white workers who voted to be represented by UPWA are unavailable, all evidence suggests that the majority of workers who favored unionization were black, simply because blacks constituted the vast majority of the workers in the plants targeted by the UPWA. White workers in these plants tended to vote for the UPWA, in spite of the heightened racial tensions of the times. Yet, as already suggested, the majority of white workers in Cambridge did not become involved in the UPWA's campaign because they did not work in the packing plants. In the 1930s and 1940s many more whites had been employed by the Phillips Packing Company, including in factories making tin cans. During the dramatic strike of 1937, they had supported establishing a biracial union. By the early 1960s, however, far fewer whites toiled in the remaining packing or canning industries. Coastal Foods no longer made its own cans, as had Phillips Packing Company. Whites who labored in factories tended to work for employers who had few black employees. In other words, the segmentation of the labor market along racial lines diluted the impact of the labor drive. As a result, the UPWA's efforts did not produce a common bond between many white and black workers. It did not compel whites to shed their sense of belonging to a privileged caste so as to attain class unity. It put few white workers in the awkward position of expressing their solidarity with blacks in the workplace and separation from them in the public sphere.[45]

In the wake of the UPWA campaign, white workers demonstrated that they could use organized labor as a means to protect their caste interests. In mid-January 1965, Sarah Stafford charged the local longshoremen's union with discriminating against black dockworkers. Robert Davis, one of the four horsemen and the president of Cargo Handlers Incorporated, adamantly denied Stafford's charge. However, when Parren Mitchell, head of the statewide Interracial Relations Commission and the son of two of the most prominent civil rights leaders in the country, Clarence and Juanita Mitchell, agreed to hold hearings on Stafford's allegations and threatened to take the case to the National Labor Relations Board, Davis modified his stance. The problem, Davis explained, lay with the union, not his company. In the eyes of Stafford and other activists, Davis's statement left the union as the primary culprit.[46]

Stafford's charge stemmed from developments that began in the summer of 1964, after two officers of the International Longshoremen's Association (ILA) organized Local 1199 in Cambridge. All the members of the new local were white. After being recognized by the company, the union assumed responsibility for hiring dockworkers. Shortly thereafter, two black men were denied employment by the hiring boss at the union's hiring hall on the grounds that they were not union members. According to the contract Local 1199 had signed with Cargo Handlers, union members automatically received priority when a ship arrived in port. Yet when blacks sought to obtain information about the union or become members, they were stonewalled by local union officials. Only after civil rights activists complained to the International about the local's discriminatory practices did officers of the International pressure the local to accept blacks as members. And not until the National Labor Relations Board ruled against the local affiliate, finding that the union "effectively barred [blacks] from obtaining the same regular work opportunities . . . as those enjoyed . . . by the unionized white stevedores," did the discriminatory practices finally come to an end.[47]

The willingness of blacks to protest against such employment discrimination demonstrated their new assertiveness in challenging white employers and white unions. The outcome of the dispute, as with the RFC case, showed that blacks could successfully break down barriers of caste. However, the way blacks gained access to the union, through the courts rather than by direct action, contributed to the deradicalization of the movement and the return of normalcy, or at least the perception that normalcy had returned. At the same time, in struggling for entry into the union, blacks grew increasingly disenchanted. Investigations by the NLRB revealed the complicity between union officials, white dockworkers, and Robert Davis, who signed a contract that recognized an all-white union. The fact that Davis signed this contract without any second thoughts provided further proof of the depth of racism and the hurdles that blacks would have to jump to attain equal employment. Because of the Civil Rights Act of 1964, companies could no longer openly deny blacks employment. Yet, the longshoremen's case in Cambridge exemplified a common practice that blacks would routinely confront all across the country as they sought entry into trades that had historically been white.[48]

In sum, between 1964 and 1966, evidence of continued racial polarization and normalcy existed side by side. Compliance with the Civil Rights Act, the continued desegregation of schools, construction of public housing, development of various War on Poverty programs, and acceptance of organized labor, all without great resistance on the part of whites or massive protests on the part of blacks, suggested that more normal or less tumultuous times had returned. Yet, continued battles with the Rescue and Fire Company, squabbling over the pace of school desegregation and construction of public housing, and the inability of War on Poverty programs and the Packinghouse Workers to reverse the legacy of past discrimination in the labor market suggested that Cambridge still faced a rough road ahead.

Nothing better revealed the contradictions of the era than the results of the 1966 gubernatorial race. Blacks overwhelmingly voted for Spiro T. Agnew, in both the primary and the final election. At the time, Agnew had a reputation as a moderate Republican. In contrast, by nearly as large a margin, whites favored George Mahoney, who campaigned on the slogan, "Your Home Is Your Castle, Protect It," an allusion to open or fair housing legislation, which he opposed. In local elections in Cambridge, moderates performed slightly better than extremists from either side of the spectrum. Charles Cornish retained his town council seat, turning back a challenge from George Kent, who received Richardson's endorsement and for whom CNAC veterans campaigned. Dizzyland owner Robert Fehsenfeld, who had gained a moment of fame by cracking a raw egg over the head of Edward Dickerson, lost by a wide margin. The DBCA's candidates for County Commission, including William Wise, failed to unseat several incumbents. Pointing to Cornish's reelection, moderate whites insisted that normalcy had returned. They added that Richardson had never represented more than a minority of malcontents.

Ironically, a year later, the new Maryland governor Spiro Agnew underwent a political transformation. Elected in 1966 as a political moderate, a supporter of the "Rockefeller wing" of the Republican Party, by 1968 Agnew had become the unofficial spokesman of the "silent majority," the personification of the new right. The key locale in Agnew's conversion proved to be Cambridge.

If This Town Don't Come Around

Like I said in the beginning, if this town don't come round, this town
should be burned down. . . . But . . . don't burn up your own stuff.
H. Rap Brown, SNCC (1967)

In the latter half of the 1960s, the eyes of the nation turned northward,
following the geographic migration of the civil rights movement from the
Deep South to the urban North. With this shift in terrain came an alter-
ation in the mood and message of the movement, from nonviolence to
black power, punctuated by the outbreak of a series of racial riots in the
"long hot summer" of 1967. For many Americans, the rise of black power
and the outbreak of racial rioting was not coincidental. While liberals cast
racial inequality as the root cause of both militancy and civil disorder,
conservatives contended that the advocates of black power caused the riots, either indirectly, by promulgating views that encouraged violence, or
directly, by inciting riots. Black radicals denied the specific charge that
they incited riots, but they celebrated these "uprisings" as evidence of the
imminence of a revolution, which they deemed a necessary step in the
eradication of racism in America.

Cambridge figured prominently in the contemporary interpretation of
and reaction to the urban disorders of the latter half of the 1960s. Most
important, Cambridge played a pivotal role in the transformation of Spiro
Agnew from an obscure moderate Republican governor into the embodiment and voice of the new right. Cambridge also reinforced SNCC's leftward drift, from advocating nonviolence to championing a third world
revolution. Because of the "Brown riot," Cambridge became permanently
associated with the racial strife of the 1960s. Years later, nearly every
newspaper or magazine article on the city begins by identifying it as the
place where H. Rap Brown incited a riot. Ironically, if the staff of the
National Commission on Civil Disorders, or Kerner Commission, which

President Johnson established to study the causes of the race riots, had released and publicized its investigation of the disorder in Cambridge, Agnew's rise to national prominence might have been cut short, H. Rap Brown and other black radicals would have had less reason to believe that the uprisings of 1967 were a mere "dress rehearsal" for a worldwide revolution, and Cambridge might today be better known as the hometown of several governors and for its history of black political representation.[1]

The Fire This Time

In early 1967, the Justice Department surveyed hundreds of cities for their potential for violence. Based on its findings, the department predicted that the summer of 1967 would be a "hot" one. However, Justice Department officials determined that Cambridge was unlikely to experience racial violence because of a lack of leadership within the black community. The Justice Department was not alone in asserting that racial turmoil would not reappear in Cambridge. In March 1967 the Associated Press (AP) released a story contending that Cambridge had overcome its racial troubles. "Ask about racial demonstrations in Cambridge these days," began the article, "and you're likely to hear, instead, about the gleaming new housing development." "Progress is a favorite word," said the AP story, "and there has undoubtedly been progress." In the past few years, the piece continued, Cambridge had witnessed the erection of a 150-unit public housing project, a sharp decline in the unemployment rate, the establishment of several War on Poverty programs, and the peaceful desegregation of public accommodations. Even former members of the Cambridge Nonviolent Action Committee, such as Frederick Jackson, recognized the change. "If you look at the entire county today," Jackson informed the AP, "it doesn't even seem like the same place as 1963." While not all of Cambridge's racial problems had been solved, Jackson continued, undeniably "a big overall improvement in the racial climate" had occurred.[2]

In the early spring of 1967, the Maryland Interracial Relations Commission offered a similar judgment of the situation. The commission found that Cambridge had made significant progress in five crucial areas, including jobs and housing. The "only serious remaining needs," the commission asserted, was a recreational center for black youths, a need the town council and other public leaders were addressing.[3] While the pace of school desegregation remained a sore spot, both the AP and the commission could have noted, as the *Daily Banner* did, that the U.S. Office of Education had endorsed the county's freedom of choice plan. Even "if desegregation had not come overnight," the local paper editorialized, the schools were "steadily moving in the right direction."[4]

One of the keys to a cool summer was the Rescue and Fire Company, CNAC's long-standing nemesis.[5] In the summer of 1966, the Fire Company chose to close its pool rather than comply with a federal desegregation court order. This action aggravated an already dire recreational situation. In mid-February 1967, however, the RFC sold its pool and indoor arena to Brice Kinnamon, the police chief and former head of the RFC, for an estimated $100,000. (The pool was initially valued at $300,000 when it opened in 1958.) In March, Kinnamon opened the arena for use as a roller-skating rink, allegedly on a desegregated basis, although he admitted that no blacks used the facility. Not long afterward, the town council and several community leaders met with officials of the Office of Economic Opportunity to discuss a proposal for obtaining federal funds for a summer educational and recreational program, centered on the pool. On June 24, the federal government announced approval of the summer program; the pool opened several days later. (Kinnamon did not run the pool; rather he leased it to the county, making a nice return on his original investment in the process.) While the pool was technically open to all, School Superintendent James Busick made clear that students enrolled in the summer program, mostly black children, had priority use of it. Having sold the pool, the RFC acquiesced to this development without public protest. (Few of the pool club's white members chose to swim at their old pool, preferring instead to swim at other pools, such as one recently opened by the all-white chapter of the Veterans of Foreign Wars.)[6]

In spite of the opening of the pool to black children, evidence of discontent within the black community began to appear. As the details for the opening of the pool were being finalized, Cambridge experienced a rash of fires. Authorities quickly established arson as the cause of all but one of them. The first three fires took place on the night of June 26, 1967, at the White Owl Inn and Murphy's Store, two white-owned businesses in the Second Ward, and at the Pine Street Elementary School. The Pine Street school was a symbol of the of the inequities that blacks faced in the field of education. It was dilapidated, overcrowded, and segregated. Rather than demolish the school, which would have sped up the process of desegregation, the school board decided to build temporary classrooms at the all-black St. Clair Elementary School five blocks away, where some of the Pine Street students were sent. Rapid responses by the Rescue and Fire Company limited the damage to the Pine Street Elementary School and the two businesses. Another fire erupted on the night of June 27 at Schroeder's grocery store, another white-owned business in the Second Ward, allegedly caused by a Molotov cocktail thrown through the store's rear window.[7]

Seeing the fires as an ominous sign, State's Attorney William B. Yates vowed "to use any means . . . to apprehend" the arsonists and to punish the perpetrators "as severely as the law will allow."[8] To this end, he offered a reward of $1,000 for information leading to the arrest and conviction of anyone involved in setting the fires. A day after this pronouncement, local authorities arrested civil rights activist Dwight Cromwell for reporting a false alarm. Upon his arrest Cromwell declared, "Gloria Richardson is back and she is going to tear this town down." Cromwell added that he had been appointed youth secretary of the recently reactivated NAACP chapter. While Richardson continued to live in New York City, she maintained contact with local activists. Several weeks after Cromwell boasted that Richardson was back, she visited Cambridge. During her visit, she informed reporters that the "situation could not remain stable much longer." She went on to explain, "Now I think they're in for a lot of trouble because for three years they have *not* kept the faith [my emphasis]. They were supposed to, day by day, make progress and . . . they have not done it."[9]

While he employed tough language to counter the fires, Yates's reluctance to act against two young white men accused of assaulting a young black man aggravated racial tensions. On the last day of the 1966–67 school year a fight broke out between Herbert Parks and Albert Jones, two students at the formerly all-white Cambridge High School. Parks was white and Jones was black. During the fight Parks's older brother, Joseph Nelson (Nicky), age nineteen, commanded the family dog to attack Jones. Jones's wounds were severe enough to lead to the arrest and trial of Nicky Parks for assault. Even though Vice Principal John H. Hall and former sheriff Waldo H. Robinson, both white, testified that Parks's dog had not bitten Jones, the Parks boys were convicted.[10]

Nevertheless, the verdict did not quell growing black anger, in large part because of the apparently disparate treatment received by Parks and Cromwell. At first, State's Attorney Yates did not take the dog attack seriously, even refusing to talk to Jones's parents about the incident. Only after blacks in Cambridge turned for help to Juanita Jackson Mitchell, the leader of the Baltimore branch of the NAACP, and after the Joneses filed a complaint, did Yates pursue the case. At Parks's trial, Judge Robert E. Farnell angered blacks by denying Juanita Mitchell's request to represent Jones and by clearing the courtroom of all spectators. In spite of Yates's and Farnell's statements regarding the seriousness of the offense, Parks received only a thirty-day suspended jail sentence and was fined twenty-five dollars and costs. In contrast, Yates made an example of Cromwell, initially setting his bail at $5,000, but rumors spread that it was as high as $25,000. Either was a far cry from the $100 bond that Parks posted, even though Cromwell was charged with turning in a false alarm, not setting a fire. Yates justified Cromwell's high bail on the grounds that the arson had to be stopped. This prompted George Jones, the father of the dog-attack victim Albert Jones, to cry out: "What kind of a public defender [state's attorney] have we got—an equal right and a just one, or a just [a] white one?"[11] The fact that Vice Principal Hall testified in defense of Parks exacerbated the situation as well, confirming the widely held belief on the part of blacks that school administrators opposed school desegregation, regardless of the official school board policy to comply with the *Brown* decision.[12]

Clearly, the nationwide cry for black power and stories of riots elsewhere added to the growing sense of unease in Cambridge. Lemuel Chester, for one, recalled that in 1963 when he was sixteen, he felt that blacks could end segregation through peaceful means, but by 1967 he no longer believed so. "A knife and a gun were part of my wardrobe when I got dressed." In tune with the tenor of the times, Chester and Elaine Adams founded the Black Action Federation (BAF). Made up largely of former CNAC members, the BAF kept an eye on the first black power conference held in Newark, New Jersey, in mid-July 1967. They even endorsed its pronouncement that blacks had "the right to revolt when they deem it necessary and in their interest."[13]

Rivalries within Cambridge's black community, as much as the emergence of a new set of problems, affected the racial situation in the city as well. In the wake of the Parks incident and Cromwell's arrest and trial, a number of black ministers and businessmen, representing the moderate wing of the black population, formed the Cambridge Action Council. At the core of this new organization were blacks associated with the NAACP and black and white moderates who belonged to the Ministerial Alliance. Many members of the new council had criticized Richardson when she called for a boycott of the special referendum on the public accommodations measure in 1963. They had also remained supportive of Charles Cornish and the politics of moderation. The Action Council saw the Parks incident as an opportunity to reassert its leadership role in the community and hoped to channel the anger of the black community constructively and away from the streets.[14]

Not wanting to be eclipsed by the Action Council and the politics of moderation, the BAF decided it had to respond to this challenge. Specifically, it organized a counter-demonstration against a previously announced rally by the white supremacist National States Rights Party in Cambridge. On July 16, 1967, at the rally, Joe Carroll, the leader of the ultra right-wing organization, delivered a provocative address in which he championed white supremacy. Before Carroll completed his speech, however, Chester and the BAF began to heckle him and demanded equal time. Concerned that this open confrontation between blacks and whites could escalate into a riot, Yates directed the state police to break up the rally and to place Carroll in "protective custody." Carroll complained about Yates's orders and announced plans for a second States Rights rally. None was ever held. Reasoning that it had achieved its objective of countering white supremacy and gaining notoriety, the BAF came away from the event emboldened and convinced it should sponsor more confrontational actions.[15]

From her home in New York, Gloria Richardson arranged for H. Rap Brown to speak in Cambridge. She did so in response to a BAF request that she bring either Stokely Carmichael or Brown to Cambridge to help revive the local movement. Richardson did not expect Brown's appearance to cause any trouble. As she later recalled, "Rap gave the same speech [in Cambridge] that he gave everywhere else." By implication, since violence had not erupted following his appearances in these other cities, nothing out of the ordinary should take place in Cambridge.[16]

A couple of days before Brown's address, another fire erupted at the Elks Lodge, consuming the popular all-black gathering place. Rumors spread that a white arsonist who wanted the Elks' property for a parking lot had set the fire. The fire department ruled the fire an accident. Subsequent reports suggested that a disgruntled member had started the blaze. Regardless of the cause, the incident added to growing tensions between the white and black citizens of Cambridge, convincing many that their city was ripe for a riot.[17]

H. Rap Brown and the Cambridge "Riot"

Born in Louisiana and introduced into SNCC by his older brother Ed, a veteran of the organization's activities, H. Rap Brown began questioning the goals of the mainstream civil rights movement as early as 1963 when he journeyed with other SNCC members to Cambridge. There he witnessed and was impressed by the willingness of local blacks to defend themselves with guns and by Richardson's forthrightness. Time spent in Mississippi as a participant in Freedom Summer, as a member of the SNCC affiliate called the National Action Group in Washington, D.C., and then as a field worker in rural Alabama reinforced his disdain for the vision of Martin Luther King, Jr., not to mention the NAACP. Nicknamed "Rap" as a youth, due to his ability to speak quickly and spontaneously, Brown had demonstrated his penchant for bravado before becoming SNCC's chair in the spring of 1967. Ironically, many hoped he would tone down the group's message and concentrate instead on "organizing," a goal he endorsed in his first public statements after taking over leadership of SNCC from Stokely Carmichael, who had popularized the slogan "black power" in 1966.[18]

On the morning of July 24, the date of Brown's scheduled speech, the *Daily Banner* ran headline stories on race riots in Detroit and on yet another fire at the Pine Street Elementary School. These new stories heightened tensions in Cambridge and helped set the stage for Brown's appearance and the events that followed. The Detroit riot, larger than the Newark riot a week earlier, alarmed citizens across the nation, who feared similar conflagrations in their communities. The fire at the Pine Street Elementary School, which fire chief Charles Dodson ruled arson, suggested that someone was already trying to spark one in Cambridge. Unbeknownst to authorities and the public at large, the Black Action Federation had sent a letter to the editor of the *Daily Banner* warning that Cambridge had reached the point of ignition. "You are so right when you say that Cambridge is no longer a sleepy fishing village," the BAF declared. "The black people has woke up and we intend to stay awoke [sic]."[19]

H. Rap Brown arrived in Cambridge at 9:00 P.M., on July 24, over an hour late, having missed his bus in Washington, D.C. A crowd of between two and four hundred anxiously awaited his arrival, as did local and state police and a National Guard unit that had been stationed in town for a "training session." From atop a car located across from the Pine Street Elementary School, Brown set the tone of his speech with his opening lines. Paraphrasing Langston Hughes, Brown began: "'What happens to a dream deferred? Does it dry up like a raisin in the sun? . . . Or does it explode?' . . . Detroit exploded, Newark exploded . . . It's time for Cambridge to explode."[20]

For nearly an hour Brown rambled through a vitriolic speech. He lambasted "white honkies," extolled "black power," admonished "Uncle Toms" such as Cambridge's black policemen who stood on the edge of the crowd, and demanded retribution. Peppered with calls for blacks to "get some guns" and to control their own communities, Brown's speech aroused the emotions of some and bored others.[21] Once during his speech, Brown pointed to the Pine Street Elementary School, which showed the scars of two fires, and declared: "You see that school, over there—I don't know whether the honkey burned that school or not but you all should have burned that school a long time ago. You should have burned it down to the ground. Ain't no need in the world, in 1967, to see a school like that sitting over there. You should have burned it down and then go take over the honkey's school." Following this inflammatory remark, Brown digressed into a discussion of white control of the black community, including several statements regarding the ways in which whites fooled blacks into believing they were making progress.[22]

Brown completed his speech with typical bravado, sharply setting himself off from King and the tradition of nonviolence and integration. "Don't be trying to love the honkey to death. Shoot him to death," Brown exclaimed. "Shoot him to death, brother. Cause that's what he's out to do to you." Alluding to the golden rule, Brown added: "Do to him like he would do to you, but do it to him first." Yet, at the very end of his speech, Brown offered a word of caution. "So when you move to get him, don't tear up your stuff, don't tear up your brother's stuff, hear?"[23]

While the exact sequence of events that followed remains a matter of some debate, an in-depth analysis conducted by the Kerner Commission provides the most accurate indications of what took place.[24] Drawing on police and state trooper logs compiled at the time, the Kerner Commission established that the Maryland State Police and Cambridge were well prepared for Brown's appearance. By late afternoon on the twenty-fourth, the state police had dispatched twenty-eight men and three canine units to Cambridge, with additional reserves stationed nearby in Easton. Already, the Cambridge Company of the National Guard had been mustered, to carry out a previously scheduled "routine" training session. All of Cambridge's police were ordered into duty; the force's five black policemen were stationed on the edge of the crowd that assembled to hear Brown speak. The remainder of local and state law enforcement personnel were deployed along Race Street, to protect the white section of town.[25]

At 10:00 P.M., immediately upon its conclusion, a newscaster returned to police headquarters with a tape of Brown's speech, where Kinnamon and other law enforcement officials and political leaders proceeded to listen to it. Kinnamon became especially agitated by the address. While the officers listened to the tape-recording, Brown and several members of the BAF conferred in SNCC's old headquarters. Simultaneously, a small crowd of blacks milled around Pine and Cedar streets. One BAF member, Elaine Adams, subsequently stated that Brown and the BAF members had exchanged addresses and discussed the best ways to organize blacks in Cambridge in the future. Independently, several young black women marched toward Race Street, in defiance of an alleged order to remain within the Second Ward. The police turned them back without any incidences of violence. Another teenager, Pamela Waters, decided to return home. Fearing the presence of police on Elm Street, which ran perpendicular to Race and Pine streets, she requested an escort. Brown agreed to accompany her to her home. About twenty-five to thirty others followed. From the perspective of police, this march took place immediately following Brown's address. Police stationed in the area ordered the group to stop. Then, without warning, Deputy Sheriff Wesley Burton fired two shotgun blasts, one into the ground and the other over the heads of the crowd. Some of the buckshot from one of the blasts ricocheted off the pavement and struck Brown. Although police reported that Brown urged the crowd to "burn, loot and shoot any officer white or black that stood in their way," no violence in fact took place. Instead, the group scampered back to Pine Street. Brown was rushed to the hospital, and after being treated for a superficial wound, he was secreted out of town.[26]

Not long after Brown was shot, a white sedan carrying four to six white male teenagers sped down Pine Street. Some reported that the occupants either fired buckshot or threw firecrackers from the car. The night-riders made one more pass through the Second Ward. Most of the black crowd dispersed to the safety of their homes, some to arm themselves. Fifteen minutes later the same car made another pass along Pine Street; this time it encountered hostile gunfire.[27] Meanwhile, rookie officer Russell Wrotten was shot while responding to a report that a window had been broken at a Laundromat in the Second Ward. Upon hearing of this,

Kinnamon exploded in anger. He grabbed his rifle and, according to a state police report, shouted: "We're going to get every son-of-a-bitch down there. I'm getting tired of fooling around." News that Wrotten's wound was minor calmed Kinnamon somewhat. Still, Attorney General Burch, General Gelston, and Captain Randall of the state police had to plead with Kinnamon to seal off the Second Ward, the standard operating procedure, rather than "clean[ing] out the area," Kinnamon's personal preference.[28]

About twenty minutes later, two black officers investigated a report of breaking and entering at a store near where Wrotten had been shot. They encountered a group of approximately one hundred black youths who poured gasoline into the street and set it afire. The officers uncovered no evidence of looting and saw no danger of the fire spreading. While they were assessing the situation, the white sedan made a final run along Pine Street. After state police stopped and searched the car, the driver and passengers were released. No weapons were found; nor were any arrests made, although officers observed that the car had been hit by two gunshots. The situation calmed to the point that General Gelston ordered the National Guard to go home, although the police continued to patrol the streets, and reports of at least one more fire and of blacks with guns continued to arrive at police headquarters.[29]

At approximately 1:00 A.M., after the Guard had dispersed, a fire erupted at the Pine Street Elementary School. The fire siren, however, did not sound for another forty-five minutes. In the interim, Charles Cornish, Hansel Greene, and other black residents unsuccessfully implored the RFC to put out the fire. The following morning Greene told the *Afro-American* that one "lousy truck" could have stopped the blaze. When BAF leader Lemuel Chester sought to get the Fire Company to move in, Chief Kinnamon allegedly retorted: "You goddamn niggers started the fire, now you goddamn niggers watch it burn. I don't give a damn if the entire Second Ward burns." Fire trucks did not pull out of the station house until 1:45 A.M., and the RFC merely stationed its equipment on the edge of the Second Ward so as to protect the business district.[30]

Even after thirty-two state troopers moved into position to protect the firemen, the RFC's trucks remained outside the Second Ward, in part because of police reports of a group of about thirty armed young blacks on the roof of a building. In spite of Kinnamon's and at least some of the firemen's claims, however, the crowd remained nonviolent, allowing four white linemen employed by the local utility company to clip electrical wiring without harm. Some residents borrowed a firehose from the RFC, only to find that they could not attach it to the fire hydrant. Ironically, police reported the hose as stolen. Others tried to douse the fire with buckets of water and garden hoses. In response to the lack of action by the RFC, Captain Randall of the state police fumed: "Where the hell were the fire trucks?" Not until at least 2:30 A.M., nearly two hours after the fire began, did the Rescue and Fire Company proceed into the area, and it did so at this point only because Attorney General Burch personally commandeered one of the fire trucks. When the firemen finally arrived, the crowd did not harm or impede them. On the contrary, black youths helped them water down the area. But by then the fire had spread, not to be fully extinguished until dawn. During the wait, Hansel Greene allowed members of the crowd to take perishables from his grocery store, which was destroyed by the fire. Police inaccurately reported this action as looting.[31]

As the sun rose, residents began to assess the damage, which was considerable. By then two square blocks and more than twenty buildings, including a dance hall, a grocery store, a record shop, two shoe-shine proprietors, the local Democratic Club, two barber shops, a bar-poolroom, a motel, a tailor's shop, and the Zion Baptist Church had been consumed by the blaze. Forty residents lost their homes; and at least $300,000 in property damage was incurred.[32] Arguably things could have been much worse if Kinnamon had gotten his way. If local police had sought to clear out the Second Ward rather than cordon off the area, more violence could have taken place. As Captain Randall put it, "There would have been hell to pay."[33]

In response, the National Guard rushed seven hundred strong to Cambridge, reestablishing posts they had deserted following the turmoil of 1963–64. For the next several days, Cambridge shared headlines with Detroit, the site of the worst racial riot of the decade. One *New York Times* front-page headline declared: "CHIEF OF SNCC HUNTED BY F.B.I.: Missing Leader Accused of 'Inciting to Riot' in Arson and Gunfire in Maryland." Above the headline a photograph showed the National Guard patrolling the smoke-filled streets of Cambridge, cluttered with the debris of burned buildings. Still another newspaper article described the incident as "a night of gunfire and arson . . . a night of incendiarism and sniping." Many other national newspapers carried similar front-page stories.[34]

Ten days after the Guard arrived, Hansel Greene, a Cambridge native and fifty-seven-year-old black businessman, descended from his upstairs bedroom to his downstairs den, grabbed his shotgun, and shot himself fatally in the heart. Greene had been "very depressed," his bookkeeper Elaine S. Bennett explained to a reporter. On the night of July 24, Greene's entire business—a popular poolroom, dance hall, and bar-night-club complex known as the Green Savoy, had burned to the ground. "When you see a lifetime of work go up in flames, it gets to you," explained his wife Lena, who had been in their upstairs bedroom when her husband took his life. Greene lacked insurance to offset his extensive losses, estimated at between $150,000 and $200,000, and as he told the local newspaper, he could not understand why "such a tragedy should happen to him," adding, "I tried to be nice to everybody." Greene was the only fatality of the period.[35]

Conflicting Interpretations

The "riots" in Cambridge and elsewhere prompted a flurry of investigations by government officials, journalists, and others to determine their causes and the nation's proper response to them. Cambridge figured prominently in these investigations, and in many ways, conflicting interpretations of what took place in Cambridge and why paralleled the general debate about the cause of racial rioting. Some blamed black radicals; others saw white racism as the root cause; still others found an assortment of culprits. Differences existed over what to call the events themselves, with some preferring the term *riots*, others the term *disorders*, and still others *uprisings*.[36]

About a month after the so-called riot in Cambridge, the Senate Judiciary Committee, headed by staunchly conservative Mississippi senator James Eastland, held special hearings to investigate the causes of the urban riots and to consider antiriot legislation. Proclaiming that the violence of the summer of 1967 was part of a vast communist conspiracy to take over America, Eastland invited Cambridge's police chief Brice Kinnamon to serve as one of his stellar witnesses. Kinnamon testified that H. Rap Brown was the sole cause of the riot in Cambridge. Upon completion of his "inflammatory speech," Kinnamon explained, Brown had led a group of people toward the business district, "instructing them to burn and tear Cambridge down [and] to shoot any policeman who tried to interfere." To substantiate his claim, Kinnamon played a tape of Brown's speech to the committee. After they had listened to the recording, Kinnamon contended that violence had broken out "immediately" following the speech and that the Pine Street Elementary School had been set ablaze shortly thereafter. He described the relationship between the "Negro community and the white community" as "excellent" and expressed no regrets for ordering the RFC to remain on the perimeter of the Second Ward, since the threat to their safety had been real.[37]

Even if one challenged the particulars of Kinnamon's testimony, as other witnesses would, the essence of his argument—that black radicals caused the riots—enjoyed a great deal of support. Even if Brown did not cause the riot in the precise way that Kinnamon detailed events, the police chief and others felt that Brown nonetheless caused the riot. Were Brown's words inflammatory? Did a riot take place? Would a riot have taken place had Brown not spoken? From Kinnamon's perspective the answer to the first two questions was clearly yes. Just as clearly, the answer to the last question was no. A large number of opinion makers and politicians agreed. By calling for the passage of a new law to "make it a crime to travel from state to state to incite violence," future president Gerald Ford, then the leader of the Republican Party in the House of Representatives, endorsed the view that Brown and other radicals had caused the riots. The law became known as the Brown amendment, after H. Rap Brown. A poll of Congress revealed that whereas only 14 percent of northern Democrats felt that "outside agitators" were of "great importance" in causing the riots, 69 percent of Republicans felt they were. Southern conservative Democrats, like Eastland, agreed with Republicans, a sign of the realignment of national politics that was beginning to take place.[38] By going forward with their plans to prosecute Brown for inciting a riot, Maryland's prosecutors lent weight to Kinnamon's claims. So too did many journalists and the mass media. Even when journalists disagreed with the conservative claim that radicals were the sole cause of the riots, their sensational coverage of the disorders and of black power tended to reinforce in the public mind the connection between black power and rioting. Gary Wills, one of the most prominent left-liberal journalists, began his article "The Second Civil War" by identifying Cambridge as "one of the first towns where modern demonstrations turned to rioting." Ironically, the bulk of Wills's article was critical of Kinnamon's police methods and sought to portray General George Gelston as a model for other law enforcement officials.[39]

More influential on the response of the law enforcement community to the riots than Wills's piece was *The Riot Makers*. This widely distributed film, which law enforcement recruits routinely viewed, was based on a book written by Eugene Methvin. While Methvin acknowledged the existence of multiple factors, his book and the film insisted that the "real" causes of the riots were the "riot makers." Comparing the riot makers to chemical catalysts, the film contended that the riot makers followed Leninist tactics, that they purposely set out to provoke riots so as to foster a crisis that would lead to a revolution. The film specifically named H. Rap Brown as a prime example of the modern riot maker, along with New Left stalwarts Abbie Hoffman, Rennie Davis, and Tom Hayden, all of whom were indicted on charges of conspiring to incite a riot during the 1968 Democratic Convention in Chicago.[40]

Conservatives bolstered this interpretation by noting that blacks had made gains during the 1960s; they had not fallen farther and farther behind economically and had toppled Jim Crow. Indeed, Kinnamon did not have to invent evidence of black progress to support his claim that Cambridge enjoyed good race relations. Nearly every public figure in Cambridge could rattle off a list of improvements and had done so, as had the Associated Press earlier that spring, describing advances ranging from declining unemployment to the gradual and voluntary desegregation of public schools. While most whites did not go as far as Kinnamon in denying that racial problems existed, they sided with him by arguing that Brown had played the key role in sparking the riot. For instance, one month after the riot, the *Daily Banner* published a detailed list of the city's accomplishments, from a dramatic drop in the unemployment rate to the construction of public housing. The editorial also took aim those who overlooked these gains.[41]

To counter Kinnamon's testimony and Eastland's interpretation of the riots as a by-product of a communist or black radical conspiracy, liberal Democrats called National Guard general George Gelston before the Judiciary Committee. Gelston, as mentioned, had been the commander of the National Guard when it was called to Cambridge in 1963 and again in 1967. Noting that prior appearances of "outside agitators" in Cambridge had not resulted in rioting, Gelston insisted that the cause of the disorder lay much deeper than the fiery address of a single individual. The blame, Gelston continued, lay with deep-rooted racial problems, of which Kinnamon had testified there were none. "Were there no problem," Gelston asserted, "there would be no need for an invitation" in the first place. In response to the friendly questions of liberal Democrats on the Judiciary Committee, Gelston disputed Kinnamon's specific recollection of the events. To counter the claim of black progress, Gelston read at length from a letter written by a third party, William Adkins, a prominent white attorney and politician from Talbot County. "Race relations in Cambridge are not excellent," wrote Adkins. "There are deep-seated feelings of hostility on both sides. . . . Such progress as has been made . . . has done little to improve feelings, since much that was done following 1963 was done not as a recognition of the justice of the Negroes' claims and grievances, but ostensively as a result of the violence itself." Many racial problems remained, Adkins continued. Blacks in Cambridge still lived largely in a ghetto, schools were "a continuing aggravation," and "little comment need be made about Chief Kinnamon's own swimming pool, which was operated as a totally segregated facility by the Cambridge Volunteer Fire Department."[42]

Given the chance, Kinnamon would undoubtedly have defended himself and the RFC against Adkins's suggestion, and by inference Gelston's, that the RFC shared culpability. Unlike black activists, who viewed the RFC in negative terms, Kinnamon held positive feelings toward the organization to which he had devoted much of his life. Like the RFC's other members, he considered it to represent the best of small town America, a place where people joined together in the interest of the community. Even the *Daily Banner*, which at times broached the idea of establishing a paid fire force, expressed its admiration for the "esprit de corps" of the RFC. "The members are bound together with a kind of fellowship that no other local organization enjoys," the paper wrote. "City Council members sometimes shake their heads in amazement when a question concerning the fire company comes to the surface," it continued. Or, as one of Kinnamon's fellow volunteers put it: "This organization [RFC] has always been one of the few self-sacrificing, dedicated bodies in our county. I wish and pray for many more such dedicated citizens to help foster and preserve our city, county, state and nation, especially now, when so many citizens care only for self interest and greed and are trying to grab everything for themselves and contributing nothing."[43] As a former chief of the RFC, Mayor Osvrey Pritchett would have shared these views. So too would most if not all the members of the DBCA, many of whom belonged to the RFC.

To a degree, Kinnamon's views paralleled those of many northern urban working-class whites. Historian John McGreevy argues that men and women in northern cities felt that the racial protests of the latter half of the 1960s endangered their identity and institutions, particularly those associated with Catholicism. Holding deep attachments to neighborhoods that served as the home of their churches, schools, and heritage, they fought fiercely to keep out outsiders who threatened these institutions. Similarly, the RFC had a much larger meaning than simply as a fire company. Its members saw the RFC as a symbol of a value system that was threatened by the forces of modernization. Whereas Catholicism united many lower- and working-class whites in Chicago and other northern cities, the RFC glued together a similar stratum of whites in Cambridge.[44]

This said, one reason that Kinnamon and the RFC had cause to fear for their safety was that historically, whites had benefited both economically and psychologically from the persistence of caste lines in Cambridge. Put differently, the response of the RFC to the so-called riot was rooted in the persistence of caste in Cambridge. In general, caste barriers that kept blacks out of its social facilities had not prevented the RFC from serving all of Cambridge when the fire alarm bell rang. Nevertheless, in 1967 the all-white makeup of the RFC affected its judgment and response, or lack thereof. Without a doubt, a desegregated fire company would have enjoyed much better relations with the black community and would have been much less fearful about entering the Second Ward on the night of July 24, if only for the reason that it had some filial relations to the black community.

One contemporary who held the RFC culpable was the novelist John Barth, a native of Cambridge. Barth's father "Whitey" had been a long-time member of the RFC. In one of his novels, Barth had expressed sympathy for the volunteer spirit of the fire association and its members. Yet Barth, who had moved from Cambridge upon entering college, had taken on many of the liberal ideals of the broader metropolises in which he lived and had developed dislike, if not contempt, for some of the provincial mores of America's small towns. Drawing on Gelston's testimony as well as reportage by several national newspapers, Barth rhetorically inquired: "Mustn't the responsibility of his [Greene's] losses and subsequent suicide be laid as much at the door of Chief Kinnamon and those of his way of thinking as at the door of H. Rap Brown & Co.?" After all, Barth observed, Kinnamon had prevented the Rescue and Fire Company from entering the Second Ward to put out the fire before it spread. As another Cambridge resident remarked, Kinnamon had been one of many who had kept blacks dependent on the all-white fire company, which for years had been at loggerheads with the civil rights movement in Cambridge.[45]

By holding white racism responsible, the Kerner Commission's overall interpretation of the riots complemented those put forth by Gelston and

Barth. Ironically, in a detailed analysis of the specific disturbance in Cambridge, staff members of the Kerner Commission suggested an alternative or third interpretation of the cause of the particular incident there. This interpretation, which was never released to the public, ultimately held neither Brown nor the RFC responsible because, according to its authors, Cambridge experienced a "low level civil disturbance"—not a riot, as almost all other parties presumed.[46] Rather than highlighting the impact of black radicals or institutional white racism, the staff of the Kerner Commission emphasized the themes of misperceptions and misinterpretations. Had it not been for the misperceptions between whites and blacks about each others' intentions, the commission concluded, the disturbance in Cambridge would have caught hardly anyone's attention.[47] For example, the staff reported, Officer Wrotten was shot by youths who feared that the police intended to fire on them. They felt this way because the police entered the area with their rifles drawn and because Brown had already been shot without warning. In turn, Wrotten, a rookie, had drawn his rifle because he feared snipers, based upon reports of snipers in the area and the incidences of sniper fire at other riots. Yet no one, except for Wrotten's assailant, was ever convicted of anything resembling sniper activity. Even before this shooting, the mere announcement that Brown, who had a reputation for militancy, intended to speak, had set the white community on edge, putting the police in particular in a "state of siege" mood. Some law enforcement officials, the Kerner staff argued, believed that Brown's appearance was aimed at setting a trap or an ambush for them, and one of the reasons that they shot at Brown in the first place was to prevent such an ambush. The fear of a trap and snipers also influenced the RFC's decision not to enter the Second Ward. "This view of impending events and anticipatory counter-measures" accumulated like a snowball, the Kerner staff concluded, creating the belief that a riot had taken place when in fact none did.[48]

Few in Cambridge or elsewhere, however, accepted this interpretation. Indeed, since it did not become part of the official report of the Kerner Commission, it did not receive much attention. On the contrary, the combination of two square blocks of burned buildings, the indictment of one of the most prominent militants in the nation for inciting a riot, and national headlines that placed the disturbances in Cambridge alongside those in Detroit convinced nearly all that Cambridge had experienced the most traumatic event in its history. Hansel Greene's tragic death only added to the community's sense of the gravity of the event.

Like Cambridge's residents, historians have accepted this mythical view of the disturbance. For instance, in *Freedom Bound: A History of America's Civil Rights Movement*, Robert Weisbrot writes: "Although the old guard of the civil rights movement still signaled its revulsion toward urban violence, news coverage focused on blacks like H. Rap Brown of SNCC, who gloried in destruction. In early August," Weisbrot asserts, "Brown went to Cambridge, Maryland, site of white racist demonstrations and a vigorous Ku Klux Klan chapter, and urged three hundred furious Negro youths, 'Burn this town down.' . . . Later that night blacks rioted in downtown Cambridge." (Weisbrot did not discuss the civil rights movement in Cambridge during the first half of the 1960s and provides no evidence of KKK involvement in the area.) In *The Struggle for Black Equality*, Harvard Sitkoff states that just a month after H. Rap Brown became the new chairman of SNCC, he "addressed an African-American rally in Cambridge, Maryland, during the week that the Detroit riot raged. Brown urged his audience to 'get you some guns.' . . . Brown implored, 'It's time for Cambridge to explode.' It did," Sitkoff concludes, "several hours after Brown's speech."[49]

The 1967 "riot" even became a part of one of the great epics of historical fiction, James A. Michener's *Chesapeake*. Although the events in Cambridge did not need to be embellished, Michener embellished them nonetheless. Michener's fictional protagonist LeRoy, who represented H. Rap Brown, declared of the elementary school: "We ought to burn the damned thing down!" In Michener's rendering, immediately after LeRoy had uttered these words "the gang" marched on the school, "where fires were lit and wild cries uttered as dry timbers flamed upwards in the night. The effect was intoxicating," Michener adds, "and many blacks rushed blazing fagots to ignite other buildings. . . The town fire engines clanged down the narrow road to the Neck [Michener's term for the Second Ward], but rioting blacks held them off, so after two frustrated attempts the firemen departed with the threat: 'We'll let the whole damned place go up.'" At least the last line had a kernel of truth to it. This is not to argue that historians and writers of historical fiction have exaggerated the gravity of all the riots of the 1960s or the cause of some of the larger riots of the era. But this account of events in Cambridge should caution us against misusing specific examples so as to fit general theories about the past or accepting self-serving testimony and purposely dramatic accounts of the past as the truth.[50]

This analysis also reveals the danger of relying too heavily on mass media accounts of contemporary events to reconstruct the past. As Jenny Walker has demonstrated, the mass media tended to underrepresent acts of violence during the first half of the 1960s and exaggerated the degree of violence during the latter half of the decade. This in turn helps explain why so many historians have mischaracterized the civil rights movement as being committed to nonviolence prior to 1965 and willing to resort to violence afterward, when in fact nonviolence and violence (or at least a belief in self-defense) existed side by side throughout the civil rights years.[51]

Cambridge and America

Regardless of whether Cambridge experienced a riot or just a low-level disturbance, events there and in other urban centers in the long hot summer of 1967 "changed the nation's course of racial politics," as Clayborne Carson and Tom Hamburger asserted.[52] Cambridge catapulted Spiro T. Agnew to national prominence and reinforced the politics of racial polarization. Agnew, who was elected governor of Maryland in 1966, was virtually unknown outside the state until the summer of 1967. Until the "Brown riot," he had a reputation as a moderate Republican in a state where many blacks still viewed the Republican Party as the party of Lincoln. As county executive of Baltimore County, Agnew had garnered a reputation as a "liberal," according to his biographer Jules Witcover. In the spring of 1964, Agnew urged Marylanders to vote for Senator Daniel Brewster, Lyndon B. Johnson's proxy in the Democratic Party's presidential primary, rather than supporting Alabama governor George Wallace, whom Agnew termed a fomenter of hatred and bigotry. Agnew's sharp criticism of Wallace, in fact, drew the ire of the National States Rights Party, which accused Agnew of being a communist. Agnew's support for urban renewal reinforced his reputation as a liberal on racial matters, as did his support for New York governor Nelson Rockefeller, Barry Goldwater's main opponent for the Republican presidential nomination in 1964.[53]

Agnew consolidated his reputation as a Rockefeller Republican during his gubernatorial campaign in 1966. His Democratic opponent, George Mahoney, ran on the slogan "Your Home Is Your Castle—Protect It," a thinly veiled reference to proposed open housing legislation, which Mahoney opposed. In contrast, Agnew cast himself as a responsible moderate who would stand up to the hate mongers. Based on his record and promises, Agnew won the endorsement of the *New York Times*, the Americans for Democratic Action, and the Baltimore *Afro-American*, all liberal institutions. He also won the overwhelming support of Cambridge's black voters.[54]

In his first year as governor, Agnew maintained his reputation as a moderate and the support of Maryland's African-American community. A week before Brown spoke in Cambridge, Agnew held a joint news conference in Annapolis with NAACP president Roy Wilkins. At the conference, Agnew praised Wilkins for his leadership, and Wilkins made clear his support for the governor. Nearby stood Dr. Gilbert Ware, a former professor at Morgan State University and a member of the U.S. Civil Rights Commission. Ware was the first black person to be appointed to the staff of a Maryland governor. At the time of Ware's appointment, Agnew garnered much praise from Maryland's civil rights leadership. Parren Mitchell, the son of NAACP official Clarence Mitchell, for one, called the appointment "tremendously exciting." Baltimore Urban League director Dr. Furman Templeton asserted that Ware's appointment "gives status as has never been given to Negroes before and will serve to win continued support for the [Agnew] administration."[55]

Brown's appearance in Cambridge and the fire that followed can thus be seen as a pivotal moment in Agnew's career. On the morning of July 25, Agnew rushed to Cambridge from his vacation home in Ocean City, Maryland. He immediately issued a statement expressing his "grief and perplexity at this senseless destruction precipitated by a professional agitator whose inflammatory statements deliberately provoked the outbreak of violence." After pledging to provide aid to the black citizens of Cambridge, Agnew announced that he had "directed the authorities to seek out H. Rap Brown and bring him to justice." "Such a person," Agnew continued, "cannot be permitted to enter a State with the intention to destroy and then sneak away." Several days later, Agnew exclaimed that while he deplored slum conditions and persistent discrimination, these problems did not "give any person or group a license to commit crimes." While promising to work for racial reforms, he announced he would not meet with those who "engage in or urge riots." In spite of evidence that the upheavals in Cambridge had more complex origins, Agnew maintained that irresponsible militants, like Brown, caused them. Agnew responded similarly to riots that erupted in Baltimore following the assassination of Martin Luther King, Jr., admonishing moderate civil rights leaders for not censuring black militants.[56]

When the Kerner Commission issued its report in the spring of 1968, Agnew became one of its most visible critics. In a speech to the National Governors' Conference, Agnew termed the report "compelling" in revealing "more about the mind of our nation than the nature of violence." Tragically, Agnew asserted, "like the violence it examined, the Kerner Report was self-defeating as a result of an amorphous, if not fallacious, first premise." By setting out to show that the riots had racial causes, the commission had overlooked an obvious point, namely that the majority of poor people in America were white. This fact, Agnew asserted, "opens the way to new and deeply disturbing questions. Why don't impoverished white Americans riot? Could it be that they know they will not meet with sympathy, that collective white lawlessness will not be tolerated?" Lest the audience draw the wrong conclusion, Agnew made clear his views. "They [the Kerner Commission] seem to blame everybody but the people who did it! This masochistic group guilt for white racism pervades every facet of the Report's reasoning." Drawing on his own experiences with the Cambridge "riot," Agnew lambasted the commission for neglecting to highlight "inflammatory" statements such as H. Rap Brown's 'Violence is as American as cherry pie'" as prime causes of the riots. (Brown did not utter this statement in Cambridge, although he did on another occasion.) Agnew suggested that white liberals were just as guilty as Brown. Their permissive attitudes, Agnew stated, and not white racism, stood as the "precipitating cause" of the riots. The Kerner Commission's proposed remedy of massive social programs, Agnew concluded, would produce another round of violence by rewarding the rioters.[57]

One of the reasons Agnew moved to the right was because his political instincts informed him that he would benefit by doing so. Indeed, Agnew's reaction to the riots helped convince Richard Nixon to nominate Agnew as his running mate in 1968. Agnew's rise to power was meteoric; had he not pleaded *nolo contendere* to a charge of accepting a bribe while a county commissioner, he might well have become president of the United States. Nixon nominated Agnew as his running mate because he hoped that the governor could serve as a constructive foil to George Wallace, who threatened to garner the vote of many "middle Americans." As a Marylander, Agnew also helped the Republican Party make inroads in the South.[58]

Even voters in Cambridge who had opposed him for governor in 1966 found Agnew's message attractive. In 1960, John F. Kennedy, the Democratic Party's nominee, won the state of Maryland and the majority of votes in Dorchester County. Kennedy defeated Nixon by 51.8 percent to 48.2 percent, a margin of victory slightly larger than he enjoyed nation-wide. Four years later, President Johnson swept the state, although the Republican nominee, Barry Goldwater, garnered a slim victory in Dorchester County, breaking the county's long-standing record of voting for the national winner. In 1968, the Republican Nixon-Agnew ticket outpolled George Wallace's American Independent Party ticket 41.4 per-cent to 31.8 percent in Dorchester County (Humphrey received 26.8 per-cent of the vote), although Humphrey won the state. Four years later, a whopping 75 percent of Dorchester County voters backed Nixon and Agnew. The Republican ticket also won the state.[59]

But Agnew's transformation should be seen as more than the move of an opportunistic politician. Agnew's reaction personified the reaction of many Americans to the urban riots of the time as well as their reaction to the antiwar movement, the counterculture, and other movements of the era. He both reflected and articulated the white backlash taking place in the North among much of the "silent majority." Like this silent majority, Agnew felt betrayed and besieged by the civil rights movement and liber-alism in general. To state it differently, the political shift between 1964 and 1968 was not about Agnew per se but about the issues and views that he came to personify.

Part of Agnew's allure grew out of the fact that unlike the Alabama governor, he had not championed segregation or massive resistance. He was not crudely bigoted like George Wallace. On the contrary, Agnew supported the essential goals of the civil rights movement. Yet while ad-mitting that America's system had its flaws, he insisted that the American way was the best one in the world, and he defended the U.S. government passionately against those who deemed it illegitimate and who considered violence a necessary means toward achieving a more just society. Having served in the military during World War II and having worked hard to make a successful career, he resented those who condemned him as a sym-bol of white privilege. Raised in a world in which civility mattered a great deal—his father owned and operated a small restaurant—he was aghast at its rapid decline. As much as any other leader of the time, Agnew enabled the Republican Party to wedge whites, especially working- and middle-class males, away from the Democratic Party, which helped transform the GOP from a minority into a majority party. He did so by casting himself as part of the broad white middle class that opposed reactionaries and radicals. Even though the press consistently belittled him because of his blunders on the campaign trail—as well as his disdain for the liberal press—many saw him as a more legitimate representative of their views than was Wallace. Indeed, Agnew's blunders probably helped endear him to many so-called middle Americans, because they reinforced his image as being part of the middle class rather than a representative of the elite liberal establishment.[60]

At the same time that Spiro Agnew was profitably capitalizing on white backlash against the riots in Cambridge and elsewhere (and the liberal responses to them), H. Rap Brown and other black radicals were attempting unsuccessfully to use the riots and white backlash as a springboard to launch a revolutionary challenge to the status quo.[61] While Brown denied the specific charges that he had incited a riot in Cambridge, he grew ever more bombastic in the months that followed. Upon learning that he was wanted for inciting a riot, he sought to arrange his surrender through William Kunstler, a prominent radical attorney. On July 26, while at National Airport just outside Washington, D.C., awaiting a flight to New York (where he had agreed to surrender), he was arrested by the FBI. In a strange sequence of events, the FBI took Brown to a federal courthouse in Alexandria, Virginia, the site of the arraignment, dropped charges, and then allowed Virginia authorities to rearrest him on state fugitive charges, after which he posted bail and was released. Shortly before his release, Brown issued a statement in which he declared that he considered himself neither "morally nor legally bound to obey laws made by a body in which I have no representation." Adding fuel to the fire, he proclaimed: "These rebellions are but a dress rehearsal for real revolution. Neither imprisonment nor threats of death will sway me from the path that I have taken, nor will they sway others like me."[62]

In the weeks that followed, Brown maintained this line. He told a large crowd in Detroit, "You did a good job here," predicting that if blacks united they could "make the Detroit 'rebellion' look like a 'picnic.'" In an interview with a Cuban radio station he contended: "It can be confidently predicted that every city in America which has a large colored population will have a great rebellion."[63] Concomitantly, Brown continued to deny the specific charges of inciting a riot in Cambridge, and his attorneys embarked on the long and complicated task of getting all charges dropped. Thus, ironically, Brown described the legal system as illegitimate yet crafted a sophisticated legal response to absolve him of the state's charges. For example, in a legal brief, Brown's attorneys not only denied the state's charges; they countered that the civil disturbance had been "precipitated by the act of a deputy sheriff" who had fired a shotgun blast that had hit Brown on the forehead after he had completed his speech. Cambridge's chief of police and fire chief, the state's attorney, and the sheriff of Dorchester County, the brief asserted, had "purposely conspired together and entered into a plan or scheme of concerted and joint action" aimed at harassing and deterring civil rights activists from "exercising their constitutional rights."[64]

As absurd as Brown's retort sounded, it had a grain of truth to it. Following the wave of riots in the summer of 1967, the FBI embarked on its own concerted effort, in J. Edgar Hoover's words, to "expose, disrupt, misdirect, or otherwise neutralize the activities of black nationalist, hate-type organizations and groupings, their leadership, spokesman, membership and supporters." Brown, who had been monitored by the FBI since at least late April, was one of those targeted.[65] Brown faced constant harassment from federal and state authorities stemming from his Cambridge speech. On August 18, 1967, he was arrested in Louisiana for carrying a gun across state lines. Brown was in Louisiana to visit his family, had a permit to carry the gun, and had registered it with authorities on his flight from New York to New Orleans. However, while he was en route to New Orleans, a grand jury in Maryland indicted him on the riot and arson charges. Since it was illegal for someone under indictment to transport weapons across state lines, authorities arrested him upon his arrival in New Orleans, in spite of the fact that he had not been under indictment upon his departure. Rather than recognize these special circumstances, Judge Lansing Mitchell, who prior to the trial had privately stated his intention to "get that nigger," sentenced Brown to five years in jail and fined him $2,000 for illegally transporting a weapon. Upon his release on bail of $25,000, pending appeal, Mitchell confined Brown to New York City. SNCC termed this restriction "house arrest." After speaking at a black power rally in California, Brown was arrested again for violating the terms of his release.[66]

On April 18, 1968, Brown was formally arraigned in Cambridge, under heavy guard. Afterward he was released on bond and State's Attorney Yates filed for a change of venue on the grounds that Brown could not receive a fair trial in Dorchester County. Ironically, Brown and his attorneys opposed this motion, claiming that he could not receive a fair trial anywhere and that at least in Cambridge he would enjoy the "logistical assistance and moral support" of a "large and active black community." Following a bevy of legal maneuvers, Yates's motion to remove the trial from Cambridge was granted and Brown's trial was slated to begin on March 10, 1970, in a state court located in Bel Air, Hartford County, Maryland. Brown unsuccessfully opposed this venue on the grounds that Hartford County, unlike Dorchester County, was almost entirely white. The day before the trial began, however, a bomb blew up in a car carrying two of Brown's longtime SNCC colleagues, Ralph Featherstone and William (Che) Payne, killing them both. Fearing for his life, Brown fled to Canada. Claiming that the two had intended to plant a bomb at the Bel Air courthouse, the FBI placed Brown on its "most wanted" list. Over a year later, on October 16, 1971, Brown was arrested following a robbery and shootout with police at a New York City bar and restaurant. Two years later he was convicted of armed robbery and assaulting police and sentenced to five to fifteen years in prison. Shortly thereafter, Brown pled guilty to charges of failing to show up for the 1970 trial. In exchange the state's attorney of Maryland agreed to drop the initial riot and arson charges. Most figured that he was no longer a danger anyway; by the early 1970s SNCC had disintegrated into a shell of its former self, and the black power movement had declined nearly as quickly as it had arisen. Citing the Kerner Commission's staff findings, which had never been released but which had been leaked to the press, Howard County State's Attorney Richard J. Kinlen, to whose jurisdiction the case had been moved, offered a different explanation. He argued that the state's case had always been weak, a position that hurt him politically and resulted in his loss of the post.[67]

Even though Brown was never convicted of inciting a riot, his legal travails confirmed the widespread view that he was a troublemaker and hindered his ability to provide effective leadership, something SNCC recognized when it made Phil Hutchings chair in June 1968. Notwithstanding proclamations that the United States was on the eve of a revolution, Brown's power was on the wane from July 24, 1967. Ironically, during the early 1960s, SNCC had criticized Martin Luther King, Jr., for making rash visits to various communities, delivering charismatic speeches, and then leaving for appearances elsewhere. SNCC, in contrast, sought to organize communities and to develop indigenous leadership. In fact, SNCC played this role in Cambridge in 1962. Yet in July 1967, Brown played the part of the charismatic leader who delivered rash speeches and then left town. Exhausted from years of organizing, tantalized by the mass media, harassed by law enforcement authorities, and caught up in the emotion of the moment, Brown and many of his SNCC colleagues fooled themselves into believing that radical change or a revolution was around the corner. Subsequent events, ranging from the election and reelection of Richard Nixon and Spiro Agnew to the rise of the new right, showed that nothing was farther from the truth.[68]

Equally important, the riots of the mid-1960s added to the problems of the civil rights movement. As earlier noted, when Congress finally enacted weak open housing legislation in 1968, it attached to the legislation a rider known as the Brown amendment. This rider made it illegal to cross state lines to incite a riot. The Democratic Congress passed no new civil rights legislation after 1968. Nor did Democrats, who maintained control of the House and Senate, follow up on the Kerner Commission's recommendations to develop large federal programs aimed at eradicating the ghetto conditions that in the commission's analysis underlay the riots. To make matters worse, as the economy stalled, black economic gains, which had been impressive, diminished. The economic downturn undercut the public's belief that the federal government could develop large-scale programs aimed at overcoming poverty.[69]

Moreover, in the wake of the riots of 1967 and 1968, black radicals like Brown were arrested and jailed or in some cases shot, either by police or by rival political factions. After serving several years in prison and converting to Islam, Brown changed his name to Jamil Abdullah Al-Amin. The former SNCC leader settled in Atlanta, Georgia, established a grocery store and a mosque, and laid plans for building a community center. While insisting that he remained a radical and a separatist, he drifted from the public limelight, focusing much of his time on the religious teaching of Allah and fostering a private revolution among those who attended his mosque. In 1996 he was arrested on drug charges. Although absolved of these charges, he was arrested again in 2000 and charged with the much more serious crime of fatally shooting a policeman after police attempted to arrest him for failing to show up in court on an outstanding theft charge. A smattering of radicals, including many SNCC veterans, insisted that Brown was being framed, emphasizing the long-standing hatred that the police held for him stemming from his days as chair of SNCC. They even argued that the original theft charge was part of a broader trap aimed at provoking Brown into engaging in a shootout. A jury of nine blacks, two whites, and one Hispanic, however, disagreed, convicting Brown of first degree murder. Shortly before Brown's arrest, Spiro T. Agnew emerged from years of private anonymity, largely to remark upon the life and legacy of Richard Nixon, who had recently died. Somewhat similarly,

Agnew cast himself as a victim of forces that had never wanted him to become president. Few paid much attention to Agnew's statements or to Brown's arrest, but there could be little doubt as to who had had the greater impact. Black power was a relic of the past, while the politics of racial backlash as practiced by Agnew had became a mainstay of the American political scene.[70]

The Final Act

Let the lightning flash and let the thunder roar
But Dear God Almighty let nonviolence soar
Step in and let this dark cloud cease
So we O God can live here in peace.
Cloud of hatred don't make us hate one another
Black and white together—each other's brother
We together helped build what you see
This great nation striving for freedom and equality.
Gregory Meekins, August 1967

We are not militant but tired. We are tired of being nonviolent. . . .
This is our country. We intend to live here. I intend to die here. I don't
see why we have to live like tramps.
Octavene Saunders, Afro-Aggressors, 1968

To dream the impossible dream, to fight the impossible foe . . . to reach
the unreachable star.
Cambridge High School Yearbook, 1968

An examination of the final act or chapter in the history of the civil rights
movement in Cambridge allows us to answer better the questions of what
happened to the movement and what it achieved. While in their discussion of what happened to the movement many studies highlight the assassination of Dr. Martin Luther King, Jr., the repression of black radicals,
and the developing schisms, the present study suggests that structural
forces played a greater role in bringing the movement to an end in Cambridge than did internal or accidental developments. This concluding
chapter also warns against seeing the early movement, or the fight to
topple Jim Crow, as the successful phase of the movement, and the latter
black power effort to attain greater economic, social, and political power
and personal empowerment as the unsuccessful phase. As we have seen, in
Cambridge, efforts to topple Jim Crow did not produce absolute victories.
On the contrary, in the only referendum in the nation on whether to de-

segregate public accommodations, Cambridge citizens voted to uphold Jim Crow, and the local civil rights movement orchestrated a boycott of the referendum rather than mobilize the black vote behind the anti-discriminatory measure. Nonetheless, as we shall see, the movement produced significant if incomplete economic, social, and personal gains—in other words, the very objectives championed by black power advocates nationwide in the latter part of the 1960s.[1]

After the Fire

In the immediate aftermath of the "Brown riot," Cambridge looked much like many other northern cities. It shared headlines with Detroit, Newark, and other sites of civil disorder, and tensions remained high. At 9:00 P.M. on the twenty-fifth of July, 1967, the Black Action Federation (BAF) organized a rally, which climaxed when some youths overturned a telephone booth, stoned cars, and vandalized parking meters. Following the arrest of several speakers, including Stuart Wechsler, a CORE activist from Baltimore, the commander of the National Guard warned that the Guard would use tear gas if the ralliers did not return home. They did. On the evening of the twenty-sixth the BAF held another protest, where Lemuel Chester and Elaine Adams delivered emotional speeches. Afterward a National Guard truck was stoned and some in the crowd sought to set fire to the telephone company and several other buildings. At this point the National Guard sealed off the area and commanded the crowd to disperse. When several blacks did not, the battalion commander ordered units to fire a round of gas at them. Within five minutes the streets were cleared. No further disturbances took place, and the National Guard departed on July 29.[2]

Prior to the guardsmen's departure, local authorities arrested James Lewis, Leon Lewis, and Chauncy Askins, all of Cambridge, and charged them with shooting Officer Wrotten on the night of the twenty-fourth. In addition, Chester Lewis and Johnny Lee Wilson, both of Dover, were arrested and charged with "disrespecting" the National Guard, and Lemuel Chester was arrested and charged with inciting a riot. Several juveniles were also charged with setting the Pine Street Elementary School on fire.[3]

To a degree, these arrests were aimed at sending a message to the local movement and reflected the broader national crackdown by law enforcement authorities against the Black Panther Party and other radicals. Yet, the BAF remained unapologetic about its actions. In a speech she delivered in Cambridge on August 2, four days after the Guard departed, Gloria Richardson defended H. Rap Brown, largely on the grounds that he had delivered the same speech elsewhere without provoking a riot. After a brief respite, in part due to the tragic suicide death of Hansel Greene, the Black Action Federation announced plans to hold still another black power rally. Fearing another round of violence, Governor Agnew ordered the state police to monitor the situation and to stop the speech of anyone who sought to incite a riot. The governor pressured church officials to prevent the BAF from making use of their facilities. Bishop James Leonard Eure, of Salisbury, for one, padlocked the church of the Reverend Ernest Dupree. Dupree had agreed to allow the BAF to hold its rally in his Church of God. Other ministers, associated with the larger Methodist and Baptist churches, made clear that the BAF was not welcome in their houses of worship. The destruction of the Elks Lodge eliminated the other traditional meeting place. As a result, the BAF had to hold its rally in the garage of Herbert St. Clair's house. On the day of the gathering, police and state troopers outnumbered demonstrators by a ratio of more than two to one —two hundred to seventy-five, by some estimates.[4]

In spite of fiery addresses by Gloria Richardson Dandridge and Dino Prettyman of the Baltimore-based Civic Interest Group, no violence took place at this rally. Nor did violence erupt during a subsequent nighttime march, which climaxed when state troopers blocked protesters from proceeding outside the Second Ward. However, emotions remained heated. For instance, during the latter protest Reverend Dupree declared that he would speak out on civil rights in spite of opposition from his superiors. "If I can't stand by my convictions, I'm less than a preacher," Dupree exclaimed. "Either I feel like we ought to have justice or I don't," he added. "Like I told my bishop, you can put me out of my building but you can't put me out of town." Coming from a minister, in a community where ministers had tended to play a minor role in the civil rights movement, these were heady words.[5]

Several days after this rally, representatives of the BAF appeared before a town council meeting, where they demanded better housing, jobs, and recreational facilities. "We should have representatives in city jobs. We feel the city owes them to us," declared Elaine Adams, one of the BAF's leaders. "I would like to walk into a city office . . . and see a black face sitting behind the desk, all ready to greet me," Emerson Stafford added. "The black people pay taxes too." While neither council head Charles

Cornish nor Mayor Pritchett dismissed the BAF's demands outright, Pritchett retorted that he would "never consent to laying off one person in order to take another one in his place," and Cornish complained that too often grievances had been expressed on "street corners" rather than at council meetings.[6]

Meanwhile, plans to construct more public housing stalled, in part because of a somewhat paradoxical development. For several years the federal government had pledged funds to build more units. The riots of 1967 sped up the application process, with both federal and state officials expediting the approval of a grant. Local moderates, such as the editor of the *Daily Banner* and Charles Cornish, insisted that they supported the goal of constructing public housing. Only the DBCA publicly opposed public housing, calling instead for the enactment of a home ownership initiative. However, a ruling by the federal government that not all of the new units could be located in the Second Ward, since this would entail a violation of the Civil Rights Act of 1964, complicated matters. In a strange twist, town officials now asserted that the federal government was to blame for the lack of construction of public housing. As in the past, black activists retorted that influential white landlords, including County Commissioner Roscoe Wiley, stood in the way. Concomitantly, blacks complained that the housing code, which had been written to improve conditions in existent housing, was not being enforced for many of the same reasons that new public housing was not being built. Town officials replied that they did not have the staffing or funds to inspect homes effectively and that authorities sought to avoid fining landlords, lest they board up their properties and throw their black tenants out on the streets.[7]

This atmosphere of acrimony gave rise to a new wave of fires, which accompanied the trial of the first group of alleged arsonists and assailants. Less than a month after the first black power rally, a white-owned grocery store in the Second Ward was set on fire for the second time in a year. Two days later State's Attorney William Yates reported a second case of arson, this time at a vacant house adjoining the St. Clair Elementary school, also in the Second Ward. In both cases, the RFC responded rapidly enough to extinguish the fires before they spread or caused much damage. A week after the second fire came Dwight Cromwell's trial for making a false alarm on the eve of Brown's appearance. Even though Cromwell denied the charges, the jury found him guilty, and Judge C. Burnham Mace sentenced him to prison for a year and fined him $250 and costs. Several days later two young black men, Arrenda Sharp, twenty-one, and James Maddox, twenty, were arrested on charges of arson. During grand jury hearings over this case, the *Daily Banner* reported that Lemuel Chester, the head of the BAF, "was paying out money to set the fires." A day later, in a small story, the *Daily Banner* retracted this specific allegation but left alive the rumor that the fires were part of a larger conspiracy. Whether Chester actively promoted arson remains unclear. He insisted that he did not. Yet those who were arrested hinted that they did not act alone. Nonetheless, the city did not feel it had the evidence to prosecute Chester on conspiracy charges.[8]

Around the same time, the UAW and the United Steelworkers of America lost elections to represent workers at Airpax Industries and Cambridge Wire and Cloth, respectively. Both companies employed all-white workforces, with the exception of a couple of token custodial positions held by blacks. The desire to keep blacks out and a distrust of outsiders, both reinforced by recent events, played a role in labor's defeat. The experience of the longshoremen's union several years earlier suggested that ultimately, unionization would lead to the hiring of black workers. Local activists did not initiate employment discrimination suits against either the unions that had lost or the two companies, although they continued to pressure the federal government to compel the companies, both of which held sizable defense contracts, to hire more black workers.[9]

In January 1968, members of the Black Action Federation presented a list of grievances to the Cambridge Community Relations Commission, chaired by William Chaffinch. As in the past, black radicals placed poor housing conditions in the Second Ward, inadequate recreational facilities, and discriminatory job practices at the top of their list. In reference to the ongoing debate over the cause of the previous summer's riot, Elaine Adams declared: "It's not H. Rap Brown or Stokely Carmichael but these conditions which cause disturbances." Suggesting that more trouble lay ahead, Emerson Stafford added, "March is just about the beginning of the long hot summer [and] if there are no changes as spring shapes up, people begin to make other plans."[10] Not long afterward, the BAF repeated its demands before the State Human Relations Council and in a meeting with Governor Agnew's top aides. While the council issued a statement suggesting sympathy for the BAF and accused local moderates of stalling, especially on housing, Agnew responded more ambiguously. Perhaps out of political calculation, he defended the work of Chaffinch and other Cambridge authorities, including State Senator Frederick Malkus. He rebuffed demands to drop charges against Brown in spite of a Kerner Commission memo suggesting that the specific charges would not hold up in court. In addition, Agnew privately agreed with an aide who wrote that most of the BAF's demands were "exaggerated." Yet, at the same time, Agnew lobbied the federal government to provide funding for both the War on Poverty and economic development projects in Cambridge, and his aides continued to pressure local officials to upgrade housing in the Second Ward. This behind-the-scenes lobbying suggested that Agnew, like many conservative politicians, often appeared more conservative on race relations than he was in reality. Agnew's response to the BAF also prefigured the civil rights policy of the Nixon Administration, which publicly coddled southern conservative whites and urban ethnics via anti–civil rights statements, while at the same time implementing affirmative action and overseeing the desegregation of public schools.[11]

During the early months of 1968, as the debate over public housing festered, several more blacks were tried and convicted on charges stemming from events related to the "riot" of 1967. Leon Lewis and James Lewis were sentenced to six and seven years in prison, respectively, on charges of assaulting Officer Wrotten on the night of the riot. Observing that Leon Lewis showed "no signs of animosity" and that the assault (shooting) could be attributed to the "excitement and emotion of the moment," Judge C. Burnham Mace expressed his hope that Lewis would rehabilitate himself. Still, Mace added, "The streets are not going to be safe for you or me if we permit this to continue." Lewis admitted he was armed the night of the twenty-fourth but denied shooting Wrotten. "I told them ain't no way I could have shot anyone from where I was at but they didn't want to listen to it no way. . . . Somebody had to be the fall card." The other defendants denied the charges as well. Not long afterward, Arrenda Sharp was sentenced to three years in prison for setting fire to a building in the Second Ward in October. James Maddox was convicted on a separate arson charge and sentenced to up to two years in prison. Maddox "undoubtedly got caught up in the surge of crime being committed at the time," stated the prosecutor. Nonetheless, Judge Mace argued that he could not suspend the sentence.[12]

On the national level, the crackdown on leading black radicals, from Black Panther Party leaders Huey Newton and Fred Hampton to SNCC activist H. Rap Brown, dampened the strength and viability of the civil rights movement. The impact of local prosecutions was more ambiguous. With the exception of Cromwell, none of those convicted were movement leaders. Lemuel Chester's ability to escape prosecution suggests that authorities pursued cases based upon their desire to solve real crimes rather than simply to "neutralize" the civil rights movement. Still, the series of prosecutions did send a message to civil rights forces that local authorities would not tolerate violence or arson.[13]

As with the movement in general, the movement in Cambridge was hurt by the schism of its major civil rights group. In early 1968, the BAF split in two. One group retained the name BAF and the other called itself the Afro-Aggressors. Unlike SNCC, in which schism followed lengthy debates, the BAF split into factions without undergoing any similar process. Personality differences, some of which may have been rooted in long-standing family conflicts, accounted for the split as much as did any ideological or tactical dispute. Since both organizations derived from the already diminished ranks of CNAC, neither counted many people as members, and certainly neither organization displayed the ability CNAC had shown during the early 1960s to mobilize hundreds of Cambridge's black citizens. In spite of its name, the Afro-Aggressors proved more willing to work with moderates than the BAF and included more veteran activists.[14]

The Return of Stability

By the end of 1968, the BAF had ceased to exist; the Afro-Aggressors disappeared shortly thereafter. The lack of any news coverage of their demise makes it difficult to determine the exact causes of their disbanding and reflects the decrease in racial tensions in Cambridge in the final two years of the 1960s.[15] While cities across America erupted following King's assassination, Cambridge experienced only a very small disturbance after his death. H. Rap Brown's reappearance in Cambridge for a court hearing less than two weeks after King's assassination did not produce any disruptions. Evidence of a new willingness to cooperate came in the form of interracial religious services; the construction of rent-subsidy housing and low-cost units for sale, built with the help of private funding; and the establishment of a community center. Whereas in the aftermath of the Brown riot Lemuel Chester was accused of inciting a spree of fires, in late 1968 the city appointed him director of the new community center. The community center's board of directors also included several leaders of the Afro-Aggressors, namely Elaine Adams, Emerson Stafford, and Alphonso Fitchett.[16]

Even though conservatives continued to win at the polls—Pritchett was reelected mayor by a four-to-one margin over Leon Webster, the runaway favorite of the Second Ward—in general the local government followed a centrist course in the years that followed. The County Commission, traditionally much more conservative than the town council, restored a food stamp program it had long opposed. More important, city officials responded constructively to an October 29 meeting with the Afro-Aggressors. At the meeting, four of the Afro-Aggressors' leaders delivered passionate prepared statements. "We are not militant but tired," Octavene Saunders began. "We are tired of being nonviolent." After repeating complaints about poor housing and the lack of economic opportunities, Saunders exclaimed, "This is our country. We intend to live here. I intend to die here. I don't see why we have to live like tramps."[17]

In the early 1960s and in the wake of the 1967 riots, officials responded defensively to such charges, reciting the usual litany of Cambridge's history of progressive racial relations. Time and again, they countered that radical demands were either without merit or counterproductive. In contrast, this time Mayor Pritchett promised a major development "within 60 days." The following day, in fact, the city council approved a resolution favoring the construction of seventy-five new housing units. Even though all these units were to be built in the Second Ward, William Chaffinch reported that the federal government would approve them as long as some of the proposed total of 150 units were built outside the Second Ward. Chaffinch added that the "appeal made by Second Ward delegates" had had a significant impact on the council's decision to authorize the new units. The change in views was also reflected in the editorial comments of the *Daily Banner.* which used Saunders's speech as the occasion to demand a shift in attitudes. "The time has come to think as highly of human values as we have of property values," said one editorial. In language that legitimized the Afro-Aggressors' charges, the paper added: "It is common knowledge that some of the slum landlords have been getting away with murder."[18]

Further evidence of a new, less polarized mood came in the high schools. In the early 1960s, when Donna Richardson and several others had enrolled at the all-white Cambridge High School, they encountered open hostility from white students and teachers. As a result, they returned to an all-black school. The following fall, a handful of blacks enrolled at Cambridge High School, and in the next two years a few more did so. Tensions remained high, as evidenced by the fight that broke out between Nicky Parks and Albert Jones at the end of the 1966–67 school year.

Throughout this period, white and black youths often were at the forefront of many of the confrontations that took place. Dizzyland, as noted,
was a white student hangout and one of the centers of black-white conflict. The movie theater, roller-skating rink, and pool, three spaces that
catered disproportionately to youths, were sites of constant conflict.

Following the upheavals of 1967, however, the mood began to change.
An increasing number of blacks enrolled at Cambridge High School and,
for the first time, began to participate in a growing number of integrated
activities, from sports and cheerleading to the band. For the first time
blacks joined the faculty, including George Kent, who taught French and
coached the junior varsity football squad. The motto of the *Yearling*,
adopted by the student editors of the yearbook, illustrated this shift in
attitudes. In 1964 the yearbook began by citing the chamber of commerce
motto: "Cambridge is not just a place, it's a place making progress." At the
time, the yearbook's editors praised their community's progressive record,
leaving out any mention of the town's racial discord or the presence of the
National Guard. In contrast, in 1968 the yearbook began: "To dream the
impossible dream, to fight the impossible foe . . . to reach the unreachable
star." Drawn from the popular Broadway musical, *Man of La Mancha*, and
indirectly from King's "I Have a Dream" speech, this motto reflected a
shifting zeitgeist among many youths nationwide. Even the advertisements in the yearbook illustrated the shift in racial (and gender) attitudes.
In 1966 one of the largest advertisements in the *Yearling*, for Leggett's
department store, depicted several white girls modeling two-piece bath-
ing suits before a couple of leering white boys. Three years later, the
Leggett's advertisement showed two couples, one white and one black,
jointly modeling formal wear—suggesting that they intended to go to the
senior prom together. While Cambridge's youths were not impervious to
the racial prejudices that had a long history in their community, they
could not help but be affected by the counterculture and its overall message of breaking down racial, sexual, and other boundaries. The concept
of a generational split has often been exaggerated, yet the counterculture
did wedge youths away from their parents and create a common bond
among the young, black and white.[19]

But shifting zeitgeist alone does not fully explain the lessening of tensions and the end of organized civil rights protest in Cambridge. Rather,
one needs to consider the structural changes or conditions that initially
helped give rise to the civil rights movement and ultimately fostered a
restoration of racial moderation. As already noted, the civil rights move-

ment and the white reaction to it in Cambridge were rooted in the desta-
bilization of Cambridge. The collapse of the Phillips Packing Company
created a political vacuum or void and an economic crisis. Into this void
rushed various contenders for political power, including those on the left
and right who eschewed the traditional politics of moderation. The severity of the economic crisis strengthened the appeal of those who favored
radical rather than gradual or moderate approaches. The concomitant
completion of the Chesapeake Bay Bridge, which put Cambridge within
easy reach of thousands of college students and the national media, contributed to the community's disequilibrium. Unaccustomed to responding to radical demands, from either blacks or working-class whites—in
part because they had traditionally had the power to crush such insurgen-
cies—the moderate white elite did not react in a constructive manner to
the civil rights movement, and their response exacerbated the situation.

By the end of the 1960s, however, Cambridge had returned to a state of
equilibrium. The community had digested the collapse of the Phillips
Packing Company, and the economy, although not booming, had regained some stability. Likewise, while the rise of new political factions
initially shocked the system, in time the outsiders gained legitimacy and
acted much like the traditional insiders. Put differently, once new political
leaders gained power, they charted a more centrist course than they had
espoused in order to attain power in the first place. Those most closely
identified with political agitation, namely Robert Fehsenfeld and William
Wise, lost at the polls. In turn, the economic and political restabilization
of the community allowed the new right to reach out to the Afro-Aggressors, who, in spite of their name, proved more willing to accommodate
themselves to a moderate political agenda than had the Cambridge Nonviolent Action Committee. Concomitantly, the enactment of civil rights
reforms contributed to the stabilization of the community by removing
disputes from the streets and putting them in the courts. Perhaps more
capable leaders and stronger organizations could have revitalized the civil
rights movement in Cambridge, but certainly the founders and early leaders of CNAC prospered in part because they had more fertile ground to
work.

An Assessment

Looking back at the era of the civil rights years from the vantage point of
the early twenty-first century, it is easy to downplay the accomplishments

of the civil rights movement. Scholarly studies, routine stories in the daily press, and recurrent incidences of racial strife document that race still matters a great deal in America. Great disparities between blacks and whites persist in Cambridge as well. Much evidence exists, nonetheless, that the civil rights movement had a significant impact on blacks and whites in Cambridge. Although the movement did not result in a radical restructuring of the community, it did foster a gradual improvement in the lives of many African Americans and had a lasting impact, especially on those for whom the movement was a key component of their lives. The movement also gradually altered white views of the "proper place" for blacks in society.

By the end of the 1960s, Cambridge's economy had improved considerably from its condition at the dawn of the decade. In Dorchester County, median income for all black families stood at $5,335, up from $2,450 in 1960. During the same period, the unemployment rate for black males declined dramatically from about 30 percent to 6.8 percent, largely because the economy of the community rebounded. Whereas in 1960, blacks in Cambridge faced a much bleaker employment picture than those across the nation or even than those in Salisbury, Maryland, by 1970 this was no longer the case. When the national economy stagnated during the 1970s and 1980s, particularly the economies of rural and industrial areas, the unemployment rates in Cambridge rose. Yet, as the economy rebounded in the 1990s, the employment picture brightened.[20]

More important, as the economy recovered, the range of jobs open to blacks expanded considerably. In 1960, approximately one in five black females in Cambridge worked in private households as domestics. Ten years later, less than one in ten did. By 1990 only 2 percent of all black females were employed as domestics. In 1960, the majority of black males worked as unskilled or semiskilled operatives or as laborers, largely manufacturing nondurable goods. As of 1990, fewer than one in four did so. Just as impressively, in 1960 only seventy-five blacks, male and female, were categorized as sales, professional, technical, managerial, or clerical workers. Thirty years later, 365 were, a 500 percent increase. (The total number of black employees grew 72 percent during this same period.)

Shifts in the economy away from manufacturing were one factor accounting for this increase in job opportunities, and the civil rights movement was another. In addition to toppling de jure segregation, the civil rights movement altered white attitudes about what jobs were proper for blacks and emboldened blacks themselves to become more assertive about their right to hold skilled jobs. This is not to deny that the Civil Rights

Table 7.1. Common occupations for nonwhites in Cambridge, 1960, 1970, and 1990

Job type	1960		1970		1990
	male	female	male	female	male and female
Total	716	716	878	912	1,968
Operatives	46%	67%	24%	51%	20%
Domestics	—	17%	—	8%	1%
Laborers	22%	2%	18%	7%	13%
Service workers	13%	9%	27%	13%	20%
Craftsmen	7%	—	18%	0.5%	15%
Professional	3%	3%	5%	10%	6%
Clerical	1%	1%	4%	6%	8%
Managers	1%	—	4%	0.5%	3%
Sales	2%	—	2%	0.5%	3%

Act of 1964, outlawing employment discrimination, had an impact. Yet the fact that only one employment discrimination suit was filed against an employer in Cambridge in the 1970s and 1980s, against the Volunteer Rescue and Fire Company, suggests that shifts in attitudes were just as important as those in the law, if not more so, or that the two reinforced each other.[21]

Housing, which stood alongside jobs at the top of CNAC's list of demands during the 1960s, also improved. Between 1967 and 1973, four hundred new homes were built in the Second Ward, including 190 public housing units. Government grants such as FHA loans made at the behest of public officials allowed for the construction of many of these. While objections to building public housing outside the Second Ward prevented construction of an additional forty units for the elderly, the gradual movement of a proportion of the black population into previously all-white sections of the town eased overcrowding. By the 1980s, the housing situation had improved even further, with the construction of hundreds of new homes. In 1960, a high percentage of all black homes lacked some or all plumbing facilities, and a significant percentage were considered dilapidated. By 1970, the situation had improved, as the government deemed 9 percent of all units substandard. By 1980, housing conditions were better yet, with only 3 percent of all units considered substandard.[22]

One area that showed less improvement was that of home ownership. Whereas home ownership rates for whites gradually increased between 1960 and 1980, the percentage of blacks who owned homes remained virtually unchanged. In addition, throughout this period the wide gap between the percentages of white and black homeowners did not narrow. In so far as home ownership is regarded as one of the benchmarks of middle-class status in American society, the fact that only about one-fourth of all African-American families in Cambridge owned a home, compared to nearly two-thirds of all white families, is telling. Exactly why this is the case remains unclear, although several hypotheses can be offered. First, even though income increased, African Americans remain disproportionately employed in poorer-paying and unstable jobs. Consequently, blacks have fewer chances to accumulate savings, which in turn provides them with fewer resources to fall back upon during economically hard times. Furthermore, many whites transfer their wealth (especially their homes) from one generation to another. Most blacks in Cambridge, in contrast, are not in a position to inherit a home or significant savings from their parents or grandparents. The persistence of residential segregation, sanctioned by the law through most of the twentieth century, further limited the chances for African Americans to own a home. The steady growth of the black population in Cambridge after 1960 compounded the housing shortage in the Second Ward. As a result, even though the number of blacks who owned homes increased from 365 in 1960 to 500 in 1990, the percent of blacks who owned a home fell slightly. Several other factors have kept black home ownership rates down, including the outmigration of educated and middle-class blacks. For instance, besides Richardson, Cambridge's most famous black native was William Jews. Born and raised in Cambridge, he left the city to attend college and then rose to the rank of chairman of Maryland Blue Cross, Blue Shield, headquartered in Baltimore. While he returned to visit family in Cambridge, like Richardson, Jews relocated to Baltimore and became a major figure in its business and philanthropic circles, not those of Cambridge. Mortgage practices, influenced by FHA guidelines that customarily dissuaded lenders from investing in black neighborhoods, played a role as well.[23]

Although desegregation did not prove the panacea that some thought it would at the time of the *Brown* decision, blacks in Cambridge enjoyed gains in the field of education as well. Between 1968 and 1970 the Department of Health, Education and Welfare pressured Dorchester County to speed up the pace of school desegregation. Throughout, Superintendent James Busick and the school board remained committed to the "freedom of choice" plan and defended the district's record of complying with *Brown*. For several years federal officials continued to reprimand Busick for his inflexibility while simultaneously granting the school board "time to carry out its latest desegregation efforts." When it became apparent at the end of the 1970–71 school year that the vast majority of black students would continue to attend all-black schools, the federal government's patience came to an end. The Republican-run HEW threatened to suspend payments of federal assistance to the county unless it charted a new course. Rather than risk the loss of badly needed funds, the school board accepted Busick's resignation and immediately appointed a replacement who did not hail from the region. The new school chief rapidly devised a plan that consolidated white and black schools. Even though a handful of schools remained majority black, and 5 to 10 percent of the white student population withdrew from the schools to attend private institutions, the new plan had a dramatic impact. When school resumed in the fall of 1971, classrooms resembled the ratio of the white and black student population in general. As the U.S. Commission on Civil Rights put it, the new head of the schools "did what the former superintendent thought . . . impossible." He developed a plan that rapidly desegregated the schools. Moreover, the new plan met little public opposition. The U.S. Commission on Civil Rights considered the plan such a success that it cited Dorchester County as an example of a school district where desegregation worked.[24]

Desegregation worked in Cambridge partly because the community's political leaders decided not to oppose it publicly. The formal decision to accept desegregation had been made following the *Brown* decision, and it would have been extremely awkward for politicians to condemn integrated education publicly after having formally accepted the principle of desegregation, if not the practice of it, more than fifteen years before. In addition, the ultimate desegregation of public schools in Dorchester County was not accompanied by busing or redistricting that threatened neighborhoods and local control. Elsewhere in the United States these issues often developed into another reason to oppose desegregation itself. Last, unlike whites in many other communities, those in Cambridge could not effectively avoid desegregation by fleeing to white suburbs because blacks constituted a sizable percentage of the population outside the city limits, which was not the case in many metropolitan areas, especially in the North. The fact that schools in Maryland are run by counties and not towns made it even more difficult to undermine desegregation by fleeing to a new jurisdiction. (The exception is Baltimore, which has its own schools. Many whites in Baltimore fled the city for the surrounding Baltimore County, which had few black residents.)

The desegregation of schools paralleled a gradual increase in educational attainment. As of 1960, blacks over twenty-five averaged 7.4 years of schooling. In 1980 this had risen to ten years. Whether desegregation caused or simply coincided with this gradual increase remains unclear. "White" schools were better funded and offered a greater range of courses. Teachers in historically all-black schools tended to have less training and had to manage with poorer facilities and resources. As of 1980, just 10 percent of all blacks in Cambridge twenty-five years old or older had any college education. In contrast, more than 25 percent of whites did. Still this marked a substantial increase from 1960, when less than 3 percent of blacks in Cambridge had any college education.[25]

The primary conflict between blacks and whites took place in the political arena, more specifically over the denial of voting rights. Ironically, prior to the 1960s this was the area of race relations to which whites in Cambridge pointed with greatest pride. The root cause of black complaints about the lack of voting rights was the persistence of residential segregation. In 1914, the city enacted an ordinance that strictly defined each block of the city according to race, as "white," "Negro," or "mixed," and prohibited a shift in designations. This ordinance remained in effect until 1957, and not until the 1970s did many blacks reside outside the Second Ward.[26] Paradoxically, whereas the ward system initially guaranteed blacks a share of power, over time it diluted their vote. By 1960, blacks constituted between 33 and 40 percent of the population, yet they held only one out of five seats on the town council because they lived in only one of the town's five wards. In 1960 the 347 residents of the white Third Ward enjoyed the same number of representatives on the town council as the 4,367 residents of the Second Ward. The Fourth and Fifth wards were underrepresented as well. In 1961, the city revised the boundaries of all the wards except the Second Ward. Eight years later it scrapped the old ward system in favor of a new system whereby the five council members were elected by the city as a whole rather than from five distinct geographic wards. At the same time, to ensure black representation on the council, the city imposed complicated residency requirements upon the candidates. Each ward had to be represented on the council. Hence, even though whites outnumbered blacks and could have elected five whites to the council, one black continued to hold a seat.[27]

Nonetheless, by the 1980s, careful observers noted that this new system also discriminated against black voters. Prior to 1969, the residents of the Second Ward chose their own representative. Under the new at-large system, one resident of the Second Ward sat on the town council, but whites, who constituted the majority of voters, determined who that black

person would be. In effect, this gave whites veto power over who represented the Second Ward. In 1972, in the first election under the new system, Edwin Watkins, a black moderate throughout the 1960s, defeated
Lemuel Chester, one of the most prominent civil rights activists, even
though Chester won 55 percent of the vote in the Second Ward. In 1984,
the "representative" of the Second Ward won only 35 percent of the black
vote.[28]

These results, as well as the inability of blacks to gain representation at
the county level, led to complaints of racial discrimination, charges lent
support by a study completed by the Maryland attorney general. The
study found "compelling" statistical evidence that whites in the county
would not support black candidates, although blacks voted for white candidates. In 1978, in a race for the County Commission, Gilbert Cephas,
James D. Smith, and Sarah M. Nichols, all black, finished ninth, tenth,
and eleventh respectively, out of twelve. Despite the fact that they received 51 percent of the Second Ward votes, they won only 8 percent of
the countywide total. Cephas, the president of a United Food and Commercial Workers' local in which membership was 65 percent white, did
not even win the votes of his own white union members. The attorney
general's report added that political underrepresentation had a significant
impact on blacks in Cambridge. Due to underrepresentation, blacks received inferior city services, an unfair share of federal revenues, and inadequate recreational facilities. The racially discriminatory political system
also contributed to the poor record of enforcement of the housing code
and made it more difficult for blacks than for whites to obtain employment with the city and county.[29]

In December 1984, the Justice Department filed a suit against the City
of Cambridge charging that the at-large system of electing town councilmen violated the Voting Rights Act of 1965. The suit grew out of a similar
complaint filed against Dorchester County by the Reagan Administration, which otherwise had a very conservative record on civil rights.
While the county signed a consent decree acknowledging its fault and
agreed to redraw election districts so as to increase the chances of blacks
gaining representation, the city decided to defend its record, largely on
technical grounds. After reviewing the city's argument, a federal court ordered Cambridge to scrap its at-large system of electing councilmen and
to establish new voting districts or a return to the ward system. This provided blacks with a better chance of gaining additional representation on
the town council, particularly since the ward lines were redrawn more in

accordance with the actual population. Within a short period of time, the impact of this decision (along with the consent decree signed by the county) became clear. In 1986, Lemuel Chester became the first black to win an election for county commissioner and Octavene Saunders became the second black representative on the five-person town council. Several years later, similar suits compelled the state to redraw legislative districts on the Eastern Shore so as to increase the chances of electing a black to the state legislature.[30]

Alongside these gains appeared several symbolic examples of shifts in racial attitudes. Local officials designated Harriet Tubman's birthplace as a historical landmark, and the city opened a Harriet Tubman Center in honor of what one official source termed the community's "most famous citizen." The center contains exhibits on Tubman's life and on slavery in the region and sponsors an annual community celebration of African-American history and culture. In addition, in 1995 the Episcopal Church officially recognized Tubman as a "saint."[31] (A proposal for Cedar Street to be renamed Harriet Tubman Boulevard was defeated, four to one, with supporters of the renaming agreeing with the proposal's opponents that economic revitalization of the road had to take priority over its renaming.)[32] In the sports arena, black and white high school athletes now compete together against teams from other communities, and when Cambridge's teams win, the city celebrates their victories without reference to the race of the players. Reflecting on these developments during a ceremony commemorating the Brown riot, Gloria Richardson commented that even though the changes "took a long time . . . they're welcome just the same."[33]

One institution that resisted change was the Rescue and Fire Company. It remained all white until the mid-1980s. It desegregated only after the Justice Department filed a suit that charged the RFC with discriminating against blacks and women. While the fire company denied these allegations, it finally admitted its first black member, Gregory Meekins, the president of the local NAACP. At the time, Meekins expressed his hope that the RFC would soon accept other blacks as members so as to make a costly court case unnecessary. When one-time CNAC leader Enez Grubb applied for membership, however, the RFC balked, allegedly because of her criminal record. The RFC's attorney, Harry Walsh, also insisted that Grubb had no real desire to become a firefighter, that she was "just doing it for the cause." An angry Grubb responded that her criminal record consisted of "going into stores and asking to be served Coca-

Colas" during the civil rights protests of the 1960s. A spokesman for the Justice Department added that twelve of the RFC's white members had criminal records. Ultimately, Grubb's application was accepted, but the process of desegregating the RFC, much like the process of desegregating the schools and building public housing during the 1960s, left many blacks angry in spite of the final results and displayed the resilience of racist attitudes, particularly in matters that affect the private sphere or personal identity.[34] Perhaps as the institutions that shape private identities—churches, voluntary associations, schools, workplaces, and neighborhoods—gradually desegregate, caste lines will disappear. The integration of Cambridge into a broader world, which has an ever-increasing impact on the formation of social identities, enhances the likelihood that caste barriers will diminish even further in importance.

Looking Backward

One topic that continues to divide blacks and whites is history, particularly the history of the modern civil rights movement. Most whites in Cambridge seek to forget the struggle for civil rights rather than reflect on or commemorate it. State Senator Frederick Malkus encouraged me to discontinue the present research on the grounds that nothing positive could come from it. Malkus insisted that Cambridge had been unfairly singled out during the 1960s, and he regretted the stigma that the movement had left on the community. Edward Kinnamon, Brice Kinnamon's son and Cambridge's town clerk, commented that "most people here just want to forget it [the civil rights years]. It's not something we're proud of." Likewise, Officer Wrotten, who became the chief of police, was reluctant to discuss the Brown riot. When local whites write about the civil rights years, they tend to fall back upon the old refrain that outside agitators caused the trouble. For instance, local historian Thomas Flowers insisted that integration had been completed by 1964 and that the "demonstrations were staged for the press."[35] Novelist John Barth, who had vociferously condemned the RFC following the Brown riot, tempered his criticism of whites in Cambridge, suggesting that even if he did not want to forget about the past, he sought to remember it in a different light. In his autobiographical novel *Once upon a Time*, published in 1994, Barth wrote: "It stings me to recall what sanctimonious liberal grief I gave them during the local civil rights ruckus of the 1960s, when Whitey's Candyland (on Race Street!) and the all-white clubbiness of his beloved Rescue and Fire

Company were obvious targets; my failures of historical and personal sympathy for a man of my father's generation and position, confronting sit-ins and incendiarism face-to-face, while I tisked righteously from the bucolic white enclave of the Pennsylvania State University." Hoping to make amends for his shortcomings, Barth concluded, "Forgive me Father (and Mother), for I sure did sin; my position was correct, but not my attitude."[36]

In contrast, many blacks, especially veteran activists, seek to keep alive the history of the civil rights years and to see the 1960s in a positive light. While not condoning violence, George Ames told a reporter on the twenty-fifth anniversary of the Brown riot: "In order for things to happen, positively, sometimes terrible things have to happen." Grubb had a negative memory of the same event: "We felt as if we were in an army that suffered a great defeat. It was very dispiriting." But in general she had fond memories of the movement and wanted its history to be told. "The unity of the people working together for the common good of equality" stood out, Grubb recalled; "everybody had the dream." Similarly, both Gloria Richardson and Grubb cooperated fully with me and hold fond memories of the movement, especially the way in which it added to the community's sense of self-worth, as illustrated by a reduction of crime.[37]

In addition to the fact that they disagreed with the methods of the local movement, Malkus, Kinnamon, and others look back unfavorably on the 1960s because they assume that the stigma of the civil rights movement impacted Cambridge's economy adversely.[38] Yet it is not clear that the racial turmoil of the 1960s harmed Cambridge as much as they assumed. More reliant on manufacturing in the first place than St. Michael's or Oxford, two other nearby Eastern Shore communities, Cambridge in the 1990s found it difficult to package itself as a quaint little town attractive to the bed-and-breakfast crowd. Even before this period of gentrification, Cambridge had failed to capture the interest or dollars of those who packed Maryland's beach resorts each summer. But this was because it was located on the Choptank and Chesapeake, rather than on the Atlantic Ocean, not because of the turmoil of the 1960s. Improvements in the highway system, demanded by vacationers who sought to speed their travel, compounded the difficulties Cambridge's downtown merchants faced. While a bevy of fast-food restaurants sprang up along Route 50, establishments on Race and High streets found it difficult to attract beachgoers. Farther away from Washington, D.C., and Baltimore than towns closer to the Chesapeake Bay Bridge, Cambridge also has proven unable to capitalize on the real estate boom associated with exurban development. Without a college campus or a prison, Cambridge lacks two of the main incubators of job growth.

If racial turmoil is to be held responsible for the economic stagnation of Cambridge, then communities that avoided such turmoil should have performed better economically. But this has not been the case. Salisbury, Maryland, which the media praised for its enlightened leadership and absence of civil rights protests during the 1960s, experienced economic difficulties during the 1970s and 1980s. Whereas in the 1960s Salisbury enjoyed a much lower unemployment rate than Cambridge, both cities had virtually the same unemployment rate between 1970 and 1980. While the median income for black families increased slightly more in Salisbury than in Cambridge, this probably had more to do with the expansion of the chicken industry, which declined precipitously in the 1990s, than with the stigma of the civil rights movement.[39]

Perhaps as tourists tire of traffic jams in Ocean City, and overpriced and inauthentic restaurants in St. Michael's, and as homeowners find that they can buy neither the country life nor security by moving to the other side of the Chesapeake, Cambridge will enjoy a wave of economic good fortune. Indeed, the Hyatt Corporation recently completed construction of a large luxury resort on the outskirts of Cambridge, replete with recreational attractions from golf courses to a marina, a destination promoters hope will rival the Greenbrier resort in West Virginia. Such a facility holds promise precisely because it takes advantage of Cambridge's relatively cheap real estate, especially compared to other Eastern Shore communities that have already enjoyed a real estate boom. Lower costs combined with the community's location—close enough to big cities for an occasional jaunt but far enough away to bring a sense of security—may prove especially attractive to senior citizens, whose numbers continue to increase. As was the case when it was founded, Cambridge has the asset of a beautiful natural port. Even more so than several blossoming Eastern Shore resorts, Cambridge's underutilized manufacturing plants hold the potential to attract artists who yearn for large and open spaces.[40]

Promoters of the resort suggest that it will usher in a new golden age. William Donald Schaefer, former mayor of Baltimore and governor of Maryland, touted the Hyatt project as Cambridge's "Inner Harbor," a reference to the extremely successful entertainment development that he helped build in Baltimore. "You don't know what's going to happen; you can't imagine the changes," Schaefer told local businessmen and community leaders. "You're going to have a boom." One expert predicted that the Hyatt resort could add an additional $30 million a year to the local economy, including 1,200 new construction jobs and about 350 resort workers after construction was completed. In addition, the resort promised to have a ripple effect on the rest of the economy, to the advantage of local subcontractors, fishermen, and charter boat owners. One recent article in the *Baltimore Sun* even touted Cambridge as a "funkier" version of St. Michaels and suggested that the city could easily supplant other nearby communities as a magnet to the young and creative.[41]

In spite of these upbeat predictions, several veterans of the civil rights struggles of the 1960s remain skeptical, largely because they hold a different view of the past. "We're concerned that all this is going to benefit a small number of people in Cambridge," stated Enez Grubb. "The wealth has never been spread around," she observed. The jobs that are needed are ones that "allow people to support families," to live in dignity, she added. Previous redevelopment plans had failed either to materialize or to create the ripple effect that their promoters promised, said the Reverend Leon Hall of the AME Church. "There's always a feeling of mistrust," Hall continued. "This community is still affected by things that happened in the 60s." White boosters countered such skepticism by emphasizing that it is the future not the past that is most important. "History is important," acknowledged Gage Thomas, a white real estate agent who heads the chamber of commerce. "But we have to move forward. We're all Cambridge. We've got to decide who we are and where we need to go."[42]

One way for the community to overcome these differences is for it to embrace its past, all of it. Recently, several southern communities that experienced bitter struggles for civil rights in the 1960s decided to commemorate the civil rights years. Birmingham, Alabama, and Memphis, Tennessee, for example, constructed museums and a park (in Birmingham's case) to honor the modern black freedom struggle and its participants. The Birmingham exhibit includes moving pieces of artwork that recall "Bull" Connor's vicious use of dogs and water cannons to turn back youthful protesters. Rather than trying to hide the tragedies of its past, the Memphis museum highlights King's assassination at the Loraine hotel. By developing a similar commemoration to the black freedom struggle of the 1960s, including monuments to Gloria Richardson and the St. Clair family, the white community might bridge some of the long-standing mistrust that exists between the races and even add to the number of tourists who would want to use the Hyatt resort. Whether the community has the maturity to adopt this course remains to be seen.[43]

Conclusion

Cambridge and the History of the Movement

How does a study of Cambridge affect our broader understanding of the civil rights movement? What does it tell us about the origins, nature, course, and legacy of the movement that we have not already learned from existing works? In what ways does examination of events in Cambridge alter or reaffirm findings based upon somewhat similar community studies and specialized monographs?

Even though historians have largely ignored the civil rights movement in Cambridge, contemporary analysts did not. Some commentators focused on Cambridge because they believed it offered special insight into the nature and trajectory of the civil rights movement. Most notably, journalists Michael Durham in *Life* and L. Brent Bozell in the *National Review* compared Cambridge and the nearby Eastern Shore city of Salisbury, Maryland. In many ways their articles epitomized the conflicting liberal and conservative interpretations of the social unrest of the 1960s.[1]

Durham blamed the white leaders of Cambridge for the town's troubles. Both cities found themselves targets of freedom rides in early 1962, Durham reported. Based on Cambridge's progressive reputation as opposed to Salisbury's history of racism—it had been the site of a notorious lynching—one would have expected that Salisbury, not Cambridge, would have become the site of sustained racial protest in the 1960s. Yet in reaction to the freedom rides, Durham observed, whites in Salisbury accommodated themselves to the inevitability of racial reform. In contrast, he wrote, whites in Cambridge "reacted to the Negro demands . . . with bitter intransigence." The result was racial peace in Salisbury and "racial war" in Cambridge.[2]

In contrast to Durham, Bozell held black leaders and white liberals responsible for the Cambridge unrest, in a piece that anticipated subsequent conservative critiques of the Kerner Commission's report and other liberal tracts on the civil rights movement. Even though Bozell rejected the conventional southern refrain that no racial problems existed until outside agitators stirred them up, he condemned radical blacks for causing the violence. By stepping outside traditional political channels, he argued, they caused the strife. Bozell added that if black activists had resisted the temptation to resort to direct action protest, they would have achieved more of their goals and avoided provoking white backlash. "It was not a matter of good guys and bad guys," Bozell insisted. "Cambridge was *singled out* for violence by Negro leadership; Salisbury was not" (emphasis mine). Even if their grievances were legitimate, Bozell asserted, the source of the trouble was that "Negroes lost patience." By doing so they "shattered" the process for gaining change and poisoned a "reasonably congenial atmosphere."[3] While Durham and Bozell disagreed over the origins of the conflict in Cambridge, both forecast a similar outcome. Even before George Wallace used Cambridge as a launching pad for his forays into the North and prior to Spiro T. Agnew's metamorphosis from a moderate Republican into a darling of the new right, Durham and Bozell predicted that white backlash would result from the strife.

When I began this study nearly a decade ago, the modern civil rights movement had already received a great deal of attention, including several Pulitzer Prize–winning books and other award-winning studies. The movement had also been chronicled by one of the more celebrated television documentaries, *Eyes on the Prize*, and several widely watched movies. References in the historical literature to the Bozell and Durham articles have been few, but many students of the early civil rights movement have adopted one of their positions, with the majority following Durham's line of reasoning. Put somewhat differently, based upon their study of Cambridge, Durham and Bozell established the two most prominent paradigms for understanding the civil rights movement. Most orthodox studies of the national civil rights movement follow one of the paradigms. Nearly all discussions of the latter 1960s agree with their assertion that increasing black militancy caused white backlash.[4]

Yet, as several scholars noted around the time research on this project began, there was something unsatisfying in this interpretation. To develop a better understanding of the recent past, they suggested that the movement needed to be examined from the bottom up, preferably from a community or regional perspective. As my research proceeded and other community studies were published, a new understanding of the movement began to emerge. Without denying that key national leaders orchestrated campaigns aimed at attaining federal reforms, these studies suggested that the civil rights movement embodied much more. Looked at from the bottom up, the civil rights movement was a mass movement that empowered hundreds of thousands of ordinary people. While not going as far as Bozell or arguing that direct action protest backfired, local studies suggested that the civil rights movement was "exceedingly long, exhaustively crooked and extensively smudged"—and not as victorious as has often been presumed.[5]

Building on the national narrative and to a lesser extent on case studies, social movement scholars simultaneously added another level of sophistication to our understanding of the civil rights movement and social movements in general. Whereas contemporaries focused on the role that individual leaders played in initiating the civil rights movement, these scholars emphasized the importance of structural and long-term factors in giving rise to the civil rights movement. Scholars taking this course are considered adherents of the resource mobilization or political process/ political opportunity schools of social movement theory. Foremost, these theorists posited that the modernization of the South undermined the region's traditional political economy. With the demise of this economy, the need for a racial caste system diminished. While many white southerners clung to Jim Crow long after its primary social purpose disappeared, the collapse of the traditional plantation economy made the system susceptible to a sustained challenge.[6] By the time that the South's traditional economy began to crumble, these scholars added, African Americans had accumulated the resources, both internal and external, that made it possible for them to mount a challenge to the racial status quo. For instance, they had built a variety of black-run and black-owned institutions, from churches and colleges to newspapers and magazines. These resources allowed them to launch and sustain the movement in the 1950s and 1960s.[7]

Numerous scholars add that the Great Migration (which can be seen as a by-product of the plantation economy's collapse) and the Cold War paved the way for the civil rights movement. With their migration to the North blacks gained the vote, which they effectively leveraged in the political arena in the 1950s and early 1960s. Blacks also garnered newfound economic assets, which they used to finance many of the institutions that bolstered the movement, such as the NAACP.[8] In a somewhat similar way, the Cold War compelled the federal government to live up to the American creed lest the Soviet Union paint the United States as a nation with a racial double standard, an image America could ill afford, especially in the developing world.[9]

This study of Cambridge complements and supplements much recent scholarship by historians and social movement theorists. Most important, it demonstrates that social movements are not uniform. This is because they contain multiple (and often competing) organizations and because activity varies across geographic areas. To state it differently, this study suggests that no single paradigm explains the civil rights movement or white backlash. The civil rights movement was not neat geographically, chronologically, or ideologically. Its victories and defeats were not as dramatic or complete as they have often been portrayed. While the standard narrative commonly argues that the movement began in the South with the goal of toppling Jim Crow, and after achieving this goal climaxed in the North with the rise of black power, such was not the case in Cambridge. Multiple and often contradictory currents existed simultaneously, alongside one another. Some of these currents reinforced each other, while others clashed. This is not to argue in defense of chaos or against scholarly efforts to write works of synthesis. But such works need to portray the civil rights movement as a varied and complex social phenomenon, replete with irresolvable paradoxes and contradictions.

In terms of the origins of the local movement, Cambridge conforms to the pattern established by most political process/political opportunity theorists and accepted by most historians of the movement. Broad structural changes, accompanied by the accumulation of resources by the black community, paved the way for the emergence of the civil rights movement. Cambridge provides one more illustration of the connection between disturbances—in this case the construction of the Chesapeake Bay Bridge and the collapse of the Phillips Packing Company—and the emergence of a social movement. Still, Cambridge also shows that some of the particulars of social movement theorists, when applied to the civil rights movement, need revision. The movement in Cambridge did not arise because of the collapse of the plantation economy. On the contrary, Cambridge enjoyed a relatively smooth transition from agriculture to manufacturing in the latter decades of the nineteenth century and early decades of the twentieth, retaining some of the remnants of the old caste system, like segregation, but not others, most notably all-white political rule. Hence, rather than focusing on the demise of the plantation as the basis for the movement, the Cambridge experience suggests that we pay more attention to all types of shifts or disturbances in the political economy.[10]

Likewise, while the Cambridge story lends weight to those who emphasize the role that accumulated resources played in giving rise to and sustaining the movement, it lacks some of the particulars advanced by resource mobilization or political process theorists. Most notably, black ministers did not play a large role in Cambridge, although the black church was a factor. Black ministers offered their buildings for use by the movement only reluctantly, did not serve as leaders of the local movement, and openly opposed Gloria Richardson's leadership at a crucial juncture. While students from colleges in the region participated in the freedom rides of 1962 and demonstrations in 1963 and 1964, since Cambridge did not have its own black (or white) college, students did not play as active a role in maintaining the movement in Cambridge as they did in many other communities, such as Nashville, Albany, New Orleans, and Greensboro, all homes of black colleges. Instead, Cambridge's civil rights movement drew on a variety of informal resources, the grapevine, family and social networks, and most important, indigenous and independent black leadership. As a member of the St. Clair family, Gloria Richardson inherited a reputation that enabled her to mobilize the black community. While her situation may appear unique, it had many parallels in the border states, where blacks often retained the vote after Reconstruction. In Baltimore, for example, the Jackson-Mitchell family led the local struggle for racial equality in the 1950s and 1960s in part because it had a long-standing tradition of having played this role.[11]

In addition, the Cambridge story suggests that scholars have overstated the significance of the Great Migration. Cambridge's black population grew gradually during the middle decades of the twentieth century, and almost all this growth came from the surrounding region rather than from the Deep South. Population growth exacerbated an already bad housing situation and contributed to the gap between white and black unemployment rates. But compared to the situation in northern cities, where the Great Migration clearly underlay the rise of racial protest, it played only a minor role in Cambridge. Nor did migration destabilize the region's political economy as it did in many southern communities. Much more influential was the dramatic shift in Cambridge's cultural geography or spatial relationship to the surrounding regions. The construction of the Chesapeake Bay Bridge ended the town's isolation, putting it within easy reach of students, representatives of the mass media, and government officials. These outsiders did not migrate to or permanently relocate themselves in Cambridge; they were not individuals who uprooted themselves from the Deep South in order to live in the "promised land." Still, they arrived in Cambridge with worldviews that differed sharply from those held by most residents of the Eastern Shore. Since this spacial shift came so rapidly, longtime Cambridge residents lacked the time to prepare themselves for and digest the influx of new ideas and views. The speed of this shift in cultural geography contributed to white resistance, especially among the white elite, which had grown accustomed to making decisions outside the gaze of the national media.

Nor did the Cold War play a major role in Cambridge. Civil rights activists in Cambridge did not invoke the Cold War imperative to shame whites into enacting reforms, and attempts at red-baiting focused on the CNAC fell largely on deaf ears. The agreement hammered out and signed by Robert F. Kennedy and CNAC, ironically, came on the heels of John F. Kennedy's disparaging remarks about the movement in Cambridge, which he made following his trip to Berlin and his most famous Cold War speech. Perhaps the only connection between the Cold War and the rise of the civil rights movement in Cambridge was pure coincidence. In the early 1960s, demonstrations on the Eastern Shore commenced after freedom riders called off protests along Route 40, north of Baltimore. These protests stemmed from the refusal of restaurants along the route to serve African diplomats. To avert an international crisis, the Kennedy Administration intervened. Hence, civil rights groups turned their attention to the Eastern Shore. Clearly the Cold War imperative prodded the Kennedy Administration to negotiate a resolution of the Route 40 protest. Just as clearly, the freedom riders sought to take advantage of the nation's foreign policy concerns. But their decision to train their attention on the Eastern Shore was determined by geography, not foreign policy. African diplomats were not involved in the "testing" of sites on the Eastern Shore, and Cambridge was not a factor in the Cold War publicity battle for the allegiance of the developing world.[12]

The Vietnam War also did not have a significant impact on the course of the civil rights movement in Cambridge. The war reinforced SNCC's drift leftward and the broader split between the new left and liberals, but as we have seen, Gloria Richardson and CNAC espoused a fairly radical position prior to the escalation of the Vietnam War. There is no evidence that the Vietnam War further radicalized CNAC or further polarized Cambridge. Indeed, General George Gelston, a prominent pro-war spokesman in Maryland, remained on good terms with civil rights activists in Cambridge during the latter half of the 1960s, even defending H. Rap Brown before a U.S. Senate committee out to establish that communists and black radicals intentionally precipitated the race riots of 1967. Nor did any of the candidates for local office in either 1966 or 1968, black or white, make an issue of the Vietnam War.[13]

Cambridge, however, did not become the site of one of the most vibrant episodes in the civil rights movement by accident. As suggested, local political, social, and economic conditions paved the way for the outburst of racial strife. The collapse of the Phillips Packing Company created a political void that both working-class whites and blacks sought to fill. At the same time, the company's demise undermined the power held by the community's black and white elites. While the community briefly united behind the efforts of moderates to overcome high unemployment and unstable economic circumstances, rival political factions ultimately refused to accede to the lead of the white elite, preferring instead to assert their newfound independence from the iron grip of the Phillips Packing Company. Indeed, the Cambridge story dovetails nicely with J. Mills Thornton's theory that changing political circumstance underlay the emergence of protests for racial equality.[14]

What happened in Cambridge confirms that the orthodox interpretation of the civil rights movement, which focuses on the national movement and the drive for civil rights legislation, is in need of revision. While CNAC emerged out of protests aimed at desegregating public accommodations, it quickly displayed just as much interest in economic needs and empowering blacks. Project Eastern Shore, for example, sought to increase the political consciousness among blacks and to enhance the unity of the black community so that people could attain more jobs and better housing. Moreover, even though CNAC publicly identified itself with the philosophy of nonviolence, it displayed willingness to tolerate, if not foster, armed self-defense well before black power became a national rallying cry.

Just as important, the decision by Gloria Richardson and CNAC to call for a boycott of the town's vote on a public accommodations measure commands a rethinking of the goals of the movement. As earlier noted, Richardson did not see voting as a waste of time. She was not a modern syndicalist who considered the political process some sort of opiate that fooled the masses into believing they could peacefully topple capitalism. However, drawing on her experience with politics, she felt that electoral politics had its limitations. Foremost, she refused to participate in electoral politics if it entailed undermining her ultimate goal, namely attaining full equality. She called for boycott of a vote because she felt that voting for or against an anti-discriminatory public accommodations measure lent legitimacy to the notion that certain rights could be given to or taken away from African Americans. In addition, while Richardson saw mobilizing blacks to vote for or against certain candidates as a useful mechanism to educate and unite the black community, over time she paid less attention to the electoral process because she found that other means were more effective in achieving her primary goals, including gaining more jobs, better housing, and black empowerment.

Does this mean, as President Kennedy suggested, that Cambridge was the exception that proved the rule? Only if one adopts a monolithic or simplistic view of the rule or norm. Indeed, Cambridge adds further weight to the view that the civil rights movement was organizationally, ideologically, and geographically diverse, not a centralized and unified force. In many ways, Richardson's views prefigured those that Stokely Carmichael would espouse in the latter part of the 1960s. Moreover, if one's definition of the movement includes Malcolm X, Robert Williams, and other black nationalist figures, then Richardson and the events in Cambridge do not appear unique but rather constitute an important and sizable variation that movement scholars have begun to delineate.[15]

While the latter years of the civil rights movement have received less attention in the works of historians and social movement theorists than have the early years (and many recent studies keep adding more and more detail to the early years of the movement, pushing its origins farther and farther back), a general consensus about the causes and nature of black power and white backlash exists. The most widely accepted theories on urban disorders maintain that perceptions of economic deprivation, more than absolute poverty itself, underlay the riots of the latter half of the 1960s. Those who rioted saw themselves as deprived compared to the rest of the population. Improving economic conditions raised expectations without significantly closing large socioeconomic gaps between blacks and whites. A sparsity of constructive political channels for venting frustration and the discriminatory behavior of the police, who were often seen as the embodiment of the political elite, increased the chances of riots.[16]

In many ways, Cambridge lends credence to this general view. Economic conditions gradually improved during the mid-1960s, although the gap between blacks and whites barely narrowed, and the process of change or reform was exceedingly messy. This bred discontent. Yet, insofar as the staff of the Kerner Commission is correct that Cambridge experienced a low-level civil disturbance, not a riot—and I believe this assessment was right—Cambridge differs from the established model. Snow-balling misperceptions played a seminal role in producing the blaze that destroyed two square blocks of the Second Ward. But the fire itself was not a riot, popular belief notwithstanding.

Scholars often portray radicalism as the result of frustration or, more precisely, of the absence of constructive political channels through which a community can assert its voice. The Cambridge story adds another twist to this theory. Blacks in Cambridge had a political voice. Charles Cornish and Helen Waters may not have represented all blacks and may have been out of touch with a large segment of the population. Nonetheless, Cornish was reelected in 1958, 1962, and 1966 by sizable majorities, and he became the city council president in 1966, making him one of the highest ranking black elected officials in the nation. Paradoxically, political representation may have fostered the move to extrapolitical or extraelectoral strategies. Whites looked to Charles Cornish, and to a lesser extent to Helen Waters, to understand the concerns of the black community. Cornish's general criticism of direct action protest, as well as his endorsement of the pace of school desegregation and other governmental actions, assured them that Cambridge was making racial progress. Bozell blamed black radicals for causing the turmoil in Cambridge because they went outside traditional political channels. In a sense this is true, but Bozell missed the point that CNAC went outside traditional channels because it concluded that the political system was faulty. Paradoxically, if Cambridge had had a less progressive tradition, if blacks had not been represented on the town council and the school board, if Cornish had not been elevated to the top post of the town council, then whites might have been more attuned to the concerns of black radicals as revealed through extrapolitical protest like the fires that preceded the so-called riot of 1967. Had blacks not enjoyed any political representation, whites might have been more willing to accede to black demands when they were first made. In Salisbury, where blacks lacked political representation, local authorities compromised in order to avoid extrapolitical protest.

Strictly speaking, it was not a lack of political voice that gave rise to radicalism but imperfections in the political system, imperfections that experienced political observers like Richardson recognized and sought to rectify. As noted, at the key moment in the movement, Gloria Richardson and CNAC called on blacks to boycott the referendum vote on the local public accommodations measure because they did not feel it was right to put human rights up to a vote. As they observed, human rights were human rights, not white rights. The white majority had no right to determine whether blacks enjoyed the same inalienable rights. In a sense, these views paralleled those of Alexis de Tocqueville, who had warned about the dangers of the tyranny of the majority, especially in regard to racial minorities. To grant whites the power to favor or oppose human rights, in Richardson's mind, only legitimated tyranny. Most liberals nationwide disagreed, with some arguing that Richardson betrayed the principles of the movement by refusing to exercise her right to vote. Only the most astute understood that the struggle to enfranchise blacks in the South was but the initial step in a much larger process aimed at creating a world in which all individuals were judged as members of the human race, each with the same inalienable rights, rather than some belonging to a separate caste whose rights could be given or taken away by the white majority.

Finally, Cambridge sheds lights on the rise of the new right, suggesting that this force cannot be seen simply as a form of white backlash against the radicalism of the civil rights movement (or, by extension, the new left). Well before black power emerged, competition for political power among whites had already begun. Differences over many issues lay behind the insurgency of the new right. In Cambridge, the collapse of the old order, which preceded the arrival of the civil rights movement, unleashed latent political rivalries rooted in class differences. The election of Frederick Malkus, for instance, took place a decade before the freedom riders arrived. While the civil rights movement intensified these rivalries, racial discord often became the excuse for breaking with the traditional moderate elite—not the primary cause. Once the new right were in power, moreover, the Cambridge story suggests that they were less reactionary in actuality than their rhetoric alone would lead one to believe. White conservatives in Cambridge accommodated themselves to the desegregation of public facilities mandated by the Civil Rights Act of 1964 and applied for and disbursed federal funds, in spite of their criticism of big government. In time, rather than risk the loss of federal funds, local conservatives forced James Busick to resign and hired an outsider who rapidly desegregated the schools. Following the Brown riot of 1967, the law-and-order authorities of Cambridge even proved willing to appoint local radicals to positions of power and to construct public housing units. In many ways, the actions of local conservatives paralleled those of the Nixon-Agnew Administration, which had a fairly moderate civil rights record while at the same time casting itself as a voice for white backlash.[17]

Indeed, the relatively moderate actions of the new right in Cambridge meant that in a short time the centrist political tradition reemerged as the dominant tradition in the community. As in the pre–civil rights period, this entailed a pro-business, pro-development mentality, with some concessions to local provincial traditions and the needs of an expanding black population. Moreover, as the community stabilized or regained its political and economic equilibrium, the conditions that had given rise to the civil rights movement in the first place diminished. Not surprisingly, the movement did so as well. Whether this augured a prolonged period of stability remains to be seen, in part because if there is one thing history reveals, it is the difficulty of predicting the future.

Notes

Introduction

1. John F. Kennedy, "Address," 11 June 1963, in Levy, ed., *Let Freedom Ring*, 117–19; *Public Papers of the Presidents, John F. Kennedy, 1963*, 572; *New York Times*, 18 July 1963, 1.

2. *Public Papers... John F. Kennedy, 1963*, 572; Schlesinger, *A Thousand Days*, 965–73; Brauer, *John F. Kennedy; New York Times*, 18 July 1963, 1.

3. *Public Papers . . . John F. Kennedy, 1963*, 572; *New York Times*, 18 July 1963, 1.

4. "Agreement," 22 July 1963, in Burke Marshall Papers. In one sentence Carl Brauer notes that Robert Kennedy worked out a "short-lived truce." He does not mention JFK's remark at the press conference (*John F. Kennedy*, 288).

5. The state of California held a referendum on open housing measures in 1966, but as far as I can tell no other city held a referendum to repeal a standing measure to desegregate public accommodations.

6. CNAC, "Statement," and Gloria Richardson, "Press Release," both in Burke Marshall Papers; *Afro-American* (Baltimore), 28 September 1963.

7. *Time*, 11 October 1963, 30; *Saturday Evening Post*, 5 October 1963, 78–80; Lewis, *Portrait of a Decade*, 100–103.

8. Jones, *The Wallace Story*, 281; *Cambridge Daily Banner*, 12 May 1964.

9. Sellers, *The River of No Return*, 68; interview with Courtland Cox.

10. Brown's speech can be found in *Is Baltimore Burning?* This collection of documents is available online at www.msa.gov.

11. Witcover, *White Knight*, 126–29.

12. Williams, *Eyes on the Prize*; Branch, *Parting the Waters* and *Pillar of Fire*; Brooks, *Walls Came Tumbling Down*; Lawson, *Running for Freedom*; King, *Freedom Song*; Marable, *Race, Reform and Rebellion*; Sitkoff, *The Struggle for Black Equality*; Weisbrot, *Freedom Bond*; Blumberg, *Civil Rights*; Cook, *Sweet Land of Liberty?*

13. Lowery and Marszalek, eds., *Encyclopedia of African- American Civil Rights*. Local studies have added little to our understanding of the movement in Cambridge since they are based largely on limited and unconfirmed information. See Wennersten, *Maryland's Eastern Shore*.

14. Schlesinger, *A Thousand Days*, 965–73; Brauer, *John F. Kennedy*; Stern, *Calculating Visions*; Weisbrot, *Freedom Bond*, 264–65; Sitkoff, *The Struggle for Black Equality*, 203–4; Office of the Assistant Deputy Director for Research, "Analysis of Cambridge, Maryland, Disturbance," Staff Paper No. 4 (Draft), 29 October 1967, in *Civil Rights during the Johnson Administration*, pt. 5.

15. D'Emilio, review of *Creating a Place for Ourselves.*

16. Crawford et al., eds, *Women in the Civil Rights Movement,* esp. articles by Payne and Brock; Robnet, *How Long? How Long?*

17. Carson, "Martin Luther King, Jr.: Charismatic Leadership in Mass Struggle."

18. Tyson, *Radio Free Dixie.* Tyson argues that the nonviolent desegregationist and the black power movement sprang from the same soil and suggests that both goals held sway in the North and the South.

19. *Time,* 19 July 1963, 17–18.

Chapter 1. The Contours of History

1. Interview with Enez Grubb, 24 August 2001.

2. Jones, *New Revised History of Dorchester County;* McElvay, "Early Black Dorchester."

3. McElvay, ibid., chaps. 2 and 3; Clark, *The Eastern Shore of Maryland and Virginia.*

4. Brugger, *Maryland,* 780–81; McElvay, ibid., chaps. 1–3; Wright, *The Free Negro in Maryland, 1634–1860,* chap. 8.

5. McElvay, ibid., chaps. 2 and 3.

6. Stump, *It Happened in Dorchester County,* 52–53.

7. McElvay, "Early Black Dorchester," chaps. 2 and 3; Williams, *The Garden of American Methodism.*

8. McElvay, ibid.

9. Wright, *The Free Negro in Maryland, 1634–1860.*

10. Clark, *The Eastern Shore of Maryland and Virginia.*

11. Ibid.; Fields, *Slavery and Freedom on the Middle Ground.*

12. McElvay, "Early Black Dorchester," chap. 8.

13. Ibid.

14. Ibid.

15. Elias Jones, *New Revised History of Dorchester County.* Calvin W. Mowbray's two works on Cambridge, *The Dorchester County Fact Book* and *The Early Settlers of Dorchester County and Their Lands,* are no better. Written in the early 1980s, they contain only passing mention of slavery and nothing else on African Americans in the region. For information on the state of the black community in the early twentieth century, see Brown, "Cambridge at the Early 20th Century."

16. Brugger, *Maryland,* 318–28.

17. Jones, *New Revised History of Dorchester County,* 437–39, 495–96.

18. *Moody's Manual* (1940, 1945, 1953); Clark, *The Eastern Shore of Maryland and Virginia,* 1:857–76, 2:7–9; Phillips Packing Company, vertical file; Phillips Packing Company, "Annual Report," 1939–1956; Maryland Historical Society, *Maryland in World War II,* 44.

19. Clark, *The Eastern Shore of Maryland and Virginia,* 3:7–9; Kent, "The Negro in Politics in Dorchester County."

20. *FTA [Food and Tobacco Workers] News,* 5 January 1947.

21. Maryland State Planning Commission, *A Program for Economic Development of*

Dorchester County; Mullin-Kille, *Directory;* Bureau of Business and Economic Research, *Maryland's Eastern Shore;* Phillips Packing Company, "Annual Report," 1939–1956.

22. Mullin-Kille, ibid.; Dept. of Commerce, *County and City Data Book.*

23. Ibid.

24. Grubb, *In Spite Of;* William H. Kiah, "Black History in Dorchester County Recalled," *Cambridge Daily Banner,* 1 March 1982; interview with Enez Grubb, 24 August 2001.

25. Kent, "The Negro in Politics in Dorchester County"; Brown, "Cambridge at the Early 20th Century"; Grubb, *In Spite Of.* In a hotly contested election in 1898, St. Clair lost to Zachariah Jews, a black laborer who was backed by James Derry, a black barber and the black appointee to the Dorchester County State Central Committee of the Republican Party. Since Derry was not a resident of the Second Ward, he selected Jews as his surrogate to run for the town council against St. Clair. Jews held office for only one term, and St. Clair was reelected in 1906.

26. Interview with Gloria Richardson, 13 May 2000.

27. Kent, "The Negro in Politics in Dorchester County"; Brown, "Cambridge at the Early 20th Century."

28. Kent, ibid.; University of Maryland, "The History and Present Status of Community Organization in Cambridge, Maryland."

29. University of Maryland, ibid.

30. Interview with John Barth; Barth, *Once upon a Time,* 152; Mullikin, *A History of the Easton Volunteer Fire Department.*

31. *Joseph W. Williams et al. . . . Civil Action 16658,* case file; *Joseph W. Williams et al. v. Rescue Fire Company;* "Maryland Fire Department Accused of Bias," *Washington Post,* 26 November 1985, C5; "Racial Issue Smolders within Cambridge, Md., Fire Department," *Washington Post,* 18 August 1986, B1. On the outdoor and minstrel shows, see "Ninth Annual Outdoor Show" and "Young Talent in `Fun and Frolic' Show," *Democrat and News,* 28 January 1954, 1.

32. *Joseph W. Williams et al. . . . Civil Action 16658,* case file; *Joseph W. Williams et al. v. Rescue Fire Company;* "Maryland Fire Department Accused of Bias"; "Racial Issue Smolders within Cambridge, Md., Fire Department."

33. Barth, *Once upon a Time,* 153; Pierce, *A Boy's Eye View of World War II,* 78; Wallace quoted in Anderson, "Black Men, Blue Waters: African Americans on the Chesapeake."

34. Phillips Packing Company, vertical file; National Labor Relations Board (NLRB), Phillips Packing Company, case file, RG 625, entry 155, box 1608; NLRB, *Decisions and Orders of the National Labor Relations Board,* 5:272–87; United Cannery, Agricultural, Packing and Allied Workers of America, *Official Proceedings, First National Convention, Denver, Colorado, July 9–12, 1937;* Baltimore *News-American,* 2 March 1947.

35. Barth, *The Last Voyage of Somebody the Sailor,* 36–37; interview with John Barth.

36. For general discussions of labor during this period see Bernstein, *Turbulent Years.* On the Cambridge strike see Phillips Packing Company, vertical file; NLRB, Phillips Packing Company, case file; NLRB, *Decisions and Orders,* 5:272–87; United Cannery,

Agricultural, Packing and Allied Workers of America, *Official Proceedings, First National Convention.*

37. Phillips Packing Company, ibid.; NLRB, Phillips Packing Company, case file; NLRB, *Decisions and Orders*, ibid.; United Cannery . . . Workers of America, ibid.

38. After World War II, the left-leaning Food and Tobacco Workers (FTA) made another attempt to organize a bona fide union at Phillips Packing Company. It was easily defeated. Once again union organizers were physically attacked and imprisoned, and the company recognized the DORCO Workers Union as the collective bargaining agent for its workers. Subsequent campaigns by the AFL and Teamsters in the 1950s never succeeded. NLRB, *Decisions and Orders*, 73:447–53; *FTA News*, 15 January, 1 February 1946, 8 January 1947.

39. *Moody's Manual* (1957); Hobart Taylor, Jr., to John E. Nolan (Regarding Employment in Cambridge), 19 July 1963, Burke Marshall Papers; Connor, *Food Processing*, 374.

40. Kent, "The Negro in Politics in Dorchester County"; interview with Frederick Malkus.

41. Kent, ibid.; Sachs, "At-Large Election of County Commissioners: An Audit Conducted by the Office of the Attorney General."

42. Interview with Frederick Malkus; Thornton, "Municipal Politics and the Course of the Civil Rights Movement."

43. U.S. Department of Commerce, *Census of U.S. Population*, vol. 2, 1950 and 1960; Memo to Attorney General (Regarding Employment in Cambridge), 18 June 1963, Burke Marshall Papers.

44. Interview with Gloria Richardson, 21 March 1993. Brown, "Cambridge at the Early 20th Century," documents the existence of numerous black barbers, but by 1960 the economic health of these barbers was not good.

45. For a remarkable discussion of the reasons why new firms located in Cambridge, see George Hubley to Governor Millard Tawes, 6 November 1961, and the enclosure "Case History of a Plant Location Survey in Maryland," box 21, Economic Development, 1961–62, General File, Governor Tawes Papers. See also "The Four Horsemen of Cambridge," *Maryland Magazine* (Autumn 1972).

46. Lewis, "The Origins of the Civil Rights Movement."

47. Wennersten, *Maryland's Eastern Shore*, 3–4; Lee McCardell, "Old and New Meet beside the Choptank in Pleasant and Bustling Cambridge," *Baltimore Sun*, 23 December 1945.

48. Newhouse, *Maryland Lost and Found*, 29–32; Wennersten, ibid.

49. H.L. Mencken quoted in Wennersten, *Maryland's Eastern Shore*, 228.

50. Interview with Gloria Richardson, 13 May 2000; interview with Enez Grubb, 11 February 2000.

51. *The Yearling* (1960), Cambridge High School Yearbook, contains a photograph of this billboard; Huntley and Brinkley are quoted in *National Review*, 23 August 1963, 47.

Chapter 2. The Freedom Rides and the Birth of CNAC

1. *Afro-American*, 27 January, 7, 10 February 1962, 4; CNAC, "Study," CNAC Papers; "Cambridge Report," CORE Papers, reel 40; Bartley, *The Rise of Massive Resistance*; McMillen, *The Citizens' Councils*; Calcott, *Maryland and America*, chap. 7; Kent, "The Negro in Politics in Dorchester County." In 1955, about 300 whites met in Hurlock, a rural town in Dorchester County, to declare their opposition to the *Brown* decision. But the group did not affiliate with the Citizens' Councils that formed in the South, nor did the school board's policy alter to comply with the decision. "Upper County Group Studies Delay in School Integration," *Democrat and News*, 7 July 1955; "Anti-Integration Meeting in Hurlock," *Democrat and News*, 6 September 1956; "Elected School Board Hearing Held Monday," *Democrat and News*, 31 January 1957.

2. All from *Democrat and News*: "U.S. Sen. Kennedy in Dorchester, Sat. May 14," 5 May 1960; "Kennedy Greeted Enthusiastically," 19 May 1960; "We Go Forward or Stand Still," 20 October 1960; "Advertisement: Big Labor Has Moved to Shore," 3 November 1960; "Kennedy Elected President, Johnson Sweeps Shore," 10 November 1960.

3. *Cambridge Daily Banner*, 14 July, 31 December 1960; CNAC, "Study," CNAC Papers; Wennersten, *Maryland's Eastern Shore*, chap. 8; interview with Frederick Malkus.

4. *Cambridge Daily Banner*, 30 December 1961.

5. "Ghana Official Addresses Elks," *Democrat and News*, 29 June 1961; "Harriet Tubman Day Observed," *Democrat and News*, 9 November 1961, Clarence Logan, notes and clippings file.

6. Brauer, *John F. Kennedy*, 77–79; Calcott, *Maryland and America*, 155–56; Romano, "Diplomatic Immunity."

7. Palumbos, "Student Involvement in the Baltimore Civil Rights Movement, 1953–63"; Brugger, *Maryland*, 608–9.

8. Palumbos, ibid., and Carson, *In Struggle*, 40. Among those who chronicled CIG's actions was August Meier, a white history professor at Morgan State College and the adult advisor to CIG. Meier, who would jointly author the definitive study of CORE, observed that CIG enjoyed unusually good relations with older, well-established civil rights organizations, namely the NAACP and the National Urban League. See Garrow, ed., *We Shall Overcome*, 62.

9. Calcott, *Maryland and America*, 155–56; *New York Times*, 12 July 1961, 13; 4 September 1961, 1; 16 September 1961, 2; 21 September 1961, 20; 27 September 1961, 2; 5 October 1961, 24; 8 October 1961, 56; 28 October 1961, 24; 29 October 1961, 52; 2 November 1961, 28. On CIG see Meier, *A White Scholar and the Black Community, 1945–1965*, especially 26–27, 198, 206–207; Logan, notes and clippings file; Palumbos, "Student Involvement in the Baltimore Civil Rights Movement."

10. William Hansen to Peter Levy; interview with Gloria Richardson, 21 March 1993; interview with August Meier; Szabo, "An Interview with Gloria Richardson Dandridge"; "Six on Trial for Sit-Ins at Crisfield," *Cambridge Daily Banner*, 26 Decem-

ber 1962, 1; Logan, notes and clippings file; "Ten Sit-Iners Choose Jail for Holiday," *Baltimore Sun*, 26 December 1961, 1.

11. Zinn, *SNCC*, 66–67; Carson, *In Struggle*, 45–55.

12. Zinn, *SNCC*; *Baltimore Afro-American*, 27 January 1962, 15; "Integrationists Guilty, Fined," *Democrat and News*, 15 May 1962; Logan, notes and clippings file.

13. "Cambridge Report," 1962, CORE Papers, microfilm edition, reel 40.

14."Field Reports, 1962–63," SNCC Papers, box 96; "Second Ward Rec Program On," *Democrat and News*, 20 July 1961; "County Realtors Oppose Public Housing," *Democrat and News*, 21 December 1961.

15. "Cambridge Equal Opportunity Commission Makes Report," *Democrat and News*, 18 January 1962; Logan, notes and clippings file.

16. Logan, notes and clippings file.

17. "Cambridge Report," CORE Papers; "Integration of Restaurant Attempted Here: By Outsiders," *Democrat and News*, 18 January 1962; "Restaurant Sit-Ins Draw 61 Arrests," *Baltimore Sun*, 14 January 1962, 23.

18. "Cambridge Report," CORE Papers.

19. *The Spokesman* (Morgan State), 20 March 1962; Durand quoted in Palumbos, "Student Involvement in the Baltimore Civil Rights Movement," 472.

20. *Cambridge Daily Banner*, 15, 22, 24, 25, 29 January, 2 February 1962; Logan, notes and clippings file.

21. *Cambridge Daily Banner*, 22, 24 January 1962; Logan, notes and clippings file.

22. "Cambridge Report," CORE Papers.

23. On the makeup and motivation of the students who took part in the freedom rides, see Meier, *A White Scholar in the Black Community, 1945–1965*, 206–7; Curry, *Deep in Our Hearts*, 138–39.

24. *Afro-American*, 27 January 1962; "Cambridge Report," CORE Papers; "Field Report, 1962–63," SNCC Papers.

25. *Cambridge Daily Banner*, 22 January 1962.

26. "Cambridge Report," CORE Papers; *Cambridge Daily Banner*, 25 January 1962; Garrow, ed., *We Shall Overcome*, vol. 2, especially the article by August Meier; Logan, notes and clippings file.

27. "Field Reports, 1962–63," SNCC Papers; "Cambridge Report," CORE Papers; CNAC, "Study"; Carson, *In Struggle*, 39–43; Logan, notes and clippings file.

28. Interview with Lemuel Chester by Sandra Harney.

29. Interview with Enez Grubb, 24 August 2001.

30. Interview with Gloria Richardson, 13 May 2000; Logan, notes and clippings file.

31. CNAC, "The Negro Ward of Cambridge, Maryland: A Study in Social Character" (henceforth CNAC, "Cambridge Survey"); interview with Enez Grubb, 24 August 2001; interview with Gloria Richardson, 18 May 2002.

32. Curry, *Deep in Our Hearts*, 140.

33. Interview with John Wilson.

34. Gloria Richardson has been interviewed on numerous occasions. Nearly all of these interviews discuss her initial involvement in the movement and the affiliation of

CNAC with SNCC. On youth involvement see interviews of Donna Richardson Young, Dwight Cromwell, Enez Grubb, and Lemuel Chester, all by Sandra Harney.

35. CNAC, "Cambridge Survey," 3.

36. Interviews with Enez Grubb, 2001, and Gloria Richardson, 2000.

37. CNAC, "Study," CNAC Papers; "Marking the 30th Anniversary of Cambridge's Pine Street Fire," in "Maryland Race Relations—Eastern Shore," vertical file, Dorchester County Public Library; Grubb, *In Spite Of.*

38. Interview with Gloria Richardson, 2000.

39. Ibid., 1993, 2000.

40. *Cambridge Daily Banner,* 29 January 1962; interviews, ibid.

41. Kent, "The Negro in Politics in Dorchester County"; interview with Gloria Richardson, 1993; Brock, "Gloria Richardson and the Cambridge Movement."

42. Interview, ibid.; CNAC, "Cambridge Survey"; "Field Reports, 1962–63," SNCC Papers; "Frederick St. Clair Remembered as Unsung Hero," vertical file, Black History, Dorchester County Public Library.

43. Interviews with Gloria Richardson, 1993, 2000; Brock, "Gloria Richardson and the Cambridge Movement."

44. Interviews, ibid. and 2002; Brock, ibid.; interview with Gloria Richardson by Sandra Harney, 1997.

45. Interview with Gloria Richardson, 2000; Robnet, *How Long? How Long?*

46. Interviews with Gloria Richardson, 1993, 2000; Brock, "Gloria Richardson and the Cambridge Movement"; interview with Gloria Richardson by Sandra Harney; Szabo, "Interview with Gloria Richardson"; Grubb, *In Spite Of.*

47. Grubb, ibid.; interview with Courtland Cox; Dorothy Zellner to Peter B. Levy (e-mail), 10 August 2001.

48. Interviews with Gloria Richardson, 1993, 2000, and by Sandra Harney; "Field Reports, 1962–63," SNCC Papers.

49. Interviews, ibid.; Millner, "Recasting Civil Rights Leadership."

50. Robnet, *How Long? How Long?*

51. "Gloria Richardson," *Ebony,* July 1964, 23–30; Kempton, "Gloria, Gloria"; Liston, "Who Can We Surrender To?"; Cook, "Gloria Richardson"; CNAC, "Study," CNAC Papers; Kent, "The Negro in Politics in Dorchester County"; interview with Lemuel Chester.

52. *Afro-American,* 15 June 1962, 4, 20 April 1963; *Daily Banner,* 15 January, 4 September 1962; Editorial, WJZ-TV by Herbert Cahan, 24 July 1963, Governor Tawes Papers, S1041–1530; *Baltimore Evening Sun,* 22 January 1962; Logan, notes and clippings file.

53. Interview with Gloria Richardson, 1993; Schneider, "Summer of Fire," 10; *Daily Banner,* 18, 19 September 1962.

54. Lester, "The Angry Children of Malcolm X."

55. CNAC, "Study," CNAC Papers; Hobart Taylor, Jr., to John E. Nolan, 19 July 1963, and Memo to Attorney General [Regarding Employment in Cambridge], 18 July 1963, both in Burke Marshall Papers.

56. *Afro-American,* 15 June 1963, 24; CNAC, "Study," CNAC Papers.

57. *Cambridge Daily Banner,* 24 January, 1, 2 February 1962.

58."Analysis of the Cambridge, Maryland Disturbances," Office of the Assistant Director of Research, Staff Report No. 4 (Draft), Burke Marshall Papers; Cambridge, Maryland, 1960–69, Afro-American vertical file, Enoch Pratt Free Library, Baltimore.

59. *Joseph W. Williams et al.* v. *Rescue Fire Company; Joseph W. Williams et al. . . . Civil Action 16658,* case file; U.S. Senate,"Hearing on H.R. 421," 31–64, 730–45.

60. *Cambridge Daily Banner,* 28 June, 10 July 1962; "Voter Education Meeting," 2 October 1962, CORE Papers, A:XVII; CNAC, "Cambridge Study"; Logan, notes and clippings file.

61. "Voter Education Meeting," 25 September 1962, SNCC Papers, box 11, folder 37.

62. On Fayette County see Levy, *Let Freedom Ring,* 85–86.

63. On McComb County see Carson, *In Struggle,* chap. 4.

64. *Cambridge Daily Banner,* 26 July 1961; Rev. T. M. Murray to Legal Department of the NAACP, 2 August 1962, Papers of the NAACP (microfilm edition), part 22, reel 12.

65. "The Summer Project," CORE Papers, A:XV:170.

Chapter 3. A Cauldron of Hate

1. Jones, *The Wallace Story,* 281; Branch, *Parting the Waters,* chaps. 14–17; Carter, *The Politics of Rage,* 105–10.

2. *Cambridge Daily Banner,* 31 January 1962.

3. John F. Kennedy, "Televised Address to the Nation," 11 June 1963, in *Public Papers of the Presidents.*

4. Sitkoff, *The Struggle for Black Equality,* 133.

5. Logan, notes and clippings file; CNAC, "Study," CNAC Papers; Szabo, "Interview with Gloria Richardson"; "Integrationists Make Demands to City Council," *Democrat and News,* 28 March 1963; *Cambridge Daily Banner* 1 April 1963.

6. CNAC, "Study," CNAC Papers; Szabo, "Interview with Gloria Richardson"; "Integrationists Make Demands," *Democrat and News,* 28 March 1963; *Cambridge Daily Banner* 1 April 1963.

7. CNAC, "Study," CNAC Papers; *Cambridge Daily Banner* 1, 3, 8 April 1963; "Advertisement for Dorsett Theater," *Democrat and News,* 4 April 1963.

8. CNAC, "Study," CNAC Papers; "Cambridge Fears D-Day," *Afro-American,* 18 May 1963, 1; interview with Enez Grubb, 2001; Logan, notes and clippings file.

9. CNAC, "Study," CNAC Papers; Logan, notes and clippings file.

10. "Cambridge Report," CORE Papers; *Cambridge Daily Banner,* 4, 15, 16, 18 May 1963; MCIRPR,"Report on Racial Situation in Cambridge," 12 June 1963, in Governor Tawes Papers, S1041–1557; CNAC, "Study," CNAC Papers.

11."Cambridge Fears D-Day," *Afro-American,* 18 June 1963.

12. On the Henry family see Jones, *New Revised History of Dorchester County,* 331–37.

13. *Baltimore Sun,* 8 May 1963; "54 Demonstrators Found Guilty, Fined 1 Cent,"

Democrat and News, 9 May 1963; *Cambridge Daily Banner*, 8 May 1963, 1; Brock, "Gloria Richardson and the Cambridge Movement," 128.

14. Interview with Courtland Cox.

15. "Racial Protests Continue: Local Groups of Young Negroes Have Paraded, Picketed, and Sat-In Almost Daily," *Democrat and News*, 16 May 1963.

16. Nearly every person I interviewed mentioned the family ties between Richardson and Henry, although none went on to show how they precisely affected developments in Cambridge during the 1960s. On working-class authoritarianism, see Shostak, *Blue Collar Life*; Lipsett, "Working Class Authoritarianism," 336.

17. Millner, "Recasting Civil Rights Leadership."

18. MICRPR, "Report on Racial Situation in Cambridge," Governor Tawes Papers; "Cambridge Report," CORE Papers; *New York Times*, 5–11 June 1963; *Afro-American*, 18 May, 8 June 1963; *Cambridge Daily Banner*, 22 May 1963.

19. "Report on Racial Situation in Cambridge," 12 June 1963, Governor Tawes Papers, "Statements and Speeches, 1963–1964"; G. Roland Harper, Jr., "Letter to the Editor," *Cambridge Daily Banner*, 19 July 1963.

20. *Cambridge Daily Banner*, 2 July 1963; interview with Enez Grubb, 24 August 2001.

21. *Cambridge Daily Banner*, 24 May, 18 June 1963.

22. White's "Letter" quoted in Schneider, "Summer of Fire," 8; "Crossroads of 80s," vertical file, Dorchester County Public Library. The NAACP's appeal of Cromwell's conviction, which it won, was a precedent-setting case, enhancing the rights of juveniles in Maryland and elsewhere.

23. *Cambridge Daily Banner*, 5, 8, 10, 11 June 1963; *New York Times*, 12 June 1963, 23; *Afro-American*, 18 May 1964, 24.

24. "Cambridge Report," CORE Papers; *New York Times*, 5–11 June 1963; *Afro-American*, 18 May, 8 June 1963; Burke Marshall, "Memorandum," 17 June 1963, Burke Marshall Papers.

25. CNAC, "Study," CNAC Papers; *New York Times*, 12 June 1963; *Cambridge Daily Banner*, 12 June 1963.

26. *Cambridge Daily Banner*, 13 June 1963; *New York Times*, 13 June 1963.

27. "City Officials Study Equal Accommodations for Cambridge," *Democrat and News*, 20 June 1963.

28. *New York Times*, 11–15 June 1963; *Cambridge Daily Banner*, 11–15 June, 1963; *Afro-American*, 15 June 1963.

29. Ibid.; Governor Tawes, "Press Release," 14 June 1963, Governor Tawes Papers, S1041–1530; Millner, "Recasting Civil Rights Leadership"; Brock, "Gloria Richardson and the Cambridge Movement"; Kempton, "Gloria, Gloria."

30. Gloria Richardson to Governor Tawes, 12 June 1963, Governor Tawes Papers, "CAM-CAN"; interview with Gloria Richardson by Sandra Harney. On the tradition of self-defense see Tyson, "Robert F. Williams."

31. *New York Times* 14 July 1963, 1; 15 July 1963, 20; 18 July 1963, 14.

32. *Cambridge Daily Banner*, 26 June, 16 July 1963. Ruth Ann Pritchett, one of the

two white girls who was arrested, wrote a letter to the editor in which she expressed her strong white supremacist feelings and suggested that she had not been caught downtown by mistake; ibid., 19 June 1963.

33. CNAC, "Study," CNAC Papers; *Cambridge Daily Banner*, 2, 6 July 1963.

34. "Cambridge Report," CORE Papers; Burke Marshall, "Memorandum," 1963, Burke Marshall Papers.

35. *New York Times*, 9 July 1963, 1, and 10 July, 1963, 19; *Cambridge Daily Banner*, 7–12 July 1963; Dwight Campbell, "Report," 11 July 1963, CORE Papers, reel 21; "City Council Passes Public Accommodations Amendment," *Democrat and News*, 4 July 1963; "National Guard Moved Out Monday, Picketing Started One Hour Later," *Democrat and News*, 11 July 1963.

36. *New York Times*, 13 July 1963; "Cambridge Calms Down Again After Nine Are Shot," *Democrat and News*, 18 July 1963; Dwight Campbell, "Report," 11 July 1963, CORE Papers, reel 21; *Afro-American*, 13 July 1963, 1; Governor J. Millard Tawes, "Speech," 19 July 1963, Governor Tawes Papers, S1041–1557.

37. *Cambridge Daily Banner*, 16 July 1963.

38. Lewis, *Walking with the Wind*, 212–13; interview with Gloria Richardson, 2000.

39. CNAC, "Study," CNAC Papers.

40. Lewis, *Walking with the Wind*, 212–13; interview with Gloria Richardson, 2000; CNAC, ibid.

41. *Afro-American*, 20 July 1963; "Agreement," 22 July 1963, Burke Marshall Papers. In the fall of 1963 a total of twenty-nine blacks enrolled in previously all-white schools in Dorchester County, including three at Cambridge High School, eleven at Cambridge Junior High School, four at Academy Elementary School, and two at Peach Blossom Elementary School.

42. Logan, notes and clippings file.

43. *Afro-American*, 20 July 1963; "Agreement," 22 July 1963, Burke Marshall Papers.

44. Logan, notes and clippings file.

45. *Cambridge Daily Banner*, 24 July 1963.

Chapter 4. Good-bye to Gradualism

1. Sellers, *The River of No Return*, 68; Walker, "A Media-Made Movement?"

2. *Cambridge Daily Banner*, 24–26 July 1963.

3. *Cambridge Daily Banner*, 2, 4, 9, 10 August 1963.

4. Ibid.

5. *Cambridge Daily Banner*, 10 September 1963; "Group Pledges Accommodations Defeat," *Democrat and News*, 12 September 1963.

6. Ibid.

7. *Cambridge Daily Banner*, 24, 25 July, 23 August, and 25, 28 September 1963.

8. "Letters to the Editor," *Cambridge Daily Banner*, 18, 19 July 1963.

9. *Cambridge Daily Banner*, 20 September 1963.

10. *Cambridge Daily Banner*, 1, 3, 13 September 1963.

11. *Cambridge Daily Banner*, 4, 6 September 1963; interview with Gloria Richardson, 2000; Papers of the NAACP, part 21, reel 19.

12. Interviews with Gloria Richardson, 1993 and 2000, and Enez Grubb, 2001.

13. Ibid.

14. *Afro-American*, 28 September 1963; "Field Report," 1963, SNCC Papers (microfilm edition), reel 17; CNAC, "Statement," and Gloria Richardson, "Press Release," both in Burke Marshall Papers; CNAC, "Study," CNAC Papers; CORE Papers, A:XV:170 (microfilm edition).

15. *Cambridge Daily Banner*, 28 September 1963; CNAC, "Study," CNAC Papers; *Afro-American*, 5 October 1963; interview with Philip Savage by John Britton; NAACP Papers, especially Philip Savage folders, 1962–65; interview with Gloria Richardson, 2000.

16. Interview with Gloria Richardson, 2000. For a black woman with similar views, see Lani Guinier, *The Tyranny of the Majority*.

17. CNAC, "Study," CNAC Papers.

18. Stories on Cambridge often were placed next to stories on protests led by northern branches of CORE or the NAACP, which in many ways paralleled the protests initiated by Richardson. During the same period, Malcolm X was distancing himself from the Nation of Islam and outlining his black nationalist philosophy. See Carson, *In Struggle*.

19. Walker, "The `Gun-Toting' Gloria Richardson." Walker tends to set up a straw dog in this article. By beginning with the wrongly held view that Richardson was a "gun-toter," Walker understates Richardson's disagreements with the philosophy of nonviolence. Her views of nonviolence shifted. At times she clearly identified herself as an advocate of nonviolence, at least tactically. At other times, she verged on advocating violence. See especially John Britton's interview with Gloria Richardson Dandridge.

20. Millner, "Recasting Civil Rights Leadership"; interview with Gloria Richardson, 2000.

21. Millner, ibid.; Robnet, *How Long? How Long?*

22. See "Minutes (Notes) of (Miles) Governor Committee Meetings," Cambridge, 18 June 1964, Governor Tawes Papers, S1041–1557; Kempton, "Gloria, Gloria"; Liston, "Who Can We Surrender To?"; William Hansen to Peter B. Levy; Millner, ibid.; interview with Gloria Richardson by Sandra Harney.

23. Millner, ibid.; interview with Gloria Richardson, 2000.

24. Robnet, *How Long? How Long?* At times Robnet plays a bit loose with her evidence to fit Richardson into her argument. She relies too much on Foeman, "Gloria Richardson: Breaking the Mold," which, while valuable, contains some assertions I was unable to confirm independently.

25. On King's pragmatism, see Meier, "On the Role of Martin Luther King."

26. *Afro-American*, 5 October 1963.

27. The New Left, nationwide, may have made the same mistake as Richardson, overestimating the power of liberals and underestimating the possibility that the New Left's attacks on liberals might provide an opening to the new right to assume power.

28. See "1963 Headlines Show Community Had Strength to Ride Out Crises," *Cambridge Daily Banner*, 31 December 1967; Editorial, *Daily Banner*, 30 December 1963; "Human Relations Committee Notes Progress," *Daily Banner*, 18 December 1963.

29. *Afro-American*, 5 October 1963; interview with Philip Savage; Philip Savage folders, 1962–65, NAACP Papers, IIIC, 306; "Daisy Bates Speaks at A.M.E.," *Cambridge Daily Banner*, 11 November 1963.

30. See the *Cambridge Daily Banner*, 8 November, 30, 31 December 1963; *New York Times*, 30 November 1963; Saunders quoted in Trever, "Gloria Richardson and the Cambridge Civil Rights Movement." The fact that the integrated memorial service for the girl was arranged by General Gelston, the commander of the National Guard units that remained stationed in Cambridge, influenced Richardson's decision to support it.

31. "Rights Leader Praises Council President Choice," *Cambridge Daily Banner*, 23 July 1964; Major Jack Koulman to General Reckford, 4 February 1964, in Governor Tawes Papers, General File, "Interracial-Cambridge, 1964"; *Cambridge Daily Banner*, 8 November, 30, 31 December 1963; Alsop, "People in a Trap"; interview with Gloria Richardson by Sandra Harney.

32. Richardson quoted in Goldman, *The Death and Life of Malcolm X*, 116.

33. Bracey et al., eds., *Black Nationalism in America*, xliv–xlvii, 421–26; Sales, *From Civil Rights to Black Liberation*; Muse, *The American Negro Revolution*, 123; Szabo, "Interview with Gloria Richardson Dandridge."

34. Malcolm X files, FBI reading room.

35. Gloria Richardson, "Freedom—Here and Now."

36. "Wise and the DBCA," *Cambridge Daily Banner*, 15 November 1963; Louis Panos, "DBCA President's Views on Rights Movement Described by Newsman," *Cambridge Daily Banner* 11 May 1964, 3; "DBCA to Seek State and National Affiliates," *Democrat and News*, 17 October 1963; "DBCA Invites Lawmakers Here," *Democrat and News*, 9 January 1964.

37. *New York Times*: "New Move Slated in Cambridge, Md.," 26 January 1963, 36; "Incident Imperils Truce in Maryland," 4 March 1963; "News Control Bill," 13 February 1964; "Maryland Limits Civil Rights Bill," 14 April 1964, 10. *Cambridge Daily Banner*: "Cambridge Human Relations Committee," 22 October 1963; "Wise and the DBCA," 15 November 1963; Louis Panos, "DBCA President's Views on Rights Movement Described by Newsman," 11 May 1964, 3. See also "Wm. L. Wise Heads National Group," *Democrat and News*, 23 January 1963.

38. "Wise and the DBCA," and Panos, "DBCA President's Views," *Cambridge Daily Banner*; "Wm. L. Wise Heads National Group," *Democrat and News*.

39. Gloria Richardson, "Press Release," 1963, CNAC Papers; "Local Elected Officials Blast Gelston, Tawes, Brewster," *Democrat and News*, 5 March 1963.

40. "New Move Slated," "Incident Imperils Truce," "News Control Bill," "Maryland Limits Civil Rights Bill," *New York Times*; "Cambridge Human Relations Committee," "Wise and the DBCA," *Cambridge Daily Banner*.

41. Carter, *The Politics of Rage*, 276–80.

42. Louis G. Panos, "DBCA President's Views on Rights Movement Described by Newsman" and "Wallace to Speak in City Tonight," *Cambridge Daily Banner*, 11 May 1964.

43. Jones, *The Wallace Story*, 276–80; *Cambridge Daily Banner*, 12 May 1964; *New York Times*, 12 May 1964, 1; "DBCA Addressed by Gov. Wallace," *Democrat and News*, 14 May 1964.

44. *New York Times*, 12 May 1964, 1, and 13, 15 May 1964.

45. Sellers, *The River of No Return*, 71; *New York Times*, 13 May 1963, 1; interview with Courtland Cox.

46. Sellers, ibid.; interview with Courtland Cox.

47. *Cambridge Daily Banner*, 27, 28 May 1964.

48. Ibid.

49. *Cambridge Daily Banner*, 26, 27 May, 5 June 1964; "Minutes of Governor's Committee (Miles) Meeting," 11 June 1964, Governor Tawes Papers, S1041–1557. The Tawes papers also include tens of telegrams on the Cambridge situation, especially in the folder "Interracial-Cambridge, 1964."

50. *Cambridge Daily Banner*, 5, 30 June 1964.

51. Ibid., 13 July 1964.

52. Ibid., 8 June 1964.

53. Ibid., 13, 14 July 1964.

54. Ibid., 16 July 1964.

Chapter 5. The Paradox of Change

1. Carson, *In Struggle*. "Shuffle Along" was a famous all-black musical composed by Noble Sissel and Eubie Blake. The play opened on Broadway in 1921 and featured many songs that became hits, such as "I'm Just Wild about Harry."

2. *Cambridge Daily Banner*, 6 July 1964; "Report of the Miles Committee," Governor Tawes Papers, S1041–1557.

3. *Cambridge Daily Banner*, 6–8, 23 July 1964; "Last Troops Quit Cambridge, Maryland," *New York Times*, 12 July 1964, 54; "Negro Elected to Head Cambridge, Md., Council," *New York Times*, 21 July 1964, 20.

4. Office of the Assistant Deputy Director for Research, "Analysis of Cambridge, Maryland, Disturbance," Staff Paper No. 4 (Draft), 29 October 1967, in *Civil Rights during the Johnson Administration*, pt. 5; Clarence Mitchell to Governor Tawes, 3 July 1964, Governor Tawes Papers, "Statements, Speeches, 63–64"; interview with Gloria Richardson, 2000. For an example of the emotional strain of the movement see Moody, *Coming of Age in Mississippi*.

5. Interviews with Steve Fraser, Dwight Cromwell by Sandra Harney, and Courtland Cox.

6. On the exhaustion of SNCC see Carson, *In Struggle*; John Batiste took over SNCC's responsibilities in Cambridge. See also Gloria Richardson to Stokely Carmichael, 1 July 1966, SNCC Papers (microfilm), reel 5, no. 65.

7. There is little scholarship on this subject. While several studies detail the long

struggle to enact the Civil Rights Act of 1964, they do not delve deeply into why it did not engender massive resistance. Most overviews of the civil rights movement similarly jump from the enactment of the law to "Freedom Summer," and the Selma protest that led to the Voting Rights Act of 1965, without theorizing on why the former did not engender the sort of opposition that the *Brown* decision did. One exception is Colburn, *Racial Change and Community Crisis.*

8. "You Made Me Do It," *Cambridge Daily Banner,* 11 July 1964; Novella Baldwin, "Letter to the Editor," *Cambridge Daily Banner,* 14 July 1964.

9. *Cambridge Daily Banner,* 14 July 1964.

10. *Joseph W. Williams et al.* v. *Rescue Fire Company; Joseph W. Williams et al. . . . Civil Action 16658,* case file.

11. Ibid.

12. Ibid.

13. Ibid.

14. Ibid.

15. Lichtenstein, "From Corporatism to Collective Bargaining," traces a similar phenomenon in the labor movement.

16. *Joseph W. Williams et al.* v. *Rescue Fire Company; Joseph W. Williams et al. . . . Civil Action 16658,* case file.

17. Interview with Enez Grubb, 11 February 2000.

18. U.S. Department of Commerce, "Area Redevelopment Administration: Directory of Approved Projects," 30 September 1964; "Press Release: Redevelopment Loan, Grant Approved for Project in Cambridge, Maryland," 14 September 1961, U.S. Department of Commerce, 378–67A-4033, box 44, folder 2. For an overview of the ARA see Levitan, *Federal Aid to Depressed Areas.*

19. U.S. Department of Commerce, "ARA Field Report," November 1964; U.S. Department of Commerce, Area Redevelopment Administration, "Press Release," 27 February 1964, "Cambridge Folder."

20. Maryland Division of Economic Development, *Community Economic Inventory: Dorchester County, Maryland;* U.S. Department of Commerce, "ARA Field Report," November 1964, Office of Economic Opportunity Papers, RG 381; Housing and Urban Development Papers, RG 207.

21. "Reconnaissance Survey: Field Research Report," Inter-Office Memorandum (Draft), n.d., in *Civil Rights during the Johnson Administration,* pt. 5, reels 6, 17, 23.

22. Ibid.

23. Ibid.; interview with Albert Atkinson.

24. Interview with Steve Fraser; Piven and Cloward, *Poor People's Movements.*

25. Sources on housing are multiple. See CNAC, "Study," CNAC Papers; *Cambridge Daily Banner,* 9 February, 21 March, 15, 17 August, 4 September 1962, 4 January 1963.

26. CNAC, "Study," CNAC Papers; *Cambridge Daily Banner* (see preceding note).

27. "Agreement," Burke Marshall Papers; "Interracial-Cambridge, 1964" and "Reconnaissance Survey: Field Research Report," both in Governor Tawes Papers; Alice

Thomas to Gilbert Ware, 14 August 1968, Governor Spiro T. Agnew Papers, General File, box 11, Correspondence—Cambridge.

28. Minutes of Governor's [Miles] Committee Meeting, 11 July 1964, and James Busick to J. Millard Tawes, 11 October 1964; James Busick to J. Millard Tawes, 14 October 1964; MCIRPR, "Report on Racial Situation in Cambridge," 12 June 1963, all in Governor Tawes Papers.

29. *Cambridge Daily Banner*, 25 June, 8 September 1965, 9 September 1966; U.S. Commission on Civil Rights, "School Desegregation in Dorchester County, Maryland," September 1977.

30. Interview with Enez Grubb by Sandra Harney.

31. Minutes of Governor's [Miles] Committee, 18 June, 1964, Governor Tawes Papers. On the views of the DBCA toward housing see Louis Panos, "DBCA President's Views on Rights Movement Described by Newsman," *Cambridge Daily Banner*, 11 May 1964.

32. "Canning Offers Greatest Organizing Potential," 14 March 1957; A. T. Stephens, "Memo [Re: Canning Organizing Potential]," 16 April 1957, both in folder 4, box 527, UPWA Papers; Ruth Shields to Russ [Lasley], 27 March 1957; "Report From Meeting on UPWA Canning Caucus . . to UPWA National Conference," 3 October 1957, both in folder 4, box 376, UPWA Papers.

33. Meyer Sherman to Emerson Moseley, 8 April 1957; Meyer Stern to Russell Lasley, 4 June 1957; Clive Knowles, Hazel Hayes, and Ruth Shields to Russell Lasley, 6 June 1957; Clive Knowles to Meyer Stern, 27 May 1957; Clive Knowles to Russell Lasley, 8 June 1957; all in folder 4, box 376, UPWA Papers.

34. "Coastal Foods Co. Campaign," n.d., folder 2, box 178, UPWA Papers; "How the Union Came to Town in Troubled Cambridge, Maryland," *Packinghouse Worker*, May 1964. On the UPWA's racial record see Halpern, "Interracial Unionism in the Southwest."

35. "How the Union Came to Town"; "Campbell Kids Bring Industrial Democracy to Eastern Shore," *Packinghouse Worker*, March 1963.

36. "How the Union Came to Town"; "The View from the Eastern Shore," *Packinghouse Worker*, June 1963; "District 6 Cheers 20th Birthday," *Packinghouse Worker*, April 1964.

37. "Coastal Foods Co. Campaign"; "Win Pair of Cannery Votes on Maryland Eastern Shore" and "How the Union Came to Town," *Packinghouse Worker*, December 1963; Office of the Assistant Deputy Director for Research, "Analysis of Cambridge, Maryland, Disturbance," Staff Paper No. 4 (Draft), 29 October 1967, in *Civil Rights during the Johnson Administration*, pt. 5. This document is somewhat surprising in that it shows a representative of the Johnson Administration openly recounting the ways in which the business elite subtly cultivated racial divisions in order to fight off unions and maintain low wages.

38. CNAC, "Study," CNAC Papers.

39. "Coastal Foods Co. Campaign Election" and G. R. Hathaway to Butch, 27

August 1963, both in folder 2, box 178, UPWA Papers; "How the Union Came to Town"; CNAC, "The Negro Ward of Cambridge," CNAC Papers.

40. *Packinghouse Worker,* May 1964; interview with Enez Grubb, 11 February 2000.

41. *Packinghouse Worker,* April 1964; interview with Gloria Richardson, 1993.

42. *Cambridge Daily Banner,* 8 November 1963.

43. "Letter to the Editor," *Cambridge Daily Banner,* 14 November 1963.

44. I have been unable to access company documents confirming this argument, but local newspaper stories surmised that this was the case.

45. For a breakdown of the workforces in these plants see CNAC, "Study," CNAC Papers.

46. *Cambridge Daily Banner,* 8 January, 31 March, and 1, 13 April 1965; "Cargo Handlers, Inc. and Ronald Sampson," in NLRB, *Decisions and Orders,* vol. 159.

47. Ibid.

48. Hill and Jones, *Race in America;* Hill, "The Problem of Race in American Labor History," 189; Nelson, *Divided We Stand.*

Chapter 6. If This Town Don't Come Around

1. For an example of typical coverage of Cambridge see Chris Guy, "Hotel Project Provokes Mistrust," *Baltimore Sun,* 28 May 2000, 1. Guy begins his story on the economic revitalization of Cambridge, "where more than 30 years ago black activist H. Rap Brown helped light a fire fueled by anger and frustration." For the Kerner Commission's analysis of events in Cambridge see the following three items in *Civil Rights during the Johnson Administration,* pt. 5: "Report of Office of Investigations," 25 March 1968, reel 17; "Reconnaissance Survey: Field Research Report," Inter-Office Memorandum (Draft), n.d., reel 23; and Office of the Assistant Deputy Director for Research, "Analysis of Cambridge, Maryland, Disturbance," Staff Paper No. 4 (Draft), 29 October 1967, reel 6 (henceforth cited as "Analysis of Cambridge Disturbance"). Also see Boesel and Goldberg, "Crisis in Cambridge," 110. Brown is quoted as describing the riots of the latter part of the 1960s as a dress rehearsal for a broader revolt in "The Time Has Come," *Eyes on the Prize II,* PBS Video, Blackside, Inc., 1989.

2. Tom Stuckey, "Progress in Cambridge during Last Four Years Cited by Associated Press," *Cambridge Daily Banner,* 17 March 1967.

3. "Report Praises Cambridge," *Cambridge Daily Banner,* 13 April 1967.

4. Editorial: "Freedom of Choice," *Cambridge Daily Banner,* 1 April 1967; "Official Pleased with State's School Desegregation Progress," *Cambridge Daily Banner,* 5 April 1967; Dick Parsons to Edgar May, 22 May 1967, Office of Economic Opportunity Papers.

5. Editorial: "Keeping It Cool," *Cambridge Daily Banner,* 27 June 1967.

6. *Cambridge Daily Banner,* especially 7 October, 31 December 1966; 17 February, 7 March, 14, 21, 24, 30 June, 1, 6, 8, 10 July 1967.

7. "Fire Marshal Investigating Fires Here," "Arson Causes Fire," "Arrested for Turning in False Alarm," *Cambridge Daily Banner,* 27, 28, 29 June 1967 respectively;

"Reconnaissance Survey: Field Research Report," in *Civil Rights during the Johnson Administration.*

8. "Fire Marshal Investigating Fires Here"; "Arson Causes Fire" (source of quote); "Arrested for Turning in False Alarm."

9. Interview with Gloria Richardson Dandridge by John Britton; Page, "H. Rap Brown and the Cambridge Incident."

10. "Youth Found Guilty," *Cambridge Daily Banner,* 23 June 1967.

11. Letters to the Editor, *Cambridge Daily Banner,* 3, 26 July 1967; "Analysis of the Cambridge Disturbance."

12. Letters to the Editor, *Cambridge Daily Banner,* 16 June, 3 July 1967; "Youth Found Guilty," *Cambridge Daily Banner,* 23 June 1967.

13. Letters to the Editor, *Cambridge Daily Banner,* 26 June 1967; Chester quoted in William Thompson, "Tensions Remain in Cambridge," *Baltimore Sun,* 26 July 1992, 1C.

14. Interview with August Meier.

15. "Burch to Be Here for Rally," *Cambridge Daily Banner,* 14 July 1967; "Rights Rally Is Broken Up," *Cambridge Daily Banner,* 17 July 1967; Page, "H. Rap Brown and the Cambridge Incident"; "Reconnaissance Survey: Field Research Report."

16. Page, ibid.; "Cambridge Action Council Formed," *Cambridge Daily Banner,* 30 June 1967; "Burch to Be Here for Rally" and "Rights Rally Is Broken Up," ibid.; interview with Gloria Richardson Dandridge by John Britton.

17. "Reconnaissance Survey: Field Research Report" and "Analysis of the Cambridge Disturbance."

18. Carson, *In Struggle,* 252–55; "H. Rap 'The Lamb' Turns Erring Lion," *Afro-American,* 19 August 1967.

19. "7,000 Guardsmen Quell Race Riot in Detroit" and "Arson Termed Cause of Fire at School," *Cambridge Daily Banner,* 24 July 1967; Letter to the Editor, *Cambridge Daily Banner,* 26 July 1967.

20. H. Rap Brown, "Speech," Cambridge, Maryland, 24 July, 1967. There are various renditions of the speech. See "A Collation of Transcripts," by Lawrence Peskin and Dawn Almes, in *Is Baltimore Burning?*

21. H. Rap Brown, "Speech"; Page, "H. Rap Brown and the Cambridge Incident."

22. Ibid.

23. Ibid.

24. "Report of Office of Investigations," 25 March 1968; "Reconnaissance Survey: Field Research Report"; "Analysis of Cambridge Disturbance," all in *Civil Rights during the Johnson Administration.* See also Boesel and Goldberg, "Crisis in Cambridge." Brown's attorney, William Kunstler, sought to obtain internal Kerner Commission memos regarding Cambridge, but the commission made sure that these memos remained classified. See Nathaniel R. Jones to Victor H. Palmieri, 28 March 1968, and Henry B. Taliaferro, Jr., to David Ginsberg and Victor Palmieri, 1 November 1967, both in *Civil Rights during the Johnson Administration,* reels 14 and 18, respectively.

25. "Report of Office of Investigations," "Reconnaissance Survey: Field Research Report," and "Analysis of Cambridge Disturbance," ibid.; Boesel and Goldberg, ibid.

26. Ibid.

27. Ibid.

28. Boesel and Goldberg, ibid., 112; "Analysis of Cambridge Disturbance."

29."Report of Office of Investigations"; "Reconnaissance Survey: Field Research Report"; "Analysis of Cambridge Disturbance"; Boesel and Goldberg, ibid.

30. Ibid.

31. Ibid.

32. Ibid.; *Is Baltimore Burning?*

33. "Report of Office of Investigations," 25 March 1968; "Reconnaissance Survey: Field Research Report"; "Analysis of Cambridge Disturbance"; Boesel and Goldberg, "Crisis in Cambridge."

34. *Is Baltimore Burning?*; *New York Times*, 26 July 1967, 1; Walker, "A Media-Made Movement?"

35. "Services for Green Are Incomplete," *Cambridge Daily Banner*, 5 August 1967; "They're Bitter, Fearful, Bewildered," *Afro-American*, 5 August 1967; "Cambridge Riot Figure Takes Own Life," *Afro-American*, 13 August 1967.

36. Conservatives uniformly used the term *riots*; liberals used the terms *riots* and *civil disorders*; radicals tended to use the term *uprisings*.

37. "Second Ward Resident Gives out Statement," *Cambridge Daily Banner*, 29 July 1967; William E. Cephas, Letter to the Editor, *Cambridge Daily Banner*, 8 August 1967; "Chief Kinnamon Testifies before the Senate Judiciary Committee," *Cambridge Daily Banner*, 13 August 1967; U.S. Senate, Committee on the Judiciary, 90th Cong., 1st sess., "Hearings on H.R. 421, Anti-riot Bill—1967," esp. 31–64; "Statement by Governor Spiro T. Agnew," 25 July 1967, and "Statement," 30 July 1967, Spiro T. Agnew Papers, series II, subseries 3, box 1; John Woodfield, "Guardsmen Move into Area; White Policeman Shot," *Cambridge Daily Banner*, 25 July 1967.

38. "Ford Assails Brown and Carmichael," *New York Times*, 29 August 1967. On the political realignment that was taking place see Edsall and Edsall, *Chain Reaction*; Phillips, *The Emerging Republican Majority*; Carter, *The Politics of Rage*; Himmelstein, *To the Right*.

39. Wills, "The Second Civil War," 71.

40. Methvin, *The Riot Makers*.

41. *Cambridge Daily Banner*, 27, 28 July, 30 August 1967.

42. U.S. Senate, Judiciary Committee, "Hearings—Anti-Riot Bill," Adkins quoted on 741–44; see also *Congressional Record*, 90th Cong., 1st sess., vol. 113, part 19, 25404–6. The findings of the Kerner Commission substantiated Gelston's views. Strongly influenced by New York City Mayor John Lindsay, a moderate Republican, and by a coterie of liberal academics, the Kerner Commission assured President Johnson that the riots were neither part of a conspiracy nor caused by black radicals. Rather, the Kerner Commission concluded that the riots were fundamentally caused by divisions within American society, between blacks and whites. Even more tellingly, the

commission blamed white racism, which had created and maintained the ghettos, for the riots. Not surprisingly, the commission prescribed a healthy dose of federally funded social programs to alleviate and overcome the social conditions of the ghetto.

43. "A Paid Fire Company" and Cecil K. Applegarth, Letter to the Editor, *Cambridge Daily Banner*, 12 September 1967; "Remarkable Records," *Cambridge Daily Banner*, 22 December 1967. Kinnamon obviously had the admiration of his fellow members, as evidenced by his election as chief of the RFC in October 1967. "RFC Officers Are Elected," *Cambridge Daily Banner*, 24 October 1967.

44. McGreevy, *Parish Boundaries.*

45. John Barth, Letter to the Editor, *Cambridge Daily Banner*, 11 August 1967; *Is Baltimore Burning?*; interview with John Barth; U.S. Senate, Committee on the Judiciary, "Hearing on H.R. 421," especially 730–45; George Collins, "They're Bitter, Fearful, Bewildered," *Afro-American*, 5 August 1967.

46. "Report of Office of Investigations," 25 March 1968; "Reconnaissance Survey: Field Research Report"; "Analysis of Cambridge Disturbance." Nathaniel R. Jones to Victor H. Palmieri, 28 March 1968, and Henry B. Taliaferro, Jr., to David Ginsberg and Victor Palmieri, 1 November 1967, both in *Civil Rights during the Johnson Administration*, reels 14 and 18, respectively. "'Raw Memo' to Panel Links Cambridge Riots to Fears of Whites," *New York Times*, 6 March 1968; Boesel and Goldberg, "Crisis in Cambridge."

47. Esp. 730–45; Collins, "They're Bitter, Fearful, Bewildered."

48. "Analysis of Cambridge Disturbance"; Jones to Palmieri, 28 March 1968, and Taliaferro to Ginsberg and Palmieri, 1 November 1967; "'Raw Memo' to Panel"; Boesel and Goldberg, "Crisis in Cambridge."

49. Weisbrot, *Freedom Bound*, 264–65; Sitkoff, *The Struggle for Black Equality*, 203–4. Weisbrot incorrectly placed Brown in Cambridge in August rather than July and bases his claim that whites had organized a vigorous Ku Klux Klan on unsubstantiated rumors.

50. Michener, *Chesapeake*, 792–93.

51. Walker, "A Media-Made Movement?"; Tyson, *Radio Free Dixie.*

52. Tom Hamburger and Clayborne Carson, "The Cambridge Convergence," *Minneapolis Star Tribune*, 28 July 1997, 11A.

53. Witcover, *White Knight*, esp. chaps. 5 and 6.

54. Ibid., 126–29; "Agnew Wins, Dorchester County Favors Demos," *Cambridge Daily Banner*, 9 November 1966.

55. "Dr. Ware Eases Agnew's Burdens," *Afro-American*, 8 April 1967; "Transcript—News Conference with Roy Wilkins," 19 July 1967, Papers of Spiro T. Agnew, box 5, subseries 3; Governor Agnew to William Yates, 12 July 1967, in Governor Spiro T. Agnew Papers, S1041–1713, box 14.

56. "Statement by Governor Spiro T. Agnew: Subject Cambridge," 25 July 1967; "Statement by Governor Spiro T. Agnew—Civil Rights and Rioting," 30 July 1967; and "Conference with Civil Rights and Community Leaders," 11 April 1968, all in Governor Spiro T. Agnew Papers, box 1, subseries 3.

57. Spiro T. Agnew, "A Critique of the Kerner Commission Report," 23 July 1968, in Burdette, *Addresses and State Papers of Spiro T. Agnew.*

58. Witcover, *White Knight;* Carter, *The Politics of Rage.*

59. Scammon, *America Votes.*

60. Witcover, *White Knight.*

61. Carson, *In Struggle,* 252–55; "H. Rap `The Lamb' Turns Erring Lion," *Afro-American,* 19 August 1967.

62. "Rap Brown—Revolutionary Violence," *The Movement,* August 1967, 11; "No Formal Extradition Request Made by Maryland Yet," *Baltimore Sun,* 27 July 1967; Carson, ibid., 256–57.

63. "Report of Office of Investigations," 25 March 1968; "Rap Brown Predicts More U.S. Violence," *Afro-American,* 2 September 1967.

64. *State of Maryland* v. *H. Rap Brown* 295 F. Supp. 63 (1969).

65. Hoover directive quoted in Carson, *In Struggle,* 262; "F.B.I. Report on SNCC Travel," January 9, 1968, in *Civil Rights during the Johnson Administration,* reel 18.

66. Carson, ibid., 256–57; Brown, *Die Nigger Die,* chap. 12; "Rap Brown under `House Arrest,'" *The Movement,* August 1967.

67. Carson, ibid., 297–98; "Excerpts from the Vertical File of the Enoch Pratt Free Library," in *Is Baltimore Burning?*

68. Carson, ibid.

69. Collins, "Growth Liberalism in the Sixties," 11–14; Katz, *The Underclass Debate;* Wilson, *The Truly Disadvantaged;* Jaynes and Williams, *Common Destiny;* Matusow, *The Unravelling of America.*

70. John Lewis, "Private Revolution," *Baltimore City Paper,* 24 January 1992; Steve Viser, "In Al-Amin Trial, Both Sides Buoyed by Evidence, or Lack of It," *Atlanta Journal-Constitution,* 17 February, 2002, 1; see also http://accessatlanta.com/ajc/metro/alamin/021702.html.

Chapter 7. The Final Act

1. Gregory Lane Meekins, "Cloud of Hatred," *Cambridge Daily Banner,* 9 August 1976; *Cambridge Daily Banner,* 19 October 1968; Cambridge High School, *The Yearling,* 1968. The staff of Cambridge High School adopted this line from the hit Broadway musical "Man of La Mancha" as the motto for the class of 1968.

2. "Reconnaissance Survey: Field Research Report."

3. Ibid.; Anne Hughes, "A Look Back at Cambridge's 'Long Hot Summer' of 1967," in folder, Maryland Race Relations, Eastern Shore, vertical file, Dorchester County Public Library, Cambridge.

4. "Church Padlocked; B.P. Rally Moved," *Afro-American,* 7 October 1967; "Black Power Rally Here over Weekend," *Cambridge Daily Banner,* 2 October 1967.

5. Ibid.

6. "Negro Group Demands Better Housing, Jobs," *Cambridge Daily Banner,* 3 October 1967.

7. "For Better Housing," *Cambridge Daily Banner,* 7 October 1967; Housing and

Urban Development (HUD) Papers, Record Group 207, entry 55, box 342, folders 42–69 "HAA-Low Rent Public Housing, 1968, Md-Mn.," especially George Nesbitt to Stanley Newman, 7 September 1967, and George Nesbitt to Don Hummel, 31 August 1967. Cambridge's opposition to public housing was both similar and dissimilar to opposition in other communities. See Sugrue, *The Origins of the Urban Crisis*, especially chaps. 1–3; Hirsch, "Massive Resistance in the Urban North," 522.

8. All in the *Cambridge Daily Banner*: "Arsonists Blamed for Fire," 20 October 1967; "Another Case of Suspected Arson in Town," 23 October 1967; "Vacant House Fire Reported," 31 October 1963; "Found Guilty of Turning in a False Alarm," 11 November 1967; "Men Charged with Arson," 5 November 1967; "Two Men Facing Arson Charge Are Ordered Held for the Grand Jury," 12 December 1967; and "Misquotation in News Report," 13 December 1967.

9. "Choice Is Made," "Wire Cloth Rejects Union," "Airpax Votes Against Union," *Cambridge Daily Banner*, 27 November 1967; "Analysis of the Cambridge Disturbance."

10. *Cambridge Daily Banner*, 25 January 1968.

11. Governor Spiro T. Agnew Papers, S1041–1713, box 14, especially Charles Brewster to Gov. Spiro T. Agnew, 6 September 1967; Secretary of the Interior A. B. Trowbridge to Gov. Agnew, 2 October 1967; Gil Ware to Gov. Agnew, 1 November 1967 and 31 July 1968; Walter Lively, Danny Grant, Robert Moore, to Gov. Agnew, 13 March 1968; William Chaffinch to Gov. Agnew, 25 January 1968; Gov. Agnew to Sec. Trowbridge, 2 November 1967; and "Civil Rights Accomplishments of the Agnew Administration," n.d. See also in box 11 Alice Thomas to Gilbert Ware, 14 August 1968; Edward Van de Castle to George Tawes, 18 March 1968; and Herbert Thompson to Charles Brewster, 10 June 1968, Gov. Spiro T. Agnew Papers. Students of Richard Nixon's civil rights policies have found a similar pattern. Nixon cultivated the white "backlash" vote by condemning busing and criticizing many of the demands of the civil rights movement. Yet, during his presidency, affirmative action developed and busing spread.

12. *Cambridge Daily Banner*, 22 January, 2, 16, 20 February, 7 April, 9 July 1968.

13. Neither Chester nor Saunders admits to being influenced by these prosecutions.

14. Material documenting this history exists in the *Daily Banner*, yet its validity is problematic.

15. Governor Spiro T. Agnew Papers, S1041–1713, box 14, especially Charles Brewster to Gov. Spiro T. Agnew, 6 September 1967; Secretary of the Interior A. B. Trowbridge to Gov. Agnew, 2 October 1967; Gil Ware to Gov. Agnew, 1 November 1967, 31 July 1968; Walter Lively, Danny Grant, Robert Moore, to Gov. Agnew, 13 March 1968; William Chaffinch to Gov. Agnew, 25 January 1968; Gov. Agnew to Sec. Trowbridge, 2 November 1967; and "Civil Rights Accomplishments of the Agnew Administration," n.d. See also in box 11 Alice Thomas to Gilbert Ware, 14 August 1968; Edward Van de Castle to George Tawes, 18 March 1968; and Herbert Thompson to Charles Brewster, 10 June 1968.

16. *Cambridge Daily Banner*, 29 October, 4, 5 November 1968.

17. Ibid. At the end of the year, HUD approved part of the request, allowing for the

construction of forty new units. The town council and the federal government would continue to haggle over the placement of the remaining units for several years.

18. Ibid.

19. Cambridge High School, *The Yearling*, 1963–68, 1970, 1971. The literature on the counterculture is abundant, although little has been done on its impact on the local level, particularly outside college campuses or major metropolitan areas.

20. U.S. Department of Commerce, *1960 Census of Population: General Social and Economic Characteristics: Maryland*, and *1970 Census of Population: General Social and Economic Characteristics: Maryland*; Maryland Division of Economic Development, *Community Economic Inventory*. More recent data can be found at http://www.skipjack.net/le_shore/b-envir/accra.html.

21. Kuennan, *A Profile of Rural Delmarva*; U.S. Department of Commerce, *1960 Census of Population . . . Maryland* and *1970 Census of Population . . . Maryland*; Maryland Division of Economic Development, *Community Economic Inventory*; William Chaffinch to Members of Committee, 24 January 1969, Governor Marvin Mandel Papers, General File, "Cambridge Community Relations Committee"; Carson, "The Black Freedom Struggle." It is possible that more employment discrimination suits were filed but were settled before going to trial. In addition, it is likely that the threat of suits influenced employers to change their hiring practices.

22. "Cambridge: The Old Order Changes," *Washington Post*, 11 November 1973; Maurice P. Freedlander to Marvin Mandel, 10 May, 1969, Gov. Marvin Mandel Papers, General File, S104–1847, "Cambridge"; Maryland Department of Economic and Community Development, *Dorchester County Development Report*. On the dispute over building public housing units in the Second Ward, see Housing and Urban Development (HUD) Papers, Record Group 207, box 342, especially folders 42–69. Determining the exact conditions of homes in the Second Ward is a difficult task. Forty percent of all renter-occupied units in Cambridge lacked some or any plumbing facilities in 1960. In contrast, less than 10 percent of all owner-occupied units lacked such facilities. Three out of four blacks lived in rental units compared to less than one out of two whites. U.S. Department of Commerce, *United States Census of Housing 1960: Maryland*.

23. Farley, "Residential Segregation of Social and Economic Groups among Blacks, 1970–1980," 295; Katz, *The Underclass Debate*; Wilson, *The Truly Disadvantaged*. A particularly good case study is Sugrue, *The Origins of the Urban Crisis*. Housing data on Cambridge have been culled from U.S. Department of Commerce, *1990 Census of Housing*, vol. 1, pt. 22, 178; U.S. Department of Commerce, *United States Census of Housing 1960: Maryland*, 38.

24. U.S. Commission on Civil Rights, "School Desegregation in Dorchester County, Maryland."

25. U.S. Department of Commerce, *1960 Census of Population*, vol. 1, pt. 2, 138; Maryland Department of State Planning, *1980 Census Profile: Social, Economic and Housing Profile for Maryland*, vol. 2, *Western Maryland and Eastern Shore Counties*.

26. *United States of America v. City of Cambridge, Maryland* 799 F. 2d 137 (14th Cir. 1986); case file of *United States of America v. City of Cambridge*, No. 86–3533, RG 84–

4411, box 45, National Archives, Mid-Atlantic Region, Philadelphia; Sachs, "At-Large Election of County Commissioners."

27. Ibid.

28. Ibid.

29. Ibid.

30. Ibid.; "Black Election to Eastern Shore Post Is Praised," *Washington Post*, December 3, 1986, B7. On the civil rights record of the Justice Department see Levy, *Encyclopedia of the Reagan-Bush Years*, 310–11; Urban Institute, *Civil Rights and the Reagan Administration*.

31. Margaret Stubbs, "Album of Black Culture Day, Cambridge, Maryland" (n.p., 1974) (Dorchester County Public Library); "Harriet Tubman Honored as a Saint," *Baltimore Sun*, 20 February 1995, 1B.

32. Eugene L Meyer, "Eastern Shore Town Prefers to Put Its Racially Torn Past behind It," *Washington Post*, 10 August 1997, B3.

33. *Baltimore Sun*, 11 January 1987, 20 December 1986, 26 July 1992.

34. *Washington Post*, 26 November, 1985, C5, 18 August 1986, B1; "U.S. Bias Appalling," *Star Democrat*, 12 August 1986, 1.

35. Interview with Frederick Malkus; "Tensions Remain in Cambridge," *Baltimore Sun*, 26 July 1992, 1C; Flowers, "Dorchester County Maryland: An Interdisciplinary Study for Young People."

36. Barth, *Once upon a Time*, 155.

37. "Marking the 30th Anniversary of Cambridge Pine Street Fire," vertical file, Dorchester County Public Library; interviews with Gloria Richardson, 1993, 2000, 2002, and Enez Grubb, 2000, 2001.

38. "Working on Racial Image," *Baltimore Sun*, 19 April 1974; "Cambridge Is Overcoming Its Reputation for Racial Prejudice," *Baltimore Sun*, 10 January 1977; "Recollection by George Collins," *Baltimore Sun*, 2 March 1982; U.S. Census Bureau, *Census of Population and Housing, 1980—Maryland*. Some blacks who were active in the movement, particularly those who have government jobs in Cambridge, proved less willing to discuss the movement with me.

39. U.S. Department of Commerce, *1970 Census of Population* vol. 2, pt. 22; U.S. Department of Commerce, *1990 Census of Population and Housing*, vol. 5, pt. 22.

40. All from the *Baltimore Sun*: "Hyatt Likely to Buy Cambridge Land from State," 7 January 1998, C1; "Hyatt to Build Resort on Choptank," 8 January 1998, D1; "Hotels Reviving Shore," 28 March 1999, 1D; "Hyatt Proposes Cambridge Resort," 24 January 1996, 1A. Several years earlier, town leaders had announced plans for "Sailwinds Park," Cambridge's version of Baltimore's successful Inner Harborplace. It was supposed to include a visitors' center, a waterfront park, riverfront shops, an amphitheater, and a 300-room hotel. Promoters hoped that the development would need only limited start-up funds and that it would generate a virtuous cycle of support, attracting new investment at each stage of construction. While all of the plans did not materialize, the goal of attracting the attention of outside investors deserves at least partial credit for spark-

ing the Hyatt Corporation's decision to locate in Cambridge. See Gary Gately, "Cambridge Charts Course for Renewal," *Baltimore Sun*, 6 August 1995, E1.

41. Chris Guy, "Cambridge Expects Boost from New Resort," *Baltimore Sun*, 5 May 2000, B1; Chris Guy, "A St. Michaels, but Funkier," *Baltimore Sun*, 21 June 2002, 1.

42. Chris Guy, "Hotel Project Provokes Mistrust," *Baltimore Sun*, 28 May 2000, B1.

43. See the National Park homepage entitled "We Shall Overcome: Historic Places of the Civil Rights Movement," http:www.cr.nps.gov/nr/travel/civilrights/mainmap.htm.

Conclusion

1. Durham, "Thirty Miles Divide Folly and Reason," 18–25; Bozell, "The Lessons of Cambridge and Salisbury," 145–48. See also "Why Race Troubles Hit One City, Spare Another; A Case Study: Cambridge and Salisbury, Maryland," *U.S. News* 55 (5 August 1963): 78–80.

2. Durham, "Thirty Miles Divide Folly and Reason"; "Why Race Troubles Hit One City, Spare Another; A Case Study."

3. Bozell, "The Lessons of Cambridge and Salisbury."

4. Good review essays on the movement are Lawson, "Freedom Then, Freedom Now," and Fairclough, "State of the Art."

5. Among those who have called for a new history of the movement are Carson, "The Black Freedom Struggle," and Norell, "One Thing We Did Right." On the value of case studies in general see D'Emilio, "Review of *Creating a Place for Ourselves*." A valuable exchange on looking at the civil rights movement from the national and local perspective can be found in Lawson and Payne, *Debating the Civil Rights Movement, 1945–1968*.

6. Oberschall, *Social Conflict and Social Movements*; Piven and Cloward, *Poor People's Movements*; McAdam, *Political Process and the Development of the Black Insurgency, 1930–1970*; Morris, *The Origins of the Civil Rights Movement*.

7. For a good overview of the sociological theories on the movement's origins see Bloom, *Class, Race, and the Civil Rights Movement*, 10–15; Levy, *The Civil Rights Movement*; Lewis, "The Origins and Causes of the Civil Rights Movement"; Cook, *Sweet Land of Liberty?*

8. Lewis, "The Origins," 3.

9. Levy, *The Civil Rights Movement*, 45–47; Dudziak, "Desegregation as a Cold War Imperative."

10. As a recent study of Detroit suggests, blacks in the North were already experiencing the process of deindustrialization before the latter part of the 1960s. This deindustrialization gave rise to their dissatisfaction with the mainstream movement's focus on caste concerns and paved the way for the rise of black nationalism and the riots that came to the fore in the latter part of the decade. See Sugrue, *The Origins of the Urban Crisis*.

11. Lillie May Carroll Jackson headed an active branch of the NAACP in the 1930s and 1940s. Her daughter, Juanita Jackson Mitchell, assumed her role during the 1950s

and 1960s. Juanita's husband, Clarence Mitchell, was one of the most important figures in the NAACP, and her son became Baltimore's first black congressman. See Shoemaker, "We Shall Overcome, Someday"; Olson, "Old West Baltimore"; Levy, *The Civil Rights Movement*. Studies of Mississippi also suggest that the church played a less important role than Morris claims. See Dittmer, *Local People*, and Payne, *I've Got the Light of Freedom*.

12. Romano, "Diplomatic Immunity," details the State Department's concern with the mistreatment of African diplomats along Route 40.

13. Levy, "Blacks and the Vietnam War."

14. Thornton, "Challenge and Response in the Montgomery Bus Boycott of 1955–56"; Thornton, "Municipal Politics and the Course of the Movement."

15. Carmichael and Hamilton, *Black Power*. In his study of Robert Williams, the militant NAACP leader from Monroe, North Carolina, Timothy Tyson argues that there was broad support within the African-American community for armed self-defense well before the rise of black power. John Dittmer's and Charles Payne's studies of Mississippi similarly raise questions about the acceptance of nonviolence as *the* creed of the movement in the early 1960s. Research on the black freedom struggle outside the Deep South confirms that economic and class concerns animated civil rights activists in the early 1960s; they protested against discriminatory hiring practices from Brooklyn to San Francisco and marched in the hundreds of thousands for "jobs and freedom" in Detroit, Chicago, and Washington, D.C. See Tyson, "Robert F. Williams, 'Black Power,' and the Roots of the African American Freedom Struggle"; Tyson, *Radio Free Dixie*; Ralph, *Northern Protest*; Rorabaugh, *Berkeley at War*; Levy, *The New Left and Labor in the 1960s*, chap. 1. For an example of a synthesis that draws on the most recent scholarship without breaking from the traditional paradigm, see Cook, *Sweet Land of Liberty?*

16. Greenberg, "The Politics of Disorder"; Fogelson, *Violence as Protest*; National Advisory Commission on Civil Disorders, *Report*; Fine, *Violence in the Model City*.

17. For general works on the rise of the new right see Carter, *The Politics of Rage*; Crawford, *Thunder on the Right*; Edsall and Edsall, *Chain Reaction*; Rieder, *Canarsie*. The civil rights record of the Nixon-Agnew Administration has received little scholarly attention. Most standard works on the civil rights years cast Nixon and Agnew as reactionaries. See, for example, Sitkoff, *The Struggle for Black Equality*, 224–26. A more accurate sense of Nixon's record, including the administration's implementation of affirmative action, can be found in Graham, *The Civil Rights Era*.

Bibliography

Manuscript Collections

Agnew, Governor Spiro T. Papers. Maryland State Archives. Annapolis, Maryland.

Agnew, Spiro T. Papers. Archives and Manuscript Department, University of Maryland, College Park.

Area Redevelopment Administration (Records). U.S. Department of Commerce. Washington, D.C.

Cambridge Nonviolent Action Committee (CNAC). Papers. State Historical Society of Wisconsin. Madison.

Civil Rights during the Johnson Administration, 1963–1969. Part 1, *The White House Central Files* (microfilm edition); part 5, *Records of the National Advisory Commission on Civil Disorders* [Kerner Commission] (microfilm edition). Ed. Stephen Lawson. Frederick, Md.: University Publications of America, 1984.

Civil Rights during the Kennedy Administration, 1961–1963. Part 2, *The Papers of Burke Marshall, Assistant Attorney General for Civil Rights* (microfilm edition). Reel 26. Frederick, Md.: University Publications of America.

Congress of Racial Equality (CORE). Papers, 1944–1968. Martin Luther King, Jr. Center for Nonviolent Social Change, Atlanta, Ga. Microfilm edition, Frederick, Md.: University Publications of America.

Federal Bureau of Investigation, Cambridge Nonviolent Action Committee. Freedom of Information Act Release, 100–442079. U.S. Justice Department, Washington, D.C., n.d.

Housing and Urban Development (HUD) Papers. Record Group 207. National Archives, College Park, Md.

Is Baltimore Burning? Maryland State Archives: Documents for the Classroom. Maryland State Archives. Annapolis.

Logan, Clarence. Notes and clippings file. (Partial copy in possession of the author.)

Mandel, Governor Marvin. Papers. Maryland State Archives. Annapolis.

National Association for the Advancement of Colored People (NAACP). Papers. Library of Congress, Washington, D.C.

National Labor Relations Board (NLRB). Case files. Record Group 625. National Records Administration, Suitland, Md.

Office of Economic Opportunity (OEO). Papers. Record Group 381, National Archives. College Park, Md.

Student Nonviolent Coordinating Committee (SNCC). Papers, 1959–1972. Martin

Luther King, Jr. Center for Nonviolent Social Change, Atlanta, Ga. (microfilm edition). Frederick, Md.: University Publications of America.

Tawes, Governor J. Millard. Papers. General File. Maryland State Archives, Annapolis.

United Packinghouse Workers of America. Papers. State Historical Society of Wisconsin, Madison.

Oral Histories (by author unless otherwise noted)

Albert B. Atkinson, interview by Katherine Shannon, 8 August 1979, Civil Rights Documentation Project, Howard University, Washington, D.C.

John Barth, Baltimore, Md., 18 October 1994.

Lemuel Chester, interview by Sandra Harney, 2 August 1997 (in author's possession).

Courtland Cox, Washington, D.C., 24 March 2000.

Dwight Cromwell, interview by Sandra Harney, 27 August 1997 (in author's possession).

Steve Fraser, Chicago, Ill., 30 March 1996.

Enez Grubb, Cambridge, Md., 11 February 2000; 24 August 2001; interview by Sandra Harney, 6 August 1997 (in author's possession).

William Hansen (written interview), 2 April 1992.

Frederick Malkus, Annapolis, Md., 2 February 1993.

August Meier (telephone interview), 29 April 1996.

Donna Richardson, interview by Sandra Harney, 6 August 1997 (in author's possession).

Gloria Richardson (telephone interview), 21 March 1993; New York, 13 May 2000; 18 May 2000 (e-mail interview); interview by Sandra Harney, 7 July 1997 (in author's possession).

Gloria Richardson (Dandridge), interview by John Britton, 1967, Civil Rights Documentation Project, Howard University, Washington, D.C.

Philip Savage, interview by John Britton, 20 September 1967, Civil Rights Documentation Project, Howard University, Washington, D.C.

J. Millard Tawes, interview by Barry Lanham, 24 August 1970, OH 8169, Maryland Historical Society, Baltimore.

John Wilson, interview by Robert Wright, 18 February 1968, Civil Rights Documentation Project, Howard University, Washington, D.C.

Government Publications and Court Cases

Cambridge and Dorchester County Industrial and Business Development and Maryland State Planning Commission. "A Program for Economic Development of Dorchester County." 1950.

Congressional Record, 90th Cong., 1st sess., vol. 113, part 19. Washington, D.C.: GPO, 1967.

Maryland Department of State Planning. *1980 Census Profile: Social, Economic and Housing Profile for Maryland*, vol. 2, *Western Maryland and Eastern Shore Counties*. Baltimore: Maryland State Department of Planning, 1983.

Maryland Division of Economic Development. *Community Economic Inventory: Dorchester County, Maryland.* Annapolis: Division of Economic Development, 1971.

National Advisory Commission on Civil Disorders (Kerner Commission). *Report of the National Advisory Commission on Civil Disorders.* Washington, D.C.: GPO, 1968.

National Labor Relations Board (NLRB). *Decisions and Orders of the National Labor Relations Board.* Vol. 5 (1 February 1938–15 March 1938). Washington, D.C.: GPO, 1938.

———. *Decisions and Orders of the National Labor Relations Board.* Vol. 73 (31 March 1947–6 June 1947). Washington, D.C.: GPO, 1947.

———. *Decisions and Orders of the National Labor Relations Board.* Vol 159 (10–30 June 1966). Washington, D.C.: GPO, 1966.

Sachs, Stephen. "At-Large Election of County Commissioners: An Audit Conducted by the Office of the Attorney General." Baltimore, Md.: Office of the Attorney General, 1985.

State of Maryland v. *H. Rap Brown,* 295 Supp. 63 (1969).

United States of America v. *City of Cambridge, Maryland,* 799 F. 2nd 137 (1986).

United States of America v. *City of Cambridge, Maryland No. 86–3533.* Case file. Record Group 84–4411. National Archives, Mid-Atlantic Division. Philadelphia, Pa.

U.S. Commission on Civil Rights. "Report: Voting Rights." Washington, D.C.: GPO, 1961.

———. "School Desegregation in Dorchester County, Maryland." Washington, D.C.: GPO, 1977.

U.S. Department of Commerce. *1950 Census of Population: General Social and Economic Characteristics: Maryland.* Washington, D.C.: GPO, 1951.

———. *1960 Census of Population: General Social and Economic Characteristics: Maryland.* Washington, D.C.: GPO, 1961.

———. *United States Census of Housing 1960: Maryland.* Washington, D.C.: GPO, 1962.

———. *1970 Census of Population: General Social and Economic Characteristics: Maryland.* Washington, D.C.: GPO, 1971.

———. *1980 Census of Population and Housing: Maryland.* Washington, D.C.: GPO, 1982.

———. *1990 Census of Population and Housing.* Washington, D.C.: GPO, 1992,

———, Bureau of Census. *County and City Data Book.* Washington, D.C.: GPO, 1952.

U.S. Senate. Committee on the Judiciary. "Hearings on H.R. 421, Anti-riot Bill—1967." 90th Cong., 1st sess. Washington, D.C.: GPO, 1967.

Joseph W. Williams et al. v. *Rescue and Fire Company,* 242 F. Supp. 556 (1966).

Joseph W. Williams et al., United States District Court, District of Maryland, Civil Action 16658. Case file. Record Group 21. National Archives, Mid-Atlantic Region. Philadelphia, Pa.

Books, Theses, Articles, and Miscellaneous Sources

Alsop, Stewart. "People in a Trap," *Saturday Evening Post,* 6 June 1964, 12.

Anderson, Harold. "Black Men, Blue Waters: African Americans on the Chesapeake." *Maryland Maritime Notes* 2 (March–April 1998).

Barth, John. *Once Upon a Time: A Floating Opera.* Boston: Little Brown, 1994.

———. *The Last Voyage of Somebody the Sailor.* Boston: Little Brown, 1991.

Bartley, Numan V. *The Rise of Massive Resistance: Race and Politics in the South during the 1950s.* Baton Rouge: Louisiana State University Press, 1969.

Bernstein, Irving. *Turbulent Years: A History of the American Worker, 1933–1941.* Boston: Houghton Mifflin, 1970.

Bloom, Jack M. *Class, Race, and the Civil Rights Movement.* Bloomington: Indiana University Press, 1987.

Blumberg, Rhoda Lewis. *Civil Rights.* New York: Twayne, 1984.

Boesel, David, and Louis Goldberg. "Crisis in Cambridge." In *Cities Under Siege: An Anatomy of the Ghetto Riots, 1964–1968,* ed. David Boesel and Peter Rossi, 110. New York: Basic Books, 1971.

Bozell, L. Brent. "The Lessons of Cambridge and Salisbury: Was Violence Necessary?" *National Review* 15 (27 August 1963): 145–48.

Bracey, John, Jr., August Meier, and Elliot Rudwick, eds. *Black Nationalism in America.* Indianapolis: Bobbs-Merrill, 1970.

Branch, Taylor. *Parting the Waters: America in the King Years, 1954–63.* New York: Simon & Schuster, 1988.

———. *Pillar of Fire: America in the King Years, 1963–65.* New York: Simon & Schuster, 1998.

Brauer, Carl. *John F. Kennedy and the Second Reconstruction.* New York: Columbia University Press, 1977.

Brock, Annette K. "Gloria Richardson and the Cambridge Movement." In *Women in the Civil Rights Movement: Trailblazers and Torchbearers,* ed. Vicki Crawford et al., 121–44, q.v.

Brooks, Thomas. *Walls Came Tumbling Down.* Englewood, N.J.: Prentice Hall, 1974.

Brown, C. Christopher. "Cambridge at Early 20th Century." N.p., n.d. (in author's posssession).

Brown, H. Rap. *Die, Nigger, Die.* New York: Dial Press, 1969.

Brugger, Robert J. *Maryland: A Middle Temperament, 1634–1980.* Baltimore: Johns Hopkins University Press, 1988.

Burdette, Frank, ed. *Addresses and State Papers of Spiro T. Agnew.* Annapolis: State of Maryland, 1975.

Bureau of Business and Economic Research. *Maryland's Eastern Shore.* College Park: University of Maryland, 1952.

Calcott, George H. *Maryland and America, 1940 to 1980.* Baltimore: Johns Hopkins University Press, 1985.

Cambridge, Maryland. Vertical file. Enoch Pratt Free Library. Baltimore.

Carmichael, Stokely, and Charles Hamilton. *Black Power: The Politics of Liberation in America.* New York: Vintage, 1967.

Carson, Clayborne. *In Struggle: SNCC and the Black Awakening.* Cambridge: Harvard University Press, 1981.

———. "The Black Freedom Struggle." In *The Civil Rights Movement in America,* ed. Charles Eagles, 19–38. Jackson: University Press of Mississippi, 1986.

———. "Martin Luther King, Jr.: Charismatic Leadership in Mass Struggle." *Journal of American History* 74 (September 1987).

Carter, Dan. *The Politics of Rage: George Wallace, the Origins of the New Conservatism, and the Transformation of American Politics.* Baton Rouge: Louisiana State University Press, 1995.

Chafe, William. *Civilities and Civil Rights: Greensboro, North Carolina, and the Black Freedom Struggle for Freedom.* New York: Oxford University Press, 1980.

Clark, Charles B. *The Eastern Shore of Maryland and Virginia.* 3 vols. New York: Lewis Historical, 1950.

Colburn, David. *Racial Change and Community Crisis: St. Augustine, Florida, 1877–1980.* New York: Columbia University Press, 1985. Reprint, Gainesville: University Press of Florida, 1991.

Collins, Robert. "Growth Liberalism in the Sixties." In *The Sixties: From Memory to History,* ed. David Farber. Chapel Hill: University of North Carolina Press, 1994.

Connor, John M. *Food Processing: An Industiral Powerhouse in Transition.* Lexington, Mass.: D. C. Heath, 1998.

Cook, Melanie B. "Gloria Richardson." *SAGE* [Student Supplement], 1988.

Cook, Robert. *Sweet Land of Liberty? The African-American Struggle for Civil Rights in the Twentieth Century.* London: Longman, 1998.

Crawford, Alan. *Thunder on the Right: The "New Right" and the Politics of Resentment.* New York: Pantheon, 1980.

Crawford, Vicki L., et al., eds. *Women in the Civil Rights Movement: Trailblazers and Torchbearers.* Bloomington: Indiana University Press, 1993.

Curry, Constance, et al. *Deep in Our Hearts: Nine White Women in the Freedom Movement.* Athens: University of Georgia Press, 2000.

D'Emilio, John D. Review of *Creating a Place for Ourselves,* by Brett Beemyn. *Journal of American History* 85 (September 1998): 540.

Dittmer, John. *Local People: The Struggle for Civil Rights in Mississippi.* Urbana: University of Illinois Press, 1995.

Dudziak, Mary L. "Desegregation as a Cold War Imperative." *Stanford Law Review* 41 (November 1988): 66–120.

Durham, Michael. "Thirty Miles Divide Folly and Reason: Cambridge and Salisbury, Maryland." *Life,* July 1963, 18–25.

"The Eastern Shore—A Challenge to Maryland," Washington, D.C.: U.S. Department of Labor Library, n.d.

Edsall, Thomas Byrne, and Mary Edsall. *Chain Reaction: The Impact of Race, Rights, and Taxes on American Politics.* New York: W. W. Norton, 1991.

Fairclough, Adam. *Race and Democracy: The Civil Rights Struggle in Louisiana, 1915–1972.* Athens: University of Georgia Press, 1995.

————. "State of the Art: Historians and the Civil Rights Movement." *Journal of American Studies* 24 (December 1990): 387–90.

Farley, Reynolds. "Residential Segregation of Social and Economic Groups among Blacks, 1970–1980." In *The Urban Underclass: Views from History*, ed. Christopher Jencks and Paul E. Peterson. Washington D.C.: Brookings Institute, 1991.

Fields, Barbara. *Slavery and Freedom on the Middle Ground: Maryland during the Nineteenth Century.* New Haven: Yale University Press, 1985.

Fine, Sidney. *Violence in the Model City: The Cavanaugh Administration, Race Relations, and the Detroit Race Riot of 1967.* Ann Arbor: University of Michigan Press, 1989.

Flowers, Thomas A. "Dorchester County Maryland: An Interdisciplinary Study for Young People." Ed.D. diss., University of Maryland, 1982.

Foeman, Anita K. "Gloria Richardson: Breaking the Mold." *Journal of Black Studies* 26 (1996): 604–15.

Fogelson, Robert M. *Violence as Protest: A Study of Riots and Ghettos.* New York: Anchor Books, 1971.

Garrow, David, ed. *We Shall Overcome: The Civil Rights Movement in the United States in the 1950s and 1960s.* Vol. 2. Brooklyn: Carlson Press, 1989.

Goldman, Peter. *The Death and Life of Malcolm X.* 2d ed. Urbana: University of Illinois Press, 1976.

Graham, Hugh Davis. *The Civil Rights Era: Origins and Development of a National Policy.* New York: Oxford University Press, 1990.

Greenberg, Cheryl. "The Politics of Disorder: Reexamining Harlem's Riots of 1935 and 1943." *Journal of Urban History* 18 (August 1992): 395–441.

Grubb, Enez, et al. *In Spite Of.* Cambridge, Md., 1999 (photocopy, Dorchester County Public Library).

Guinier, Lani. *The Tyranny of the Majority: Fundamental Fairness in Representative Democracy.* New York: Free Press, 1994.

Halpern, Rick. "Interracial Unionism in the Southwest." In *Organized Labor in the Twentieth Century South*, ed. Robert Zeigler, 158–82. Knoxville: University of Tennessee Press.

Hill, Herbert. "The Problem of Race in American Labor History." *Reviews in American History* 24 (June 1966): 189.

Hill, Herbert, and James E. Jones, eds. *Race in America: The Struggle for Equality.* Madison: University of Wisconsin Press, 1993.

Himmelstein, Jerome. *To the Right: The Transformation of American Conservatism.* Berkeley: University of California Press, 1990.

Hirsch, Arnold. "Massive Resistance in the Urban North: Chicago's Trumball Park, 1953–1966." *Journal of American History* 82 (1995): 522.

Jaynes, Gerald, and Robin M. Williams, eds. *Common Destiny: Blacks and American Society.* Washington, D.C.: National Academy Press, 1989.

Jencks, Christopher, and Paul E. Peterson, eds. *The Urban Underclass: Views from History.* Washington, D.C.: Brookings Institute, 1991.

Jones, Elias. *New Revised History of Dorchester County, Maryland.* Cambridge: Tidewater Press, 1960.

Jones, William G. *The Wallace Story.* Northport, Ala.: American Southern Publishing, 1968.

Katz, Michael, ed. *The Underclass Debate.* Princeton: Princeton University Press, 1993.

Kempton, Murray. "Gloria, Gloria." *New Republic,* 11 November 1963, 15–17.

Kent, George B. "The Negro in Politics in Dorchester County, Maryland." Master's thesis, University of Maryland, 1961.

King, Mary. *Freedom Song.* New York: William Morrow, 1987.

Kuennan, Daniel S. *A Profile of Rural Delmarva.* Newark, Del.: Cooperative Extension Service, University of Delaware, 1974.

Lawson, Stephen. "Freedom Then, Freedom Now: The Historiography of the Civil Rights Movement." *American Historical Review* 96 (1991): 456.

———. *Running for Freedom: Civil Rights and Black Politics since 1946.* New York: McGraw-Hill, 1991.

Lawson, Stephen, and Charles Payne. *Debating the Civil Rights Movement, 1945–1968.* Lanham, Md.: Rowman & Littlefield, 1998.

Lester, Julius. "The Angry Children of Malcolm X." *Sing Out* (October–November 1966): 120–25.

Levitan, Sar. *Federal Aid to Depressed Areas: An Education of the Area Redevelopment Administration.* Baltimore: Johns Hopkins University Press, 1964.

Levy, Peter B. *The New Left and Labor in the 1960s.* Urbana: University of Illinois Press, 1994.

———." Blacks and the Vietnam War." In *The Legacy: The Vietnam War in the American Imagination,* ed. D. Michael Shafer, 209–32. Boston: Beacon Press, 1990.

———. *Encyclopedia of the Reagan-Bush Years.* Westport, Conn.: Greenwood, 1996.

———. *The Civil Rights Movement.* Westport, Conn.: Greenwood, 1998.

———, ed. *Let Freedom Ring: A Documentary History of the Modern Civil Rights Movement.* Westport, Conn.: Praeger, 1992.

Lewis, Anthony. *Portrait of a Decade: The Second American Revolution.* New York: Times Books, 1965.

Lewis, David. "The Origins and Causes of the Civil Rights Movement." In *The Civil Rights Movement in America,* ed. Charles Eagles, 3–18. Jackson: University of Mississippi Press, 1986.

Lewis, John, with Michael D'Orso. *Walking with the Wind: A Memoir of the Movement.* New York: Simon and Schuster, 1998.

Lichtenstein, Nelson. "From Corporatism to Collective Bargaining: Organized Labor and the Eclipse of Social Democracry in the Postwar Era." In *The Rise and Fall of the New Deal Order,* ed. Steve Fraser and Gary Gerstle, 122–52. Princeton: Princeton University Press, 1989.

Lipsett, Seymour Martin. "Working Class Authoritarianism." In *The Impact of Social Class,* ed. Paul Blumberg. New York: Thomas Crowell, 1972.

Liston, Robert. "Who Can We Surrender To?" *Saturday Evening Post*, 5 October 1963, 78–80.

Lowery, Charles, and John Marszalek, eds. *Encyclopedia of African-American Civil Rights.* Westport, Conn.: Greenwood, 1992.

Marable, Manning. *Race, Reform and Rebellion.* Jackson: University of Mississippi Press, 1989.

Maryland Historical Society. *Maryland in World War II.* Vol. 2, *Industry and Agriculture.* Baltimore: Maryland Historical Society, 1951.

Maryland State Planning Commission. *A Program for Economic Development of Dorchester County.* Baltimore: Maryland State Planning Commission, 1950.

Matusow, Allen. *The Unravelling of America: A History of Liberalism in the 1960s.* New York: Harper and Row, 1984.

McAdam, Douglass. *Political Process and the Development of the Black Insurgency, 1930–1970.* Chicago: University of Chicago Press, 1982.

McCarthy, John D., and Mayer N. Zald. "Resource Mobilization and Social Movements: A Partial Theory." *American Journal of Sociology* 82 (1977): 1212–39.

McElvay, Kay Najiyah. "Early Black Dorchester, 1776–1870." Ed.D. diss., University of Maryland, 1991.

McGreevy, John. *Parish Boundaries: The Catholic Encounter with Race in the Twentieth Century Urban North.* Chicago: University of Chicago Press, 1996.

McMillen, Neil. *The Citizens' Councils: Organized Resistance to the Second Reconstruction, 1954–64.* Urbana: University of Illinois Press, 1971.

Meier, August. "On the Role of Martin Luther King, Jr." *New Politics* 4 (Winter 1965): 52–59.

———. *A White Scholar and the Black Community, 1945–1965.* Amherst: University of Massachusetts Press, 1992.

Methvin, Eugene. *The Riot Makers: The Technology of Social Demolition.* New Rochelle, N.Y.: Arlington House, 1970.

Meyer, David, and Suzanne Staggenborg. "Movements, Countermovements, and Political Opportunity." *American Journal of Sociology* 101 (1996): 1628–60.

Michener, James A. *Chesapeake.* New York: Random House, 1978.

Millner, Sandra Y. "Recasting Civil Rights Leadership." *Journal of Black Studies* 26 (July 1996): 668–87.

Moody, Anne. *Coming of Age in Mississippi.* New York: Dell, 1968.

Moody's Manual of Investment, American and Foreign. New York: Moody, 1940, 1945, 1953, 1957, and 1963.

Morris, Aldon. *The Origins of the Civil Rights Movement.* New York: Free Press, 1984.

Mowbray, Calvin. *The Dorchester County Fact Book.* Dorchester County, Md.: C. W. Mowbray, 1980.

———. *The Early Settlers of Dorchester County and Their Land.* Woolford, Md.: C. W. Mowbray, 1981.

Mullikin, James C. *A History of the Easton Volunteer Fire Department.* Easton, Md.: Easton Volunteer Fire Department, 1962.

Mullin-Kille. Con Survey, *City Directory: Cambridge, Maryland.* N.p.: Mullin-Kille, 1947.

Muse, Benjamin. *The American Negro Revolution: From Nonviolence to Black Power, 1963–1967.* Bloomington: Indiana University Press, 1968.

National Advisory Commission on Civil Disorders. *Report of the National Advisory Commission on Civil Disorders.* New York: Bantam Books, 1968.

Nelson, Bruce. *Divided We Stand: American Workers and the Struggle for Black Equality.* Princeton: Princeton University Press, 2000.

Newhouse, Bill. *Maryland Lost and Found.* Centerville, Md.: Tidewater Press, 1981.

Norell, Robert J. *Reaping the Whirlwind: The Civil Rights Movement in Tuskegee.* New York: Alfred A. Knopf, 1985.

———. "One Thing We Did Right: Reflections on the Movement." In *New Directions in Civil Rights Studies,* ed. Amstead L. Robinson and Patricia Sullivan, 65–80. Charlottesville: University Press of Virginia, 1991.

Oberschall, Anthony. *Social Conflict and Social Movements.* Englewood Cliffs, N.J.: Prentice Hall, 1973.

Olson, Karen. "Old West Baltimore: Segregation, African-American Culture and the Struggle for Equality." In *The Baltimore Book: New Views of Local History,* ed. Elizabeth Fee, Linda Shopes, and Linda Zeidman, 57–80. Philadelphia: Temple University Press, 1991.

Page, Wayne. "H. Rap Brown and the Cambridge Incident: A Case Study." Master's thesis, University of Maryland, 1970.

Palumbos, Robert. "Student Involvement in the Baltimore Civil Rights Movement, 1953–63." *Maryland Historical Magazine* 94 (Winter 1999): 449–92.

Payne, Charles M. *I've Got the Light of Freedom: The Organizing Tradition and the Mississippi Freedom Struggle.* Berkeley: University of California Press, 1995.

Phillips, Kevin. *The Emerging Republican Majority.* New Rochelle, N.Y.: Arlington House, 1969.

Phillips Packing Company. "Annual Report," 1939–56.

———. Vertical file. Enoch Pratt Free Library, Baltimore.

Pierce, Franklin H. *A Boy's Eye View of World War II and Other Reminscences of Maryland's Eastern Shore.* Bowie, Md.: Heritage Books, 1998.

Piven, Francis Fox, and Richard A. Cloward. *Poor People's Movements.* New York: Vintage, 1979.

Public Papers of the Presidents, John F. Kennedy, 1963. Washington, D.C.: GPO, 1964.

Ralph, James R. *Northern Protest: Martin Luther King, Jr. and the Civil Rights Movement.* Cambridge, Mass.: Harvard University Press, 1994.

Richardson, Gloria. "Freedom—Here and Now." *Freedomways* 4 (Winter 1964): 32–34.

Rieder, Jonathan. *Canarsie: The Jews and Italians of Brooklyn against Liberalism.* Cambridge, Mass.: Harvard University Press, 1985.

Robnet, Belinda. *How Long? How Long? African-American Women in the Struggle for Civil Rights.* New York: Oxford University Press, 1998.

Romano, Renee. "Diplomatic Immunity: African Diplomats, the State Department, and Civil Rights, 1961–1964." *Journal of American History* 87 (September 2000): 546–79.

Rorabaugh, W. J. *Berkeley at War: The 1960s.* New York: Oxford University Press, 1989.

Sales, William, Jr. *From Civil Rights to Black Liberation: Malcolm X and the Organization of Afro-American Unity.* Boston: South End Press, 1994.

Scammon, Richard, ed. *America Votes: A Handbook of Contemporary American Election Statistics.* New York: Macmillan, 1996.

Schlesinger, Arthur M., Jr. *A Thousand Days: John F. Kennedy in the White House.* Boston: Houghton Mifflin, 1965.

Schneider, Howard. "Summer of Fire." *Washington Post Magazine.* June 26, 1992, 14.

Sellers, Cleveland. *The River of No Return.* New York: William Morrow, 1973.

Shoemaker, Sandy M. "We Shall Overcome, Someday: The Equal Rights Movement in Baltimore, 1935–1942." *Maryland Historical Magazine* 89 (Fall 1994): 261.

Shostak, Arthur. *Blue Collar Life.* New York: Random House, 1969.

Sitkoff, Harvard. *The Struggle for Black Equality, 1954–1992.* Rev. ed. New York: Hill & Wang, 1993.

Stern, Mark. *Calculating Visions: Kennedy, Johnson and Civil Rights.* New Brunswick, N.J.: Rutgers University Press. 1992.

Stubbs, Margaret. "Album of Black Culture Day, Cambridge, Maryland, 1974." Dorchester County Public Library. Cambridge.

Stump, Brice N. *It Happened in Dorchester County.* Easton: Economy Publishers, 1969.

Sugrue, Thomas. *The Origins of the Urban Crisis: Race and Inequality in Postwar Detroit.* Princeton: Princeton University Press, 1996.

Szabo, Peter. "An Interview with Gloria Richardson Dandridge." *Maryland Historical Magazine* 89 (Fall 1994): 347–49.

Thornton, J. Mills III. "Challenge and Response in the Montgomery Bus Boycott of 1955–56." *Alabama Review* 53 (1980): 163–235.

———. "Municipal Politics and the Course of the Civil Rights Movement." In *New Directions in Civil Rights Studies,* ed. Armstead Robinson and Patricia Sullivan, 38–64. Charlottesville: University Press of Virginia, 1991.

Trever, Edward K. "Gloria Richardson and the Cambridge Civil Rights Movement." Master's thesis, Morgan State University, 1994.

Tyson, Timothy. "Robert F. Williams, 'Black Power,' and the Roots of the African American Freedom Struggle." *Journal of American History* 85 (September 1998): 540.

———. *Radio Free Dixie: Robert F. Williams and the Roots of Black Power.* Chapel Hill: University of North Carolina Press, 2000.

United Cannery, Agricultural, Packing and Allied Workers of America. *Official Proceedings, First National Convention, Denver, Colorado, 9–12 July, 1937.*

University of Maryland. "The History and Present Status of Community Organization in Cambridge, Maryland." Compiled by George J. Kabat. Unpublished folio, 1 May 1942.

Urban Institute. *Civil Rights during the Reagan Administration*. Washington, D.C.: Urban Institute, 1988.

Vertical File, Miscellaneous. Dorchester County Public Library, Cambridge, Md.

Walker, Jenny. "The 'Gun-Toting' Gloria Richardson: Black Violence in Cambridge, Maryland." In *Gender in the Civil Rights Movement*, ed. Peter J. Ling and Sharon Monteith, 169–85. New York and London: Garland Publishing, 1999.

———. "A Media-Made Movement? Black Violence and Nonviolence in the Historiography of the Civil Rights Movement." In *Media, Culture, and the Modern African American Freedom Struggle*, ed. Brian Ward, 41–66. Gainesville: University Press of Florida, 2001.

Weisbrot, Robert. *Freedom Bound*. New York: W. W. Norton, 1989.

Wennersten, John R. *Maryland's Eastern Shore: A Journey in Time and Place*. Centerville, Md.: Tidewater Press, 1992.

Williams, Juan. *Eyes on the Prize: America's Civil Rights Years, 1954–1965*. New York: Viking, 1987.

Williams, William Henry. *The Garden of American Methodism: The Delmarva Peninsula*. Wilmington, Del.: Scholarly Resources, 1989.

Wills, Gary. "The Second Civil War: This Time It's Simpler, Black and White." *Esquire* 3 (March 1968): 71.

Wilson, William Julius. *The Truly Disadvantaged: The Inner City, the Underclass, and Public Policy*. Chicago: University of Chicago Press, 1987.

Witcover, Jules. *White Knight: The Rise of Spiro T. Agnew*. New York: Random House, 1972.

Wright, James M. *The Free Negro in Maryland, 1634–1860*. New York: Octagon Books, 1971.

Zinn, Howard. *SNCC: The New Abolitionists*. Boston: Beacon Press, 1964.

Index

Peter B. Levy is an associate professor at York College, York, Pennsylvania. He is the author of numerous books and articles, including *The New Left and Labor in the 1960s* (1994), *The Civil Rights Movement* (1998), and *America in the Sixties—Right, Left, and Center: A Documentary History* (1998).